Advance Praise

I was resistant to embodied learning at first, but it turns out it's not just some random hippie read-the-stars kind of thing. It's the real deal, and it's completely changed my life. Now that I know how to soften my eyes when I'm in high-stress moments, or sit in a way that feels powerful, my effectiveness as a leader has easily doubled. It sounds crazy, but it's true—and *Your Body is Your Brain* explains how and why. The business world could use a lot more of this kind of approach.
—Denise Rundle, General Manager, Microsoft

Your Body is Your Brain invites leaders of all stripes into a massive shift of their mental models, allowing them to access their highest and best selves. The book makes a compelling case for how and why we need to change on the inside in order to create powerful change in the world around us.
—Suzanne St. John-Crane, CEO, American Leadership Forum, Silicon Valley

For years I insisted that Mandy was writing a really important book—and indeed she has. A coherent and pragmatic synthesis of the new brain science and the field of human development, *Your Body is Your Brain* shows how learning happens at a biological level. The book is brilliant . . . accessible, grounded, personal, and eminently useful. Anyone involved in designing and facilitating learning needs to know what's in these pages.
—Doug Silsbee, author, *Presence-Based Leadership*

Hippocrates promoted holistic treatment in his first medical school in Kos, Greece, in about 500 BC. Our subsequent approach to helping people learn took some bad turns in the quest for professionalism. Amanda Blake brings us back! Her lyric and easy-to-read style makes this more than an intellectual process; it is a journey of purpose and meaning. Superb.
—Richard Boyatzis, Distinguished University Professor, Case Western Reserve University | co-author with Daniel Goleman and Annie McKee of the international best seller, *Primal Leadership*

A career dedicated to elite-level athletics has left me with a long-standing notion that every cell in our body has brains. But I could never quite explain what I meant by this. *Your Body is Your Brain* makes it clear. It takes the athlete's magical ability to make just the right move at just the right moment and applies that intuitive intelligence to everyday life. What if we could use non-athletic embodied practices to train for kinder conversations and smarter responses to stress? That's exactly what Mandy offers us in this extraordinary, eye-opening book. And it has the potential to change each one of us—and the whole world—for the better.

—Chris Carver, 3-time Olympic Coach, USA Synchronized Swimming

After a lifetime exploring embodiment—studying the embodied world of infants, practicing and teaching Rosen Method Bodywork, and intense engagement with athletics and music—this is one of the few books I've read that communicates the essence and the value of being fully embodied. Using engaging storytelling, digesting complex research in neuroscience and physiology, and offering simple exercises, the author brings home what embodiment is, what it is not, and how being embodied contributes to well-being, leadership, and relationships.

—Alan Fogel, Professor of Psychology Emeritus, University of Utah |
Rosen Method Bodywork Practitioner and Senior Teacher |
author of *Body Sense: The Science and Practice of Embodied Self-Awareness*

I know from both my own experience and from the burgeoning scholarship in the field that somatic approaches to learning lead to greater resilience and overall well-being. For a world in need of leaders who are able to navigate stressful situations with equanimity, I can think of no better place to begin than *Your Body is Your Brain*. Communities, workplaces, families, and organizations all benefit when their members thrive. But that thriving doesn't just happen. It can—and must—be cultivated. In this book, Amanda Blake shows you how.

—Pam Patterson, Associate Vice President, University Life, George Mason University

In *Your Body is Your Brain* Amanda Blake maps out a distinct, pragmatic, and wise path to embodying your values and what you care about. Her scientific research and narrative storytelling weave together effortlessly to make this an accessible, grounded entry into the world of somatics and embodiment. Read this and commit to the practices that introduce you to the power of living an embodied life.

—Richard Strozzi-Heckler, founder, Strozzi Institute of Embodied Leadership | author, *The Leadership Dojo* and *The Art of Somatic Coaching*

Reading *Your Body is Your Brain* is a little bit like discovering that someone you've inattentively known your whole life is actually your life partner. It takes us on a journey deep into the wisdom of the body, which, it turns out, we enormously underappreciate as a source of self-awareness, purpose, and well-being. An easy-to-read, science-based book with simple but powerful practices that can improve your life in an instant.

—Chris Laszlo, PhD, Professor of Organizational Behavior at Case Western Reserve University

Your Body is Your Brain combines up-to-date knowledge in neuroscience and the behavioral sciences in an easily accessible manner that will help its readers lead more successful, abundant lives. Amanda Blake provides new insights on the mind-body connection—and how it affects everyone—in a way that is easy to understand and apply.

—Dr. Srikanth Sola, Adjunct Cardiologist, Cleveland Clinic | CEO, Devic Earth

At last! Here is a book that illuminates the intelligence of the body in a way that is enlightening and accessible. Amanda has woven together science and story brilliantly. Her stories highlight how unconscious behaviors—blind spots—can impede our capacity for connection and fulfillment. She shares how her somatic coaching process helps clients to discover a life that is more whole, energetic, and inspired. A must-read for anyone who is interested in understanding the power of working with the body.

—Wendy Palmer, author of *Leadership Embodiment*

In this deeply engaging book, Mandy takes us on a journey of embodiment that seamlessly integrates scientific research with heartfelt human stories, all the while laying out a clear path to living with more purpose, presence and connection—in and through the body. A substantial contribution to the growing fields of somatics and mind-body science!

—Janice Gates, Past President, International Association of Yoga Therapists

This book is an absolute gem. Grounded in the body, biology, and beautiful results, it's your guide to embodying your best self, inspiring the same in others, and building a better world.

—Ginny Whitelaw, founder, Institute for Zen Leadership | author, *The Zen Leader*

your
body
is your
brain

Leverage your somatic intelligence to
find purpose, build resilience, deepen
relationships and lead more powerfully

AMANDA BLAKE

Trokay Press
An imprint of Embright, LLC

Copyright © 2018 by Amanda Blake

Disclaimer and Limits of Liability:

The purpose of this book is to educate and inspire. Extensive efforts to fact-check details and ensure accuracy went into the reporting of the stories and science included in these pages. However, neither the author nor the publisher guarantees that anyone following the techniques, suggestions, and ideas presented in this book will experience any particular result. In fact, the practices contained herein are best learned in the presence of a skilled practitioner. The author and the publisher make no representations or warranties of any kind, including any warranty of merchantability or warranty of fitness for a particular purpose. The author and the publisher shall have neither liability nor responsibility for any loss or damage caused or alleged to be caused, either directly or indirectly, by the information contained within this book. Nor shall the author or publisher be liable for your misuse of these materials. Contents are strictly for informational and educational purposes.

Cover layout and interior illustrations by Shannon B. Lattin.
Interior design by Stefan Merour.

ISBN (paperback) 978-0-9993681-0-7
ISBN (hardback) 978-0-9993681-1-4
ISBN (ebook) 978-0-9993681-2-1

Library of Congress Control Number: 2018904917

Printed and bound in the United States of America

For Dr. Gerald Besson, with love.

And for everyone who has a body.

CONTENTS

Introduction   **1**

Part I: The Embodied Self   **9**

  1: Biobehavioral Blind Spots   11

  2: Vision Restored   27

  3: Embodied Self-Awareness   43

Part II: Embody Social & Emotional Intelligence   **63**

  Section 1: Find Purpose   **65**

    4: Care   69

    5: Choose   81

    6: Commit   91

    7: Contribute   101

  Section 2: Build Resilience   **109**

    8: Courage   113

    9: Composure   131

    10: Confidence   149

    11: Credibility   157

  Section 3: Deepen Empathy   **165**

    12: Connection   169

    13: Compassion   183

  Section 4: Inspire Others   **193**

    14: Communicate   201

    15: Collaborate   215

    16: Convert Conflict to Consensus   227

Part III: Become Your Best Self • Build a Better World   **239**

  17: The Promise of Embodied Learning   241

Concluding Thoughts   **247**

  Appendix A: Putting It Into Practice   247

  Appendix B: Embodiment Versus...   266

Acknowledgments   271

About the Author   275

Endnotes   277

References   283

Index   295

Introduction

This book was born of the union of two stories. One is set on my living-room floor, close to midnight in the dark of December. Struck by one of those unexpected late-night sparks of inspiration, I found myself dashing around the house collecting my favorite books. I piled them on the floor and started sorting them into categories: books about physics and biology, spirituality and yoga, business, communication, and relationships. "What I *really* want," I muttered to myself with bright-eyed (and decidedly naïve) optimism, "is to write a book about all this stuff." It seemed to me that the reading that had fascinated me all my life could help explain some of the more mystifying aspects of the work I had chosen and come to love: the work of guiding people to embody their best self.

The other story takes place on my bodywork table in the bright light of day. Following a particularly moving session, my client sat up with a look of wonder in her eyes. Her face had softened, and she was beaming with joy. After decades of shouldering a heavy burden of insufficiency, she had finally opened up to a new level of self-respect. "What just happened?" she asked quietly. "I mean, seriously. I know something in me has profoundly changed. But really, what just happened? And how did you *do* that?"

This book is an attempt to answer that question.

My passion to discover this answer stems in part from a love of the work and in part from a lifelong fascination with science, but mostly from a deep desire to see a new kind of leadership emerge in the world. The tongue-in-cheek curse "May you live in interesting times" is tragically apt today. The complexity and intransigence of our current problems—from environmental degradation to violently divisive rhetoric to economic disparity and beyond—defy easy or pat solutions. If we're going to make it to the other side of this mess, we need more leaders from all walks of life who embody the commitment, courage, and capacity to fight for a livable future on behalf of all sentient beings.

Einstein wisely said you can't solve a problem with the same sort of thinking that created it. In my view, one of the primary notions underlying the biggest breakdowns of our era lies in a fundamental misunderstanding about the nature of interconnectedness. This innocent but misguided thinking has led us to value intellect and reason over love and compassion, to view human communities as separate from animal and plant communities, to see ourselves as separate from those we love (and especially from those we don't), and to mistakenly imagine that our minds are disconnected from our bodies.

For the last several decades, physics, biology, and ecology have put the lie to these assumptions again and again. Now more than ever, we are beginning to see how deeply interwoven we are with one another and with the world around us. And yet while our thinking is gradually catching up with scientific reality, our pressing problems still remain.

We need more than new thinking and different ideas to address today's ills. As Einstein pointed out, we actually need a different *kind* of thinking. We need leaders and everyday folks who truly *embody* a felt sense of interconnectedness, who have both the care and the skills to act with responsibility to the whole. These are people who have the courage to pursue what they believe in and take a strong stand for it, who are consistently able to bring their best to even the most challenging of circumstances, and who can work effectively with others—often across traditional boundaries—to create a new vision of the future. These skills have nothing to do with positional power and everything to do with personal presence.

And the path to greater presence entails a journey deep into the wisdom of your body.

One of the things that drew me to this embodied approach to leadership training is that it was discovered, not deduced. Typically, frameworks for leadership development are pulled together by incredibly bright academics who study what good leaders do and distill the common themes into models and tools that the rest of us can learn from. This is useful, insofar as it goes.

The history of embodied leadership is quite different. In the mid-1980s, the Army Special Forces invited a psychologist named Dr. Richard Strozzi-Heckler to help them improve mental and physical performance. With a doctorate in psychology, a seventh-degree black belt in the martial art aikido, and a military background himself, he certainly had the qualifications for the job. And indeed the project was an astounding success: On average, participants improved their abilities by 75 percent across the program's stated goals, which included areas such as fitness, psychological well-being, stress management, and concentration.[1]

But the training had an unexpected result. In the months and years following the program, Strozzi began to receive letters and calls from the soldiers who had participated. They spoke of how the program had affected them: They were more accountable and less combative. They had better relationships at work and at home. They were more deeply connected to their own sense of spirituality. And by the records of their promotions, their own self-reports, and the reports of their commanding officers, they were better leaders overall. While this wasn't one of the originally stated aims of the program, it was certainly a welcome outcome for everyone involved.

Following that discovery, Strozzi went on to refine his methodology with an explicit focus on leadership. He culled the best of what he had learned about honorable, ethical living and incorporated management theory into his mash-up of martial arts, meditation, and body-oriented psychology. The outcome was a holistic mind-body-spirit approach that reliably develops qualities essential for leadership and for life: integrity, accountability, vision, commitment, equanimity, clarity, persistence, and more.

Now, new research in the life sciences and particularly in neuroscience is beginning to illuminate how and why this holistic approach gets such consistent, lasting, and indisputable results. It is this synthesis of science, psychology, and body-oriented leadership learning that I wish to explore with this book.

As my endearingly curmudgeonly editor was reading the final draft of *Your Body is Your Brain*, he sent me an unexpected email. "So much popular self-improvement literature has the kind of soft, abstract, new-agey baloney that turns off a hard-headed skeptic like me," he wrote. "But your arguments are down to earth and grounded in legitimate research. Your scientific examples and anecdotal illustrations are, in fact, so solid that they've defused my expectations for a book like this."

I hope this book will do the same for you. What I share in these pages is the real deal—practical actions that generate reliable results, grounded in research from over twenty-five different scientific disciplines.[†] But my aim with this book is not so much to "prove" claims according to rigorous scientific standards as it is to peer through multiple lenses at a central question: What role does the body play in our success and satisfaction in life? And might it be more influential than we've ever imagined?

Answers to those questions are hiding in plain sight—obvious in some ways and yet altogether invisible in others. In fact they're so

---

[†] *Your Body is Your Brain* incorporates research from dozens of scientific disciplines. There is no possible way I—or any single individual—can be an expert in all of them. I have done my best to vet the validity of my claims; in many cases I've spoken directly with the researchers whose work I've included. I've also had this material reviewed by doctors and scientists. At every turn I've tried to stay as true to the scientific findings as I possibly can. That said, the ideas presented here are my own, and any errors are mine. I welcome corrections and conversations offered in a spirit of curiosity, inquiry, and collective learning.

well hidden that discovering them can come as a shock. As one of my students put it, "What you're describing makes so much sense. But at the same time... I feel like you just told me gravity doesn't exist!"

Taken as a whole, what you'll see here is a swelling tide of empirical and experiential evidence for the part your body plays in your everyday life and relationships. Ultimately my purpose is to further the conversation about how we can live our best lives and make a meaningful contribution to building a better world.

When I first set about writing *Your Body is Your Brain*, I expected to focus exclusively on leadership and professional life. I quickly discovered that to be an impossible task. Because you take your body with you everywhere you go, writing about body, brain, and behavior means writing about life in all its dimensions.

Throughout the book, I touch on personal, community, and workplace-based stories. We'll hear from entrepreneurs, corporate leaders, and aid workers, as well as military leaders, educators, parents, and partners. Some of their experiences are quite dramatic, others more subtle. No matter how wild or tame your life may seem by comparison, each of these people has something to teach us about how to live well and lead powerfully.

So while this book contains many lessons relevant to leadership, it is not written exclusively for leaders in the traditional sense. And the kind of leadership I explore here is not about position, title, or level of responsibility—in fact it's often not even tied to employment. Rather, I view leadership as a process of connecting to what matters, envisioning what could be, and taking action to bring that vision to life. When you care about something enough to ask others to care about it with you and you effectively collaborate with others to co-create a new future, then you are leading.

Because this is an inherently relational process, your capacity as a leader emerges from the personal and interpersonal qualities that make you uniquely you. Whatever actions you do or don't take, there is one inescapable fact: *You* are the instrument through which you act. And everything you do is affected by that instrument. *Everything*.

Leadership guru Warren Bennis puts it beautifully:

"Becoming a leader is synonymous with becoming yourself. It is precisely that simple, and it's also that difficult."[2]

Although this is deeply personal work, it's far from self-involved navel-gazing. Rather, it's about becoming your best self so you can build a better world. It's about building the capacity to take skillful action in a wide range of circumstances, so that you can be as effective as possible with whatever stated aims you choose.

As you train your *whole* self to be your *best* self, you reclaim long-overlooked aspects of your inherent worth, dignity, and personal power. You come to embody clarity of purpose, steady resilience, greater compassion, and more effective communication. Naturally this affects your own life. By extension it also affects the world we all share. Which means the more of us that engage in this journey, the better off we'll all be.

Picture a really accomplished extreme skier who can descend impossibly steep slopes, jump cliffs, outrun avalanches, melt through moguls, and run gates. His body responds immediately to what the moment requires without having to think about it for even a nanosecond. This skier has _embodied_ the skills of skiing. "What comes next" is simply second nature to him. He reacts appropriately to what the moment calls for, at least most of the time.

You may not be an extreme skier, but you have embodied skills, too. Can you type without looking at the keyboard? Skateboard, ride a bike, or play an instrument? Drive around a corner on a winding road without looking at your speedometer? More than likely, you've been driving long enough that you can just *feel* what speed would be appropriate for the curve, without calculating angles or looking at street signs. You might even be talking on the phone or drinking a cup of coffee as you do.

As you'll discover in these pages, you've also embodied ways of experiencing emotions and relating to others. These embodied skills, habits, and default behaviors affect how you go about pursuing your dreams, how you handle yourself in difficult situations, how you ask for help when you need it, how you move into conflict or avoid it, and so on. These ways of being are to a large extent learned, and to a much larger degree than you might expect, your body is involved in the learning. In the same way the skier embodies the ability to make the right move at the right moment, you embody certain behavioral and relational "moves." Depending on how well-matched your embodied skills are to any given relationship terrain, you'll either sail through beautifully or crash and burn.†

As I use the term "embodiment" throughout this book, it's this phenomenon that I'm referring to: our extraordinary ability to put complex actions and interactions on autopilot, so that "what comes next" or "how to respond" become second nature. It makes no difference whether you are large or small, short or tall, graceful or awkward. I'm not talking about body image and beauty, or the body as an assemblage of medical parts, or the body as an athletic machine. I'm talking about the body as a reflection of the person who lives within it.

For instance, Part I explores how one man embodied a habit of distancing himself from friends and lovers, and how physical practices opened him up to a previously invisible world of true intimacy. I'll show you how biobehavioral blind spots like this affect all of us, and I'll explain how they develop and what you can do about them.

In Part II we'll explore the four foundational skills necessary for embodying emotional and social intelligence: the capacity to *sense, center, get present,* and *galvanize others.* We'll hear from dozens of

---

† As you read, you'll almost certainly find yourself asking how you can learn to embody some of the qualities described in this book. You'll find exercises and practices to help you do so in Appendix A and also at yourbodyisyourbrain.com.

people about how building these skills changed their lives, from a banking executive who found more meaning in his work to an Army Ranger who helps fellow veterans recover from PTSD, from a graduate student nervous about networking to a physical therapist who turned around a struggling rehab center, from a young professional standing up to a bullying colleague to a retired homeowner negotiating with a general contractor. We'll also hear about several companies that improved both employee engagement and bottom-line results through embodied practice. Current research across multiple scientific disciplines will show you why cultivating embodied self-awareness leads to the kind of revolutionary insights, lasting personal growth, and measurable outcomes you'll hear about in these stories and more.

In Part III we'll take a look at how it all adds up. What happens when you discover your own biobehavioral blind spots, train to embody greater social and emotional intelligence, and learn how to exercise embodied mindfulness while interacting with others? Ultimately, these practices allow you to embody your fullest humanity and contribute in the ways you are uniquely suited to. By the end of the book, it will be unmistakably clear how your body is tied to your success and satisfaction in virtually every area of your life.

Let's dive in.

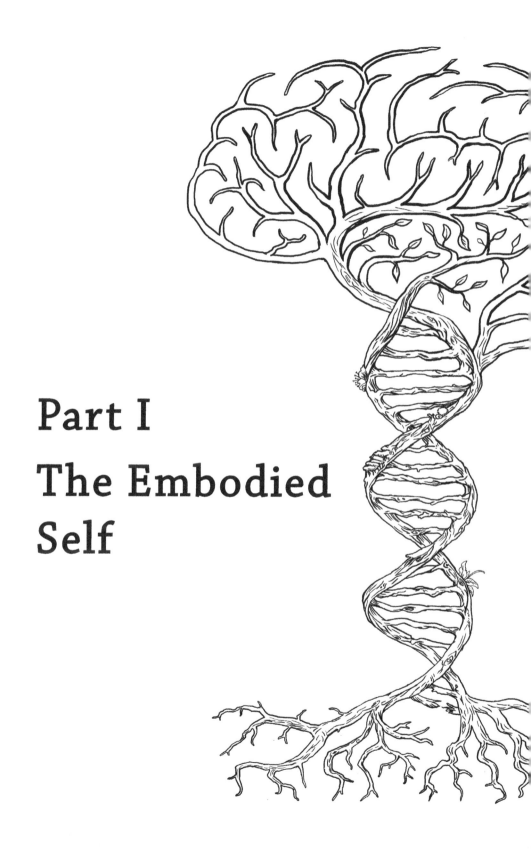

Part I
The Embodied
Self

1

Biobehavioral Blind Spots

How You Become Who You Are

The real voyage of discovery lies not in seeking new
landscapes, but in seeking through new eyes.
—Marcel Proust

Brian "Fip" Fippinger sat stunned, chest heaving, arms burning,
tears brimming. Quietly, he surveyed the scene. The oversized cushion
and the long wooden staff he had been thrashing it with were strewn
across the room. The rough-hewn barn rafters absorbed the flickering
light of the wood stove. Outside the sliding glass doors, the green hills
shone brightly in the early morning sun.

Brian's two companions sat by, respectfully hushed, as his gaze fell on first one thing and then another. His friend Luann finally broke the silence. "Fip," she asked gently, "what's going on?" Brian turned to her, his face a mixture of confusion and awe. He paused a beat, taking in the deep navy blue of her jeans. Then, *"I can see color,"* he whispered, shaking his head in amazement. After fifty-three years of black, white, and gray, Brian Fippinger's color blindness had abruptly vanished.

Normally, color blindness is a fixed trait. So how on earth did this extraordinary event come to pass?

To answer that question, we're going to enlist the help of scientists, psychologists, and philosophers. And we'll begin by laying down a few simple but radical ideas that explode many of our prevailing assumptions about our bodies and our minds.

In daily life, we tend to think about the body in terms of appearance, athletic capacity, or—hopefully infrequently—medical issues. More often than not we talk about the body as a machine, and treat it as no more than a vehicle to get us to our next activity. Rarely, if ever, do we consider the role of the body in our social and emotional life.

But really, your body is the seat of a powerful intelligence that helps you navigate your most important experiences and relationships. In a very real sense, your body is your social and emotional sense organ. It is the lens through which you perceive your relational world, and the instrument by which you act in it. As inherently social beings, that should interest us keenly.

In a manner of speaking, we're all color blind to some extent; some of us more so than others. We can't see ultraviolet light, for example, but bees can. That doesn't mean the light waves aren't there when we're looking. It simply means that they're invisible to our eyes.

In other words, our biological apparatus filters our perceptions. We don't see the world as *it* is, so much as we see the world as *we* are. It turns out this is as true of our moods and our relationships as it is of color and light. Our bodies, our brains, and even our behavior take shape—quite literally—in response to our life experiences. And that biobehavioral shape ultimately affects the possibilities we see, the options we choose, and the actions we take. This is true for every single one of us, not just the color blind.

If you stop to think about it, every action you take involves the body. In 1997, the one-time editor in chief of French *Elle*, Jean-Dominique Bauby, published a book entitled *The Diving Bell and the Butterfly*. Paralyzed by a massive stroke and unable to speak, Bauby wrote the entire book with the one part of his body he could still move—his left eyelid. A dedicated secretary spent months by his side, reading the alphabet aloud and watching him blink in response, then painstakingly scribing each word. Had Bauby lost his capacity to blink, the book could never have been written. And the world would have missed out on his extraordinary story.

Because every action involves your body, your body affects everything you do. For reasons that turn out to be really smart and biologically adaptive, this mostly happens without your knowledge or awareness.

What this means is that inevitably, life creates biobehavioral blind spots for each one of us. But we need not be condemned to our limitations. Fortunately, there's a far greater scope for change than we typically imagine. Brian discovered a Technicolor world he couldn't have dreamt of until he saw it, even though it was right in front of him the whole time. The same is possible for each one of us.

Brian's story begins in the Oak Park Hospital in Chicago, where doctors battled to save both him and his mother from a life-threatening premature birth. A sickly child, he was in and out of the hospital often, and spent five months of the 1963 school year hospitalized with tonsillitis and pneumonia. "I went to two weeks of kindergarten," he explains, "and they weren't consecutive." When he was well enough, he enjoyed doing rounds with nurses, helping them hand out medicines to other sick children.

"My parents never visited me in the hospital," he told me. *Really?*, I thought, incredulous. *Never?* Knowing how slippery and fallible human memory can be, I asked how he was certain. "Oh, I'm sure," he said with conviction. "At the hospital, I felt safe."

With little else to keep him occupied, the small dark-haired boy with an infectious smile passed his months in the hospital immersed in workbooks. He was reading at a third grade level before he turned six—a fact he recalls thanks to an ill-fated visit by the school principal to his modest Forest Park home.

Although it was unusual for the time, the working-class Fippinger household lacked a telephone; so Principal Roy stopped in for a visit instead. Having spotted Brian's smarts during his scant two weeks of kindergarten ("I must have taken some test," Brian speculates), Mr. Roy had come to encourage Brian's parents to put him ahead by a year. Brian recalls lying on the floor during the first of these visits, which occurred annually for several years until, he supposes, Mr. Roy finally gave up.

The principal sat on the couch as his mother lounged in the easy chair, as usual a cigarette dangling from her hand. As Mr. Roy made his case, she shook her head slowly. "No," she said emphatically. "No. I don't want him to feel special."

Charlotte Winifred Rose Fippinger was unusual for her times. Twenty years earlier she had played in the All-American Girls Professional Baseball League, a forties wartime diversion that was later featured in the popular 1992 film *A League of Their Own*. Brian was her fourth child by three different husbands. "It didn't take long for me to figure out I wasn't planned," Brian says. His older siblings had a head start on him by eighteen, sixteen, and eight years. His mother thought she was post-menopausal when she unexpectedly got pregnant in her forties.

"My father no more wanted to have a kindergartner at age fifty-one than he wanted to go to the moon," says Brian with a wry smile. "My mother, by the time I came around, pretty much didn't want to be a parent. I wasn't so much raised, as I was housed."

In 1968, Brian spotted some eye-catching footage on the evening news: anti-war protesters at the Democratic National Convention. A precocious political junkie, he was utterly captivated. As he often did, he told his mother he was going for a walk, strode out into the night, and hopped the train to Grant Park. There, over 20,000 troops were gathered to patrol the event. Protesters and police clashed violently in a conflagration that would later lead to the coining of the term "police riots." Brian witnessed the entire melee firsthand, gawking in fear and fascination as nearby a man was thrown full force through a plate glass window. Brian was just nine years old.

"There really were no rules or restrictions. I could come home any time I wanted, as long as I got up for school the next day. But at the beginning of each year, my mother went to school and told the teachers to smack me if I fell asleep. And they should let her know if I did, so she could smack me again at home."

The first time Brian remembers getting "the look" was around age three. Speaking of his mother, Brian says in an expressionless voice, "From the time I was three until I was eleven, she'd get this look in her eye, and I knew exactly what it meant. It wasn't a look of anger; it wasn't even demanding. She'd just give me this impassive look and a nod, like, 'You know what to do.' Even though it happened several times a week, I could never figure out what caused it. There was never any provocation. She never said a thing, or even spoke a word."

That sinister look was invariably followed by a descent into the cinder-block gray of the basement. Charlotte would grab the closest thing to hand: a baseball mitt, a hockey mask, a hanger. One day, Brian's father's golf clubs were there by the door. "I have a scar the shape of a four-iron on my knee," Brian says flatly. "She broke the wooden shaft when she hit me."

Following the beating, Charlotte would put Brian in the basement closet. She never locked it. He knew better than to come out before she let him.

Our brains are the least differentiated organ at birth.[1] A newborn has the same basic bone structure in his hands as you do, only smaller, with more cartilage and softer bone. But his brain looks very different from yours, and very different from how his own brain will look at fifteen, thirty-five, and fifty-five.

That's because the brain is designed to take shape in response to its environment.[2] The nervous system evolved, biologists believe, to keep organisms in balance with the world around them. So naturally, we must be immersed in that world in order to best adapt to it.

As the brain develops, it serves as a pattern-detection instrument, seeking out behaviors that are vital for successful interaction with the world.[3] Through structural, chemical, and physical changes to the relevant neurons, it puts those patterns on autopilot.[4] It hooks up the word "dog" with "four-legged furry thing that barks." It connects the nerves in your arm with the muscles in your hand and fingers so you can reliably get the spoon to your mouth. It associates laughter with pleasure—or, in some sad cases, with humiliation. This is a highly adaptive process that helps us automate those behaviors that allow us to survive and thrive.

In our first few years of life as our bodies and brains are in high-gear development, billions of synapses—the neuronal connections that store these associations—are created.[†] In adolescence many are pruned away, so that only the most frequently used connections remain. This proliferation and subsequent pruning of synapses phys-

---

[†] A synapse is a gap between neurons that allows these specialized cells to communicate with one another. Neurons talk to each other across synapses by sending chemical messages from one cell to another. As neuronal connections are used again and again, the cells involved thicken and become more chemically active at the synapse through a process known as "long-term potentiation." These synapses then become more likely to be used again. This is one of the ways our habitual behaviors get wired into our brains and bodies. (It's also why Canadian neuroscientist Donald Hebb coined the catchy phrase now known as Hebb's Law: "What fires together, wires together.") This process makes certain habits and ways of thinking and being more easily accessible than others. In a very real sense, we physiologically encode our own unique view of the world.

ically encodes certain neuromuscular patterns into the entire distributed nervous system.[5]

Through this process of experience-dependent brain development, our rapidly developing bodies and brains put certain emotional responses (the trembling of fear, the heat of anger, the contraction of withdrawal) and social tendencies (the downcast eyes of the shy, the quick comeback of the domineering, the automatic smile of the people pleaser) on a kind of neuromuscular autopilot. By the time we're in our twenties, we have most of our unique associations—worldviews, ways of being, relational habits—well, firmly in mind. This makes it easier to attend to other things: poetry, sports, science. It's also how we develop our strengths and gifts—those actions that come to us so naturally that they feel effortless. Unfortunately, this experiential and embodied process of brain development can also create biobehavioral blind spots that, when we finally discover them, seem nearly impossible to break.

Nevertheless, the process is highly adaptive. Our brains have been finely honed over millions of years of evolution to carefully attend to our social and emotional environment, and to quickly adopt and always remember behaviors that help us optimize access to three essential nutrients: safety, connection, and respect. Tracing the evolutionary path of brain development makes it clear why these three "nutrients" are so essential to us today.

The earthworm embodies one of nature's earliest attempts at a nervous system, with its small clusters of nerve cells strung like beads down its long, wriggly body. This prototypical "brain" allows the worm to sense its surroundings (is it dirt? stone? water?) and respond appropriately. But faced with a flood or a looming foot, there's little an earthworm can do. To solve this problem, nature evolved a centralized group of nerve cells that clustered at one end of the spine: the brainstem. Now popularly known as the "lizard brain," the brainstem gives reptiles (and anyone else with a brainstem, including us) many more behavioral responses to threat.[6]

As mammals came along and began giving live birth, a new evolutionary pressure emerged. Because they weren't yet developed enough to make it on their own, offspring needed a way to communicate their needs to caregivers. For this, nature evolved the subcortical limbic system—often referred to as the "emotional brain"—a collection of structures that turn the symphony of body language, vocalization, and facial expression into meaningful communication.[†]

The most recently evolved layer of the brain, the cerebral cortex, has greater neural density in species that live in social groups: dolphins, whales, monkeys, elephants, humans. Biologists postulate that this layer of the brain evolved in part to help social species successfully navigate the dizzying complexities of living in a troop, tribe, or community.[7]

In other words, your brain is your social and emotional sense organ because evolutionary pressures made it so. Starting with the emphasis on sensation and motion in the earthworm brain—an emphasis that our own spinal cord replicates and expands upon—the brain evolved to optimize access to safety (brainstem), connection (limbic system), and social status, or what we might refer to as dignity or respect (cerebral cortex).

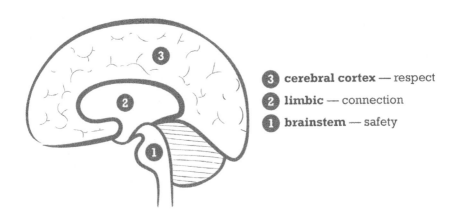

3 cerebral cortex — respect
2 limbic — connection
1 brainstem — safety

Three "essential nutrients" that influence experience-dependent brain development

---

[†] The emotional brain incorporates more than just the limbic system, but this shorthand will work well enough for our purposes. The same is true of the brainstem and cerebral cortex. The brain is so complex it is nearly impossible not to oversimplify.

Just as plants take physical shape in response to the availability of sunlight, soil, and water, the human brain evolved to take shape in response to the availability of these three essential "nutrients." Our brain captures the strategies that work to keep us as safe, connected, and respected as possible in our early life environment, and then puts those behaviors on autopilot. Just like getting the spoon to your mouth.

But of course, your brain doesn't stop at the base of your skull, and your nerves don't end in a vacuum. For you to take just about any action, your brain must communicate with the rest of your body. To "swallow your tears," you have to squeeze your eyes, your throat, your chest. To greet a friend, you open your arms for a hug or your hand for a handshake. To ask a question or to express surprise, you adopt a particular tilt of the head and tone of voice. These automatic embodied responses are a vital part of the very fabric of our everyday social and emotional experience. And each one of us has embodied our own unique set of associations, which emerge out of the culture we live in, the activities we take on, and our early relationships. So it turns out it's not just your brain that's your social and emotional sense organ. *It's your entire body.*

Because the body and brain are in rapid-growth mode when we're young, a significant percentage of this social and emotional brain shaping takes place in our early life environment. That's not because Freud said so, although it turns out he was on to something. Rather, this timeline allows the brain to mature in a way that's uniquely well-suited to its first environment. Even, and perhaps especially, when that environment includes bewildering visits to a dusty gray basement closet.

Children's brains are heavily tilted toward sensory and movement-based learning. Just as the earthworm brain was early on the evolutionary scene, children develop their capacity for sensation and motion quite young.[8] Our centers for speech and language don't come online until we're about two, and take many more years to fully mature.[9] By contrast, the somatosensory cortex, which is heavily involved in sensation and movement, is active from birth and usually fully developed by age four.[10] As children, we adopt emotional and relational patterns not as an abstraction, but primarily through what we sense and feel.

As we come to embody these social and emotional ways of being, we develop both strengths and limitations, superpowers and blind spots. For Brian, that included a literal blind spot. While most color blindness is congenital and the vast majority of color blindness is thought to be irreversible, acquired color deficiency is a known vision condition and many things can give rise to it: disease, aging, medication. And—notably in Brian's case—trauma. Trauma-induced color blindness can occur due to a blow to the head, or hypoxia, or severe emotional distress.[11] No one will ever know for sure what happened in Brian's case; he doesn't remember a time when he could see color. What we do know is that for some reason, his body and brain took on a way of seeing that matched the abusive circumstances and dusty gray closet he found himself in. Now he wonders aloud about whether he simply took on the gray of that world so that the rest of his life wouldn't seem so alarmingly bright by comparison.

This same kind of biologically-based social and emotional learning process is at play not just in cases of severe trauma, but for all of us, all the time. No matter what the nature of our upbringing, the brilliant way the brain puts behaviors on autopilot means that sometimes those once-useful ways of being become outdated. Does making an important decision cause you heart-palpitating paralysis of action? Or maybe you snap under pressure and lash out in ways you later regret. Or perhaps you hesitate to share your ideas, stomach churning as you battle with a reticence rooted in a mistaken notion about your own value.

Like trees, we take shape in response to our environment, subtly bending and twisting our physical form to match our early life circumstances. Unlike trees, we more often than not move out of that environment as we grow older. Most of the autopilot associations that get wired into our brains and bodies are helpful early on, but they can outlive their usefulness as we enter new situations.

It turns out Brian's blind spots weren't just limited to his vision. His upbringing created some less obvious—but equally powerful—blind spots that left him vulnerable to troublesome relationships as an adult.

When Fip was a junior in high school, the drama teacher recruited him and his friend Sue to inspire a lackluster class. Each day they would kick off the hour with silly antics to get the other kids engaged.

On one such day, a freshman named Diana walked in carrying a pink shag purse. It was the 1970s, after all—a forgiving time for fashion experiments. And Diana was the sort of person who, years later, would demand that her funeral be festooned with pink and blue streamers, the Monkees playing on a continuous loop in the background. She was no stranger to the flamboyant and absurd.

On this particular day, Sue and Fip exchanged a sly look as they caught sight of Diana's furry handbag.

"Did you see it move?" Sue asked in a loud stage whisper.

"Oh, yeah," Fip played along. He nudged his glasses closer to his nose and looked intently at the purse. "I think I saw it wiggle."

Sue's hand flew to her heart. "Do you think she's in *danger*?" she gasped, wide-eyed.

"Oh NO!" Brian shouted with alarm. "What are we gonna *do*?"

Together, Sue and Fip rushed at Diana, grabbed the purse, and shouted, stomped, and shook the fake furry creature until it lay dead on the ground.

Fip looked at Diana, who sat astonished in her seat. "We just saved your life," he announced without fanfare.

And that is how he met the mother of his children.

It would be another four years before they married. Brian and Diana's friendship grew through their local church youth group, but when Brian graduated from high school he left Chicago for his dream job, roaming the country with a traveling theater troupe.

When he visited home two years later, Diana had moved in with his mother. Struggling to finish school while living with a friend, Diana was juggling an alcoholic father, a developmentally delayed brother, and a mother who, according to Brian, "wasn't playing with a full deck." Brian's mother Charlotte took Diana in.

But Charlotte was in dire financial straits, and Fip felt compelled to help. He took a leave from his theater job, "one I think I'm still on," he says with a sharp laugh. He never actually quit the job. His intention was to take a short break, earn a bit of money, and get his mother back on her feet so that he could return to the road.

Instead he took an entry-level job as a clerk at Illinois Bell. Unsatisfied with the status and the pay, he kept his eyes peeled for other opportunities. Six months later he donned his best (and only) suit: a burnt-orange polyester three-piece, completed by a black shirt and white tie. Just twenty years old, he walked into a brutal and highly competitive all-day interview for the highest-paying union job available. The interviewer pointed him to a box on the desk. "That's your inbox—now go figure out what to do." Wide-eyed, Brian thought, "Uh-oh... what's an inbox?"

He managed to make it through the morning sweating bullets. Nervous and out of his depth, he downed a stiff scotch for lunch and nothing else. That afternoon, the interviewer handed him a thick binder and gave him an hour to prepare for a meeting with the "CEO" and "CFO." Suddenly it dawned on him—hey, this is a role play! His acting skills quickly kicked in. By the end of the day he had successfully bluffed his way into the job, becoming one of only two communications consultants within the entire nationwide Bell system who didn't have a college degree.[†]

Brian flourished in his new role. He took out loans to support first his mother and then Diana's parents, who were at risk of losing their

---

[†] The strength of the International Brotherhood of Electrical Workers made communications consultant into a union job in Illinois; elsewhere in the country it was management. With Brian's age, no degree, and having started at the lowest job level, he was a poster child for Illinois Bell's "Upgrade / Transfer" program.

home. He proposed to Diana. With each step, his future as a traveling dramatist fell further out of reach.

"It was young love," Fip says of marrying Diana. "But looking back on it, I can see how she fit perfectly into the caretaking tendencies I developed earlier in my life. She needed help—and a lot of it. And that was something I knew how to do."

Between the ages of nine and sixteen, Brian had been the primary caretaker for his bedridden grandfather. Mentally sharp but physically crippled by a stroke, Charles Rose spent the seven years prior to his death lying flat on his back in the front room of the Fippinger home. Most days, it was Brian's responsibility to administer medication, change diapers, and replace his grandfather's catheter. Sometimes, his parents would go out of town for the weekend, leaving the elderly Charles in young Brian's care.

Brian routinely took on responsibilities beyond his years. One sweltering July afternoon, the police visited the Fippinger household with tragic news: Brian's father Edward, a truck driver for Canada Dry, had been killed in an automobile accident. In an instant, Brian lost his father, along with all hope of affording a college education. But it was his mother who lost her grip. Crumpled in a heap on the kitchen table, she turned to Brian, eyes pleading. So it was he who—at the age of fifteen—accompanied police to identify the body, complete the paperwork, and begin funeral arrangements. He had become accustomed to taking care of everyone around him, including the person who had hurt him the most.

This pattern was deeply embodied by his early adulthood, and it continued so automatically he didn't even notice its influence. Only a few months into their marriage, Diana was already well into her first of what would ultimately be many affairs. Brian was painfully aware of what she was up to. Overcome with a furious rage, he sought out Diana's paramour outside her office. With heat pouring like lava down his arms, he slammed his fist through the man's car window, dragged him out by the collar, and threatened his life.

The assault ended the affair, but the reprieve was only temporary. Diana continued her cuckolding ways, and on one particular weekend, she excluded her husband from a trip to attend a friend's wedding. He was convinced it was because she wanted to flirt—or worse—with other men. While she was gone, Brian gave serious consideration to divorce. But just weeks after she returned, Diana announced she was pregnant. Brian decided to stay.

The affairs continued, but Diana made a lovely home for their growing family. She threw lavish parties for their children—the kind that the neighborhood mothers would simultaneously envy, compete with, and resent. The four Fippinger children woke to full-force decorations on their birthday: a house full of balloons, a ceiling full of streamers, and every wall of the dining room plastered in the birthday theme. One year it was *The Little Mermaid*, another it was a Halloween-themed birthday. At Christmas the kids busied themselves with forty-seven boxes of decorations. They needed two twelve-foot trees just to hold all the ornaments.

Brian wanted nothing more than for his children to grow up with a close family bond.

On the surface, he and Diana built a Norman Rockwell family life. Ironically, they ran a Family and Marriage Enrichment group for their church, hosting fifty people at their house every week for seven years. No one knew about the affairs, and a few years later when Diana abruptly left the family without explanation, Brian told no one why. In his words, he "never let anyone in past the foyer" of his heart; not Diana, not his children, not anyone.

Intensely private about his inner life, Brian never let his kids so much as see him with a sniffle until his eldest daughter was ten years old. Brian had become expert at hiding vulnerability and weakness and keeping everyone at arm's length. He tried in every way he could to earn love, by patiently burying his anger at his wife, working harder than anybody else, and achieving great success and recognition in his career. By then he had become a general manager for GE. "I felt I was only as good as what I brought to the table," he says. "I guess that's why I became such a good caretaker."

But he never allowed for the intimacy that creates genuine connection. Many people would have called him a close friend, but none of them truly knew the secrets of his heart. The abuse, the affairs, and virtually everything else important to him was kept locked safely away as a silent, shameful secret.

It was 1996 when Brian finally addressed the abuse he suffered as a child. He and Diana had bought a new house. During the move, Brian hoisted some boxes and walked toward the basement to put them away. Suddenly, he stopped cold. Heart pounding, he turned around, put the boxes down, and didn't go near the basement again for months.

"I don't know how I overlooked the fact that the basement had almost the same exact closet as my childhood," he says. "I guess I never went in there when we were thinking about buying the house."

One weekend Diana took the kids on an out-of-town trip. Brian stayed behind, saying he had to work. Really, he was about to face one of his most frightening demons. "I wasn't going to have a room in my house that I couldn't go into," he told me with determination. While his family was gone, he ventured onto the steps of the basement for as long as he could stand it. It was maybe twenty seconds before he felt an overwhelming urge to flee. Short of breath and hands trembling, he retreated to the kitchen until he could calm down. He did that over and over until he could stay on the steps for a few minutes, and then he ventured down another step or two. By the end of the long weekend, he was able to be in the basement for several minutes at a time.

He told no one.

Diana had her secrets, too. In 1997, she packed her bags and abruptly left the family. She tried in vain to find a doctor who would check her into a psychiatric ward; none would cooperate. In Brian's presence, one psychiatrist simply said, "Diana, there's nothing wrong with you. You're just making bad choices."

Despite this fresh betrayal, Brian tried hard to support her relationship with the children. After a couple of years apart, Diana requested full-time residential custody. Brian relented, going against the counsel of his closest advisors and even the wishes of his two older children.

What his kids knew that he didn't was that Diana had been cutting herself. Much of their time at home was spent taking care of her.

One day, Diana called and left him a message. "You'd better come get the kids directly after work. I'm leaving, and I don't intend to come back." Not long afterward, she committed suicide, tragically leaving her family one final time.

Brian was broken, but not altogether beaten. He eventually married again, but his second marriage turned out to be nearly as damaging as his first. Shelly made his children feel unwelcome in their own home, stole money from him, and never so much as asked why he chose to sleep in a separate room for the year before they divorced.

When the ordeal of his second marriage was over, his eldest daughter Jennifer asked, "Dad, why did you marry her?" He didn't have a good answer. Instead, he told her this: "I've changed my living will. If I ever say the words 'I've met someone,' you are to immediately seize all my assets and have me committed. I am **DONE**."

2

Vision Restored

Brian: Intimacy in Technicolor

Brian's results—and his relationships—began to change thanks to an ill-fated screenplay that remains unfinished to this day. In his spare time he was sketching a story that involved online dating, something he had no experience with. By way of research, he registered for a few sites, created a profile, and set about contacting women to interview them about their online dating experiences. He was always up front about his project, and he made it clear that he wasn't interested in a date. About half a dozen women took him up on his offer to buy them coffee in exchange for an interview. He was grateful to be gathering some good information for the story.

But there was one woman who kept cropping up on his newsfeed of suggested profiles. "There was something about her eyes that really drew me to her," Brian says. Even so, he ignored the profile for several weeks. He was quite clear about his purpose for being on the site, and it definitely didn't include dating.

Still, those eyes wouldn't leave him alone. Finally, he took the bait. He invited her to dinner. He said nothing about the screenplay.

The night they met, it was raining sideways. She was late. During dinner her sister called several times, but the calls kept dropping because of the storm. The phone rang and rang, and she kept answering. "This must be her 'get me out of here' call," thought Brian each time. They seemed to be enjoying one another's company, but still he kept counting up reasons for concern. She had a busy weekend coming up—she was taking her black belt test in aikido. He learned that she had a PsyD—a red flag for Brian given Diana's revolving door of psychologists. Brian felt out of his league, and he was sure this was going nowhere. But when he walked her to her car, her license plate drew a laugh: RUNUTZ2. "Huh," he thought. "Maybe she's not like all the others."

Think about your most memorable moment from high school, or your street address ten years ago, or the answer to nine plus eleven. When we talk about "remembering" something, this is what we normally mean: the autobiographical, factual information that we've already learned or experienced. This is your explicit memory.

But neuroscientists tell us that there are several different varieties of memory that are stored in different parts of our brain and body, and the kind we are most familiar with—explicit memory—is only one of them. We actually don't start laying down explicit memories until we're two or three years old, when the hippocampus—a brain structure critical to explicit memory storage—begins to mature.[1]

Before that, and indeed throughout our lives, we are constantly laying down *implicit* memories: the sensory, bodily based skills and procedures that support automatic, unconscious action.[2] Such as getting the spoon to your mouth, or keeping quiet about your pain, or taking good care of the person who harms you. Because of the way the brain matures, this implicit emotional memory develops first and foremost through sensation and movement. It's a *felt-sense* memory, as opposed to a visual, story-based, or informational memory.

Implicit memory is why you never forget how to ride a bike. If it's been a while then you might be a bit rusty, but it will never take you as long to remember how to ride a bike as it took you to learn it the first time. Once those neuromuscular patterns are in place, they're quite persistent—and that's nowhere more true than for the neuro-muscular behavioral patterns that emerged to protect those essential nutrients of safety, connection, and respect. Muscle memories that were laid down earliest have been practiced the longest and are especially tenacious. Barring major brain injury, you're not going to forget how to get the spoon to your mouth. Or, in Brian's case, how to bury his true feelings in favor of looking after others. We rely on implicit memory for our capacity to do just about anything.

But implicit memory is a tricky and fickle master. Because when implicit memory is in play, *it actually doesn't feel as though you're remembering anything at all.*[3] It feels like you just, well... act. You do what comes "naturally." In fact doing anything else usually provokes discomfort: panic, anxiety, dread. You say things like, "Oh, I couldn't possibly do *that*." You're on autopilot.

As he dipped his toe back into the dating scene, Brian was unaware that his implicit memory autopilot was lurking in the background, poised to undermine his next relationship. He had come to embody a pattern of avoiding intimacy and taking care of others at his own expense—a habit he was scarcely aware of, much less able to change. Just as many of us have experienced, without even realizing it Brian was at risk of repeating all the same mistakes from his past.

After that first date, there was a second, and then a third. One late night Brian and the woman with the haunting eyes walked out of the comedy club right into another torrential downpour. But instead of taking shelter under the trees, Dr. Chris Johnson stepped out into the middle of the street and threw her arms up to the sky, the better to take in the beauty of the rain.

"At that moment, I was enchanted," Brian said. "I didn't have words for this at the time, but it felt...." He fell quiet. "It was... kind of a ... settling," he said softly. "There was a physical manifestation of it that I had never felt before. It started in the middle of my chest, under my sternum. I felt it all the way into my spine. And everything just sort of... dropped. All my energy and weight and everything went down. I guess, as I'm thinking about it, I guess it was sort of a grounding.

"Right then I knew my life had just changed. Everything I had thought about my future had just been drastically altered." Brian and Chris hadn't even so much as kissed yet. But the following week, when Brian had breakfast with his daughter Jennifer, he brought her up to speed. "That thing I said about my living will?" he reminded her. "Forget about it."

Chris Johnson had earned her PsyD with a dissertation on trauma. For years she had worked in private clinical practice, but by the time she met Brian her focus had shifted to supporting business leaders committed to building a sustainable future. For a decade she had been studying and teaching body-oriented psychology and leadership development. As Brian and Chris continued dating and became closer, he eventually tagged along on one of her teaching gigs, sitting in to observe some of the unusual things participants were doing: walking randomly around the room, putting a hand on one another's hearts, startling one another on purpose, speaking their commitments aloud.

He was thrown by what he saw. By this point he knew Chris to be a solid, responsible professional, a remarkably grounded and intelligent woman. She spoke passionately about her body-oriented leadership work, and although he didn't quite get it, it was enough to provoke his curiosity. But when he witnessed it firsthand, he wasn't sure what to think. He wondered if he had overlooked something important about

Chris, or if she had been dishonest with him in some way. Why were all these people moving and stretching and walking and touching? This wasn't like any leadership training he had seen before.

Anything that stores information requires a physical record, whether that's zeros and ones on a microchip, hieroglyphics on stone, ink on a page, or grooves on vinyl.[4] Your implicit emotional memories have a physical record, too. They're stored in the neuromuscular patterns that affect virtually every tissue in your body.[5]

This occurs in part through a process called armoring. Wilhelm Reich originally proposed the idea of armoring in the 1930s.[6] Reich, a student of Freud's, saw connections between the body and the psyche that his contemporaries missed. In particular, he observed how people employ physical contraction to either stifle or fend off unwanted emotion.

For instance, what do you do when you're struck by something funny at an inopportune moment? In other words, how do you stifle a laugh? Probably, you tighten your chest, your jaw, your lips. Maybe you hold your breath or squeeze your eyes shut. Perhaps you cover your mouth with your hand. All of this, of course, requires muscular contraction.

Something similar occurs when we feel attacked or overwhelmed by the intense emotions of others. We cringe when someone yells at us, or literally and figuratively "pull away" when a new acquaintance becomes overly intimate. When it gets really bad, this kind of tension can leave you speechless, sputtering, and grasping for an appropriate response.

Of course what qualifies as an unacceptable emotion varies widely by culture, gender, and geography, not to mention different family norms. A woman from a boisterous Italian-American family in New Jersey will embody different gestures, expressions, and behaviors than an East Indian man studying engineering in Mumbai. The emotions we contract around are heavily influenced by cultural norms: Boys learn early to contract around their tears; many girls learn to keep their voices quiet so as not to disrupt. Ultimately, the behaviors we come to embody reflect the society we live in.

Contractions like these, when repeated often enough, ultimately change the physical structure of the entire social and emotional sense organ that is your body. If you hold in your laughter all the time, eventually you'll become stiff and rigid—both physically *and* behaviorally. If, like Brian, you continually quell your anger, the same kind of thing can happen.[†] The constellation of sensation, mood, and movement required to stifle laughter or bury anger or contain sadness gets neuromuscularly wired together and put on autopilot.

Through structural and chemical changes to neurons and the muscles, tissues, and organs they connect with, your body knows how to stifle a laugh without even having to think about it. With enough repeated use, this neuromuscular pattern can become a chronic and unconscious muscular holding—a tension that can be stubbornly resistant to the most sincere efforts to relax. In fact the tension itself may even be invisible to us. That's armoring. In this way, our everyday gestures ultimately become our physical structure. Our bodies take on the shape of our repeated emotional experience. When your mother warned you not to make those faces because your face might freeze like that, well, she was half right.

For Brian, the Technicolor world of true intimacy was rendered invisible by his automatic lean toward caretaking at any cost. In his body, this presented itself as a perpetual lean forward and a move toward others that more often than not had Brian leaving himself and his own needs behind. He had so strongly embodied this tendency that he couldn't even see how he was cutting himself off from intimacy, much less do anything about it.

A similar thing happens when you repeatedly go slack or numb out, disconnecting from your sensations. Perpetually frightened children may "escape" in the only way available to them—by going into imagination, or to a very quiet place inside. This disconnection from

---

[†] I am not advocating spewing anger everywhere as a solution to this problem. There are much more skillful ways to deal with anger—and any difficult emotion, really. We'll address these throughout Part II, especially in the section on Building Resilience.

the overwhelming sensory experience of the moment can serve as a valuable protective shield. Psychologists call this dissociation.[7] It is the flip side of armoring, but the patterns are laid down in much the same way: Repeated action physically encodes the disconnect into the muscles, tissues, and distributed brain, until it becomes far more difficult to feel your own sensations and moods.[8]

This process of biobehavioral learning is at work 24/7. And it happens especially rapidly in the presence of strong emotions: particularly fear and anger, but also pleasure and joy. That's because strong emotions flood the brain with neurotransmitters that support rapid learning.[9] *If you care about it, it must be worth remembering.* This is a highly adaptive process that allows the social and emotional sense organ that is your body to quickly automate the biobehavioral strategies that work to get us what we need.

Once these structural patterns are in place, they affect both how you see the world and how you behave. Your body is both a lens of perception and an instrument of action. And as I've pointed out before, absolutely everything you do is filtered through that instrument.

This is easy to see in Brian's case—his color blindness affected his perception quite literally. For most of us, the story is a little more subtle, closer to Brian's habit of abandoning his own needs as he leaned forward to take care of others.

It is this subtle story of embodied habits that Chris was revealing to the leaders in her workshop. Moving around the room, silently interacting with others, and paying attention to their physical responses illuminated previously invisible embodied holding patterns. Once they could see the physical manifestations of their habitual ways of relating, they were better equipped to "catch themselves in the act," as Chris puts it, and choose more resourceful ways to lead.

Brian was mystified by Chris's work, but intrigued. On the strength of his trust in her, he decided to explore further. He signed himself up for three sessions with somatic coach Madeline Wade, widely regarded as one of the preeminent bodyworkers in this relatively obscure field. Madeline is trained in the Strozzi Somatics form of bodywork, which blends Rolfing, polarity therapy, and Feldenkrais with coaching to elicit powerful embodied transformation.

Trepidatious but committed, Brian held nothing back. "I told Madeline things I had never told anyone before," he told me. "About the abuse, my dad, Diana. I told her things I hadn't even said to Chris." When they were finished talking, Madeline invited him to lie face down on her massage table, fully clothed. "It was the first time I had been on a massage table where I wasn't supposed to take my clothes off," he said. "I had no idea what I was in for."

Madeline is a soft, stocky, earth mother of a woman, the kind of person you just instinctively know you could lean your head against and cry. She pulled her long gray hair back into a clip and gently put her hands on Brian's back, behind his heart. Although she moved very little, he started to feel a vibration in his legs. After a bit, his legs started to tremble and bounce. "I remember finding it really odd that I could feel her hands on my back and I could feel my legs, but I couldn't feel anything in between," said Brian. Then, he began to cry. "I don't cry," he told her. Madeline made a soft noise of acknowledgment, and invited him to roll onto his back. She cradled his head in her hands, and he felt a familiar band of tension that ran from the bridge of his nose across his eyes and toward his ears. There was a pain behind his eyes. The tears kept flowing.

When he got up off the table he felt like a new man. "I didn't know *what* had happened," he told me in a deep, slow voice. "But," echoing what I've heard from clients again and again, "I knew that somehow, something in me had profoundly changed."

That experience drew him in even further. He enrolled in a year-long body-oriented leadership program at the Strozzi Institute.[†]

[†] Strozzi Institute has been one of the pioneers in bringing somatic education out from its healthcare roots into the world of leadership development. Several of the people mentioned in this book have studied and/or taught there, including me.

There, he was asked to sit quietly and focus his attention on his breath for the first time in his life. After just ten minutes of this, Brian found himself trembling uncontrollably.[†] He felt as if he were releasing huge amounts of energy. His mind jumped abruptly to the 1996 basement, where he had attempted to overcome his discomfort about the abuse. He thought he had dealt with it then. He saw now that he still had some distance to go.

The trembling Brian experienced while working with Madeline and during meditation is a typical example of the embodied unlearning that must take place before new learning can become second nature. Through the process of armoring, implicit memories become embedded in the beat of your heart, the shape of your shoulders, the sway of your back. To embody new ways of being, you must interrupt old habits and loosen the vise grip of unconscious armoring.

Think about what happens when your foot falls asleep. Sitting on your foot compresses nerves and impedes blood flow, so it receives less oxygen, nutrients, and nerve communication. When you stand up, your foot feels numb at first, and then tingly, like pins and needles.

When you've chronically contracted certain muscles for years and years and years, they can go a little bit (or a lot) numb. You may literally have lower blood perfusion there and a reduction of nutrients, oxygen, metabolic energy, and sensation in that part of your body. So when that muscle softens, opens up, and releases, you may feel a tingling, a rush of heat or coolness, a trembling, or some other intense sensation.

[†] Meditation is widely regarded as beneficial, and it absolutely is. However, it can sometimes be contraindicated for trauma survivors. In the quiet of focused attention, the body speaks more loudly, and sometimes intense, emotionally-laden implicit memories can surface. This can occur through powerful sensations: heat, trembling, chills, flashbacks, and many other manifestations. Without a skilled guide, this can be enormously disruptive and disconcerting for both teacher and student alike. If you have suffered trauma and you wish to take up meditation, there's no reason not to. But I strongly encourage you to find a skilled and emotionally competent practitioner to work with.

That is the feeling of more Life entering your body.

That may sound like a wonderful thing, but it can be surprisingly uncomfortable, especially if the armoring developed to help you access those essential nutrients of safety, connection, and respect. That's why our habits can sometimes be so resistant to change. And why change can sometimes be so damned disorienting when it actually comes to pass.

Unfortunately, our limited view of what the body is and does denies us the very intelligence we need (and have!) to get unstuck. The body has a limited capacity to change based on new ideas. What it really takes is practice, immersion, repetition... the same way we learned when we were kids. But as adults, we need not only the new biobehavioral learning itself. We also need to disrupt the stubborn neuromuscular patterns that keep us locked in automatic, habitual behaviors.[†] And that requires a combination of the physiological unlearning of de-armoring, along with training to embody new skills.

As part of his leadership training, Brian was asked to consider what was most important to him and what kind of future he wanted to create. He declared himself to be open to receiving love and grace from others and—perhaps most importantly—from himself.[††]

Brian entered into a series of daily embodied practices: opening his chest, lifting his chin, and paying more attention to his back. His habitual stance had always had a forward tilt to it, an anxiously eager leaning in that wordlessly and compulsively asked "What do you need? How can I help? What can I do?" As Brian brought his weight back over his hips, he started to include himself in the picture more and more.

[†] This is essential for behavioral learning as adults because we have already embodied certain ways of being. Kids typically don't need as much de-armoring, because they have fewer embodied memories and their neural pathways are more malleable.

[††] If you're wondering right now what the heck love has to do with leadership, read on. One purpose of this book is to make the answer to that question abundantly, unmistakably clear.

These practices, coupled with regular repetitions of his commitment to receiving love and grace, helped him to *embody* more openness and greater courage. He found himself more and more willing to open up to others. At one point during his training, the group focused on learning how to quit untenable situations gracefully and with dignity. "When all else fails, do you know how to walk away?" the teacher asked.

One participant objected. "I don't want to be a quitter. That means breaking a vow. Why on earth would I want to learn how to quit?" Brian asked if he could respond. He took a deep breath, dropped his shoulders, and opened his chest. And then, the man who had never let anyone in past the foyer said something he had never said out loud before, certainly not to a room full of relative strangers. "The mother of my children was a serial adulterer," he told them. His hands were trembling. "She abandoned my children, not once, but twice. I should have quit for the good of myself and my kids. I *wish* I had known how to quit."

He felt so exposed by making this statement that he nearly left the program. Luckily, one of the instructors saw his discomfort and pulled him aside. "I saw what it took for you to do that," Kathleen said. "Is there anything you need?" Brian said there wasn't, but he was grateful for the acknowledgment. He decided to stay.

While he had no idea what was happening to him, Brian could feel himself changing, and he liked the direction that change was taking. He found himself willing to open up to Chris in ways that were entirely new to him. Of course, it didn't hurt that she was a good listener. But the change he found most refreshing was his own ability to share what was in his heart. Bit by bit, he started letting her in.

Compare biobehavioral learning to language acquisition. Infants are born with the capacity to hear and to make all the sounds of any given language. But each of us is immersed in a primary language, and as we grow, the sounds of our native language become wired into our auditory nerves, language centers, and muscles for speech. If you grew up speaking Spanish, it will be easy for you to roll your Rs. If you grew up speaking English, it may be very difficult for you to hear the difference between two words in Thai that sound similar but have very different meanings. If you grew up speaking Japanese, pronouncing and hearing the difference between the English letters L and R may pose a challenge.

Notice that there's a perception piece to this—what you can *hear*—and an action piece—what you can *say*. A similar sort of process goes on with our social and emotional development. As our bodies take shape in response to our environment, our biological lens gets tuned to a particular way of seeing the world and being in it. Certain kinds of emotional responses, interpretations, and relational defaults get wired into our body. This makes some actions second nature, and others much more difficult. We could even say they're invisible to us, at times. For Brian, the path to true intimacy was as invisible as red, blue, and green.

Think about it this way: Dogs can smell and hear things that you can't. Clearly, those smells and sounds are still surrounding you all the time. You just don't have the right biological lens to perceive them. In other words, *biology is perception*. We don't see the world as *it* is—we see the world as *we* are.

As our bodies are "tuned" to certain emotional and relational ways of being, that affects both the options and possibilities that we see, as well as the actions and behaviors that are easily available. Our perceptions, interpretations, mood, and actions are all affected by our physical structure. Depending on what you've embodied, you may be "blind" to the option of standing up for yourself, for example, or trusting your intuition, or connecting more kindly to someone you're in conflict with. You can see how this would affect your daily life.

If you continually hold your shoulders high because that holding is wired into your physical structure, that can actually *generate* a sense of fear and perpetual worry. If you live your life with this ever-present background anxiety, you'll be more inclined to shout when your teenage son leaves his skateboard on the floor, rather than gently but firmly remind him to pick up after himself. Your repeated gestures and your physical structure affect your mood, and your mood affects your actions. And your actions affect both your relationships and your results, in virtually every area of your life.

Eventually, Brian and Chris decided to marry. At their wedding, he took another big step toward the authenticity that creates genuine connection. He stood before the assembled audience of friends and family and welled up as he told the story of his elderly aunt Minnie. Minnie had lived upstairs when he was a child. When he was four years old, Minnie had taught him to play poker, canasta, cribbage. In contrast with the dusty gray basement, Minnie's upstairs world was the one bright spot in young Brian's life. When he returned home from his year in the hospital, Minnie was—incomprehensibly—gone. She had been moved to a nursing home and died a short while later.

"There have only been two times in my life that I have felt unconditional love," Brian told the wedding guests. He paused to collect himself. "First with Aunt Minnie. And now," he choked up, then smiled. "Now, with Chris." He leaned in for a kiss.

Brian felt this revealing statement was a tremendous achievement along the path to being open to receiving love and grace. But his story was far from over.[†]

Brian knew he wasn't a nice guy to be around when he was angry. Mostly, he got his aggression out on the baseball field, where he played longer and worked harder than anyone else on the team. But on the day he

---

[†] As you might well imagine, for Brian to publicly share his story in this book was another huge step in the direction of openness and authenticity. Although it felt risky for him to reveal himself this way, he did so with the intention of providing hope and inspiration for you and many others. I am tremendously honored that he's entrusted me to share his story with you.

dragged Diana's lover bodily from his car, Brian came face-to-face with a part of himself he didn't like. While life gave him plenty of reasons to feel angry, after that moment he buried his anger so deep that he never truly experienced it again. So when, in the course of his leadership training, he had the opportunity to go to athletic extremes in an attempt to expel his long-suppressed fury, he jumped at the chance.

He asked instructor Tom Bepler to work with him privately one morning before the start of the program. Tom is a lithe mountaineer and leadership coach in his late fifties, healthier and more fit than most men half his age. He was happy to work with Brian, but he only agreed on one condition: He wanted a third person there. He could see that Brian's buried rage ran deep. Tom wanted someone else in the room, just to make sure they both stayed safe.

"Luann Barndt," Brian immediately requested. That wasn't exactly who Tom had in mind, but Brian quickly convinced him. "She can kick the ass of any guy in this room," he said of the retired Coast Guard Captain. Brian and Luann had become close during the course of their studies, and he was eager for her support.

That's how it came to pass that early one morning, breath condensing in the chill air, Brian, Tom, and Luann came together for a moment that would affect all of them deeply. An hour earlier Tom had fired up the wood stove, warming the cavernous carpeted barn for their arrival. With no inkling of what was about to come, they laid out the materials they would need: a firm gray cushion, three feet square; and a five-foot wooden aikido staff known as a jo. They took a solemn moment together, and Brian spoke his commitment to receiving love and grace aloud. He said a few words about what he wanted to let go of, finally and for good. And then he picked up the jo, and began.

He started by striking the bolster slowly. For the second time in his life, he felt heat like lava running down his arms, and then it turned to a freezing cold chill across his chest. He beat harder. He grunted and growled, fury and rage spilling forth. The large barn room filled with their shouts—encouragement from Tom and Luann, and wild, heartfelt "NOs!" from Brian. Tears and sweat ran together and dripped down his chin. Memories flashed across his mind's eye: Diana, his mother, the basement. Shocking new memories surfaced—ones that had long been buried below his awareness. He continued to beat the bolster, harder, and then harder still. Exhausted, he fell to his knees, but continued. With each furious strike the bolster bounced away. Brian didn't stop.

With only a few short breaks, Brian beat the cushion for nearly an hour. He was hoarse from shouting. His hands were raw. His arms burned. And yet he stopped only because it was time for the day's program to begin. It was then that he lifted his eyes from the gray of the cushion and, agape with amazement, stared through the window at the tall green grasses waving in the gentle breeze outside. All of a sudden, the world was bright and brand-new. And shockingly, overwhelmingly full of color.[†]

We now have decades of research validating embodied approaches to trauma healing as both trustworthy and powerful.[10] But what about the rest of us? Brian's story is more extreme than most, which is what makes it such a powerful illustration of things that are often quite hard to see. But all of us have biobehavioral blind spots. And just like Brian, all of us can find ways to transcend them.

Think of this for yourself. Does something in your life trip you up, limiting the future you long for, remaining stubbornly resistant to your most sincere efforts to change? Maybe you're a "fixer," anxiously trying to solve your friends' problems when really they just want you to listen. Maybe you contract in shame around money, no matter how much you have in the bank. Maybe you avoid conflict, or lash out, or push away the ones you love. Maybe you're a workaholic, sacrificing love and joy on the altar of success.

[†] Most people who are color blind are able to perceive at least some color. Brian had monochromatic color blindness—the rarest kind—which involves a total absence of color, a truly grayscale world. Brian describes regaining his vision as akin to the moment Dorothy stepped from black and white Kansas into Technicolor Oz. "It was total sensory overload," he says, "completely fascinating and overwhelming."

If so, how do you address that challenge? Perhaps you read books or blogs, listen to lectures, or talk to friends or coaches or counselors or therapists. These are all useful strategies that can be immensely helpful. But if you've ever tried any of those things and stayed stuck despite your best efforts, it may simply be that you're using the wrong tools for the job.

We don't get stuck like this because we are weak-willed, incompetent, or any number of other failings we might castigate ourselves for. We get stuck because we have come to *embody* certain ways of being that were once smart and adaptive. When we try to change simply by collecting good ideas, we often struggle.

But when you de-armor deeply embodied contractions and train to embody new skills, you open up whole new worlds. Your lens of perception changes, and you start to see—and act on—new options. In Brian's extraordinary case, his visual perception actually changed. So did his perception of the relative safety of sharing himself and his heart. And his actions changed accordingly. He became more present with Chris and others. His anxiously eager forward lean turned into a more upright and dignified stance. He became more grounded, more settled, more open, and more intimate.

Part of the process of learning new behavioral skills—adopting new perspectives, seeing new possibilities, taking new actions— means changing the lens of perception and instrument of action that is your body. Fortunately, that change is far more possible than we tend to realize. And that is what the rest of this book is about: how we can come to embody the best in ourselves, in ways that are gentle, fierce, loving, and strong... and deeply rooted in our natural embodied intelligence.

3

Embodied Self-Awareness

Meet Your Somatic Intelligence

There is one thing that, when cultivated and regularly practiced, leads to deep spiritual intention, to peace, to mindfulness and clear comprehension, to vision and knowledge, to a happy life here and now, and to the culmination of wisdom and awakening.

And what is that one thing?
It is mindfulness centered on the body.

—Gautama Buddha

Brian's story is a remarkable illustration of universal principles that operate in all of us, all the time. For most of us, though, the process of biobehavioral learning is far less dramatic. So the fact that our body plays such an influential role in our everyday lives remains invisible. Apart from athletics, we rarely think about the body as a domain of learning. But the truth is our most important personal learning inherently involves the body.

In this chapter I expand on a few of the key principles that Brian's experience so aptly illustrates and introduce some new ideas about biobehavioral learning. In order to lay a foundation for the stories to come, we'll take a slightly more technical turn here. My intention is to introduce some key concepts that will support our exploration in subsequent chapters.

Let's begin by summarizing a few main points from the last two chapters:

- Three primary evolutionary pressures drove the development of the brain: the need for physical safety, the need for emotional communication, and the need for social navigation. Your brain is your social and emotional sense organ.
- The brain takes physical shape as it learns behaviors that optimize access to three essential nutrients: safety, connection, and respect.
- Your brain is distributed throughout your entire body, and your body also subtly takes shape in response to your life experience. Through the unconscious and highly adaptive processes of implicit memory and armoring, you put successful behaviors on neuromuscular autopilot.
- This can create biobehavioral blind spots that are exceedingly resistant to change.
- Your body is a lens of perception. Everything you perceive is filtered through the medium of your body. So those blind spots affect the possibilities you see.
- Your body is an instrument of action. Every single action you take involves your body. So your biobehavioral blind spots also affect your actions.

The bottom line: Your body is a finely tuned social and emotional sense organ shaped by your life experience. And that shaping affects both the possibilities you see and the actions you take. Your results in almost every area of life are subtly but inescapably influenced by the characteristics and qualities you've come to embody.

Your Body is Your Social and Emotional Sense Organ

If your body plays such an important role in the outcomes of your life, then it would be wise to learn something about what it's telling you. Let's take a look.

Exteroception

Pause for a moment and notice what's in your direct line of sight right now. What's in your peripheral vision? Are there any smells in the air? Perhaps you didn't notice any a moment ago, but now that you stop to pay attention, you do. Are you surrounded by sound or by silence? Can you feel the texture of your clothes on your body? As I write this sentence (and many others in this book, truth be told), I'm enjoying the taste of chocolate. Perhaps you're enjoying something tasty, too.

Try to make this more than a mental exercise. Stop and take a moment to really *experience* your sensory perceptions as they're occurring, right now. Now tell me: How many senses do you have?

If you answered five, you're partially right. But you actually have a sixth sense, and a seventh... and even more beyond that. There are actually several classes of sensation, and our five senses are merely a subset of one of them.[†]

[†] There are other classes of sensation beyond those discussed in this chapter, including nociception—the sense of pain—and neuroception, a direct visceral perception of safety or danger.

That class of sensation, known as exteroception, encompasses the familiar five senses of sight, sound, smell, taste, and touch. These senses take in information from our surroundings. Because the world around us changes unpredictably, the nerves that travel from our exteroceptive sense receptors to our brains are especially large and fast.[1] This makes it easy—practically instantaneous, even—for you to sit up and take notice when a loud sound suddenly catches your attention. It's biologically adaptive for us to perceive and quickly respond to changing external circumstances, so nature has evolved a way for us to easily do that.

But the background level of sensory stimulus is so immense that we can't possibly perceive it all. If you paid attention to every sight, sound, and smell that came along as you were reading this book, you'd never be able to concentrate.

So our senses keenly filter in what's important, and screen out things that aren't relevant. This is nowhere more clearly demonstrated than in a famous experiment on selective attention, in which an actor in a gorilla suit walks slowly into a group of students passing a few basketballs back and forth, turns toward the camera, beats his chest, and walks out. If you're busy counting the number of passes, as the experimenter would have asked you to do, chances are high—50 percent, in fact—that you won't see the gorilla at all.[†]

I've mentioned before that bees see ultraviolet light and dogs smell and hear things that we can't. Those stimuli surround us even though we can't perceive them. Our senses are like our own personal radio dial, tuned first to what humans are physically capable of perceiving, and then more finely to your own unique channel. That might be limited by color blindness or dulled taste buds or years of too-loud music. If you lived your entire life on the sea, as do the Sea Gypsies of Southeast Asia, you might have developed a visual cortex that allows you to see clearly and catch your dinner thirty feet underwater.[2] Musicians with perfect pitch live in a different soundscape than people who haven't developed that skill. Celebrated sommeliers experience their wines very differently

---

[†] You can try this for yourself at www.theinvisiblegorilla.com. Although now that I've tipped you off, you may find it easier to see the gorilla.

than an elderly person with dimming taste buds. We each get access to a narrow and uniquely filtered piece of the world. In fact it's not too much to say that we are each, quite literally, living in a world of our own making.

Interoception

Interoception is essentially the inverse of exteroception. It's the term scientists use for your internal visceral experience.[3]

Get very quiet and still, and move your attention to the center of your chest. If you pay attention carefully, can you sense your heart beating? If you put your hand on your chest, does it become any easier to feel? Perhaps you notice your lungs moving with each inhale and exhale. Is there warmth anywhere in your body, or coolness? Maybe you have a relaxed sense of spaciousness on the inside. Maybe there's tension somewhere.

These are your interoceptive sensations. You may notice that it's more difficult to become aware of what you're feeling from the inside. Perhaps you had to close your eyes to do so, shutting out the exteroceptive "noise" in order to become aware of your internal state. This is common, and one reason is biological.

Interoceptive nerve cells are smaller and slower than their exteroceptive cousins. Exteroceptive nerves equip you to act quickly in response to the unpredictably changing circumstances of your environment. By contrast, processes like homeostasis allow us to exercise automatic control over our internal environment. The brain uses smaller nerve cells to process interoceptive sensations in the background, filtering them out of conscious awareness unless and until something goes wrong.[4]

Just as exteroception is divided up into five senses, the interoceptive class of sensations can be divvied up as well. Your heart, gut, lungs, skin, and connective tissue all provide unique signals to the brain about your internal state. These are the five internal senses of your social and emotional sense organ. What's known so far about these senses would fill an entire book, and scientists make new discoveries every day. Here I'll summarize just a handful of the many fascinating facts:

The Heart

- A small group of cells in the amygdala—a tiny bit of brain involved in assessing danger—fires six to eight milliseconds *after* each heartbeat. The implication: when there's something to be scared of, your rapidly beating heart lets your brain know.[5]

- In addition to pumping blood, the heart also produces oxytocin, sometimes referred to as "the love hormone." Oxytocin supports bonding during breastfeeding, sexual activity, and cuddling.[6]

- Some nerve cells in the heart resemble cells in the hippocampus, a limbic structure involved in long-term memory storage.[7] And anecdotal evidence has shown that some heart transplant patients take on characteristics of their donors. Might the heart have a memory of its own?[8]

The Gut

- The enteric nervous system in your gut operates largely independently of the brain in your head. This mini-brain is home to roughly 100 million neurons—more than either the spinal cord or the peripheral nervous system. It is the only known part of the nervous system that can override messages from the brain.[9]

- Sensations of hunger and satiety are closely tied to positive and negative mood states, especially in infancy. As we mature, this gut-mood association develops further, linking up nuanced emotional experiences with specific sensations in the gut.[10] In fact, the very same brain cells involved in feeling sensations from the gut are *also* activated when we see another person in pain, hear about a disgusting experience, or feel a relaxed sense of calm.[11] Dr. Emeran Mayer at UCLA describes the gut as "a peripheral extension of the limbic system," or, in other words, a vital part of our emotional brain.[12] In daily life, this gut-mood connection is commonly expressed in idioms like "my stomach was tied in knots," and "he made me sick to my stomach."

- The gut produces 95 percent of the body's serotonin, a vital mood-stabilizing neurotransmitter. This is one reason SSRIs—a class of depression medications that change the availability of serotonin in the brain—often have digestive side effects.[13]

The Lungs

- The muscles that support breathing are densely innervated by your autonomic nervous system, which plays a central role in your fight/flight response.[14] That's why stress dissipates when you take a deep breath and a long, slow exhale. It's also why you "catch your breath" when you're startled, or sigh deeply when you're sad.

- Different breathing patterns are correlated with different emotional states.[15] Think about sobbing or laughing and you get the idea. The same is true of more subtle emotions, too. The way you habitually breathe affects your state of mind.[16]

The Vagus Nerve

- The vagus nerve innervates the heart, gut, and lungs directly, bypassing the spinal cord to snake straight up through the middle of you. Eighty to ninety percent of vagal nerve fibers are afferent—meaning they send signals *to* the brain rather than receiving signals *from* the brain.[17] We tend to think of the brain as a top-down command center, but this is about as outdated as thinking the world is flat. The brain in your head receives vastly more "bottom-up" input from your visceral organs than the reverse. In fact, in many instances it makes more sense to say the body leads the brain.

The Skin

- Skin conductance is used as a proxy for emotional arousal in the lab. Scientists from a wide range of disciplines measure subtle changes in the skin's dampness—and therefore its ability to conduct electrical signals—to indicate changes in emotional state. This coarse but widely used measure is rooted in the vital skin-brain connection.[18]

- The skin and the brain arise from the same layer of embryonic tissue. Three weeks following conception, a human embryo divides into three layers of cells. The outermost layer is called the ectoderm, and it goes on to form the spinal cord, the brain... and the skin.[19] In fact, scientists have recently discovered how to turn skin cells into brain cells in the lab.[20]

- From birth, we automatically know the difference between kind and aggressive touch.[21] This may be due to specialized nerve fibers that travel from the skin directly into the emotional brain.[22] These unique nerve fibers may also explain why children are more quickly soothed when kind words are coupled with kind touch.

The Connective Tissue

- Fascia, or connective tissue, is the largest organ in the body.[23] It has more sensory nerve fibers than any other part of the body, including the retina, previously thought to be our richest information-gathering tissue.[24] Surrounding every organ and sheathing every muscle, fascia ranges from a viscous, fluid-like substance to a dense, fibrous one. If you're a meat eater, you will recognize fascia as the filmy white tissue that encases a chicken breast, or the gristle that attaches meat to bone. In a living body, it's what allows muscles, bones, and organs to slide by one another when you bend and move. It is also, along with the skeleton, what enables the body to maintain its shape.[25]

- Fascia is densely innervated by the autonomic nervous system, which manages automatic emotional reactions such as the fight or flight response.[26] Many fascial nerves connect to the insula, a part of the emotional brain involved in self-awareness.[27] This connection is one reason why spending an entire day making sad faces in the lab can leave you feeling blue, as Dr. Paul Ekman of UCSF discovered during his explorations of cross-cultural emotional expression.[28]

Interoception is as vital to our daily life as exteroception, and yet most of us operate completely unaware of it. That's partly by design, and partly by convention. Biologically, our interoceptive senses are designed to be on autopilot as much as possible. This frees up attention for other things: poetry, sports, science. It also allows our bodies to maintain a healthy homeostasis without our conscious involvement.

But conventionally, we don't put much stock in our interoceptive senses. We spend years—often decades—in school honing our skills of logic and reason. We spend virtually no time at all honing our capacity to wisely use our sensory intelligence. Just as it's possible to have faulty reasoning, it's possible to have faulty interoception. It's possible for your heart to jump when there's no actual danger, or for your gut to be tied in knots over something that's really of no consequence. It's possible to hold your shoulders up around your ears for decades, creating an uninterrupted fascia-to-brain communication about your background state of anxiety. So just like developing good thinking skills, getting wise about this aspect of our intelligence takes training and time.

We also tend to dismiss our sensations, urges, hunches, and gut feelings as unimportant or unreliable. We treat our bodies as vehicles to get to the next meeting, objects to polish for the next party, or machines that we hire experts to fix. Rarely do we consider that our bodies might have wisdom worth listening for.

But, like it or not, interoception affects your actions every single day. If you've ever had an itch that you reached up to scratch without thinking about it, that's interoception at work. The below-conscious nature of these sensations will drive your actions without your conscious awareness.[29] This is how you wind up making impulsive, emotionally reactive choices that you later regret. Because your interoceptive senses are so closely tied to the emotional centers of your brain, sometimes you'll feel driven to "scratch that itch" before you even realize what you're doing.[30]

In everyday life that might look like a tightening in your gut that, before you know it, has you shouting at your child. It might look like a palpable sense of yearning that drives you to compulsively call that special someone over and over until regrettably, you push them away. It might look like a blush as you shrink in embarrassment, dismissing some highly public praise at work. It might look like an email that languishes for weeks in your inbox, because every time you look at it you feel squeamish. Or, as in Brian's case, it might look like an eager-to-please forward lean that had him caretaking at any cost.

When you're flooded with uncomfortable interoceptive sensation, the intensity demands action. Usually, your immediate reaction is to say or do something to make the discomfort disappear. That's essentially the definition of a knee-jerk reaction—an irresistible compulsion to act in ways that you may later regret. These intense but often invisible interoceptive sensations drive much of our emotionally reactive behavior.[31]

In other words, your sensations often drive your actions. And because interoception is so automatic and so invisible, you're usually not even aware that's what's happening.

The good news is this oblivious state is not a life sentence. It is entirely possible to become more aware of your interoceptive sensations. When you do, you gain far more choice about your responses—a process we'll continue to explore throughout the rest of this book.

Proprioception

Proprioception, a third class of sensory experience, encompasses your sense of balance and tells you where your body is in space.

> Get still for a moment. Without looking, do you know where your left hand is in relation to your left hip? Where your left foot is in relation to the floor? What direction your head is tilted?
>
> As you're reading this, slump into your chair. Let your arms go slack. Let your chest collapse, maybe drop your head a bit. Think of the last time you felt really down about something. Let that memory take hold for a moment.
>
> Now say out loud, with as much enthusiasm as you can muster, "I'm having a fantastic day!"
>
> How was that? I'll bet your tone of voice is a dead giveaway about just exactly how "fantastic" you do (or don't) feel. When I do this exercise in groups, people often burst out laughing at the obvious and ridiculous incongruence.

This is proprioception. It is the internal intelligence that signals the position of your body and it, too, affects your social life and mood.[32]

Actors and artists know this. They learn to convey subtle emotions through the slump of the shoulders just so, the jutted chin, the crossed legs, the tapping foot. Just as Dr. Paul Ekman did in his lab, actors can make themselves feel anxious or nauseated, delighted or surprised, simply by how they inhabit their bodies.

Athletes know it, too. Proprioception is the class of sensation that allows a player to collide with a fast-moving ball at just the right direction and velocity to score. It's how gymnasts flip on the balance beam and how the New York City Ballet delights awestruck audiences night after night. Athletes rely on far more than just fitness and strength to get the job done.

While superhuman proprioception is an essential skill for athletes, actors, and artists, every one of us relies on it every day. Without proprioception, you couldn't pilot a car around a curve, ride a bicycle, drink water without spilling, or get a spoon to your mouth. Clumsy? Blame your proprioceptive sense (or lack thereof).

Proprioception relies on the vestibular system in your inner ear, which guides your sense of balance.[33] It also encompasses the nerves in fascia, as well as specialized nerve cells in your muscles known as spindle cells.[34] Combined, all of these inputs tell you where your body is in space, without your having to so much as think about it. Well, perhaps as a toddler you concentrated more intently as you discovered your limbs and learned how to use them. But as you learned how to crawl, walk, and run; how to reach and receive; how to place objects where you mean to; your sense of balance and movement became automatic.

You just experienced for yourself how shifting your body, even in minor and contrived ways, can influence mood. Biologists have long known that across species, open postures tend to signal and grant access to power and resources, whereas closed postures do the reverse. Dr. Amy Cuddy's popular research at Harvard Business School suggests that not only does this axiom apply to humans, but also that we can deliberately change our own internal sense of power—as well as others' perception of us—simply by changing our posture.[35] In Chapter 8 we'll take a closer look at what her controversial research has to say about how proprioception affects real outcomes in real life—important ones such as whether we get the job, the date, or the cooperation we've been asking for.

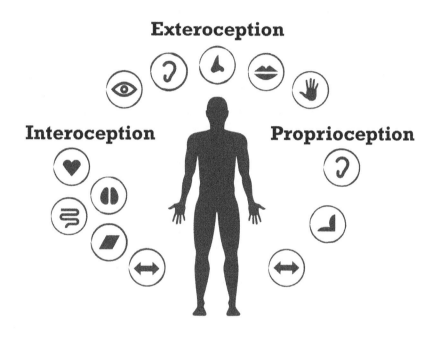

Three classes of embodied perception:
Exteroception includes sight, sound, smell, taste, touch.
Interoception involves the heart, lungs, gut, skin, and fascia.
Proprioception involves the inner ear, specialized muscle cells, and fascia.

Embodied Self-Awareness

Dr. Alan Fogel, in his excellent book *The Psychophysiology of Self-Awareness*,[36] lays out a model for two different kinds of self-awareness. Conceptual self-awareness is what you use to remember your address and construct your personal history. It relies on the body and brain areas for speech and language, including the muscles in your face.

Embodied self-awareness, on the other hand, encompasses all of interoception, exteroception, and proprioception. It is a whole-body sensory process that involves your entire extended neuromuscular system, your deepest visceral sensations, and some of the most emotionally-oriented parts of your brain.

	Conceptual Self-Awareness	Embodied Self-Awareness
	the self *thinking* about itself	**the self *experiencing* itself**
Basis	based in language and symbols rational, logical, explanatory abstract, transcends the present	based in sensing, feeling, acting spontaneous, creative, open concrete, lived in the present
Experienced As...	facts, details, information, ideas, insights narrative, perspective, story, interpretation past and future awareness	temperature, pressure, movement, pain breath, energy level, mood, emotion present-moment awareness
Nervous System	facial muscles & cranial nerves speech & language centers of the brain	entire somatosensory nervous system sensory-motor cortex, insula, ventromedial prefrontal cortex

adapted from Dr. Alan Fogel

These two types of self-awareness are both crucial for daily living. The gift of conceptual self-awareness is that it can take you anywhere in time. You can learn from your past and project inspired visions into the future. You can organize your self-understanding into a coherent story that helps you make sense of your life and make better choices as a result.

Embodied self-awareness also offers many gifts, which we'll continue to explore in the coming chapters. When people begin to build stronger embodied self-awareness, they start spontaneously saying things like "I hear the birds now—I never noticed them before," or, "I'm more aware of the warmth of the sun on my skin," or, "I don't know why, but I feel more connected to my friends and family now." More than one client has told me that the grass actually looks greener following a coaching session—and unlike Brian, those clients weren't color blind to begin with.

Whereas conceptual self-awareness takes you anywhere in time, embodied self-awareness takes you to *this* moment in time. Because sensation can only be experienced in the present moment, embodied self-awareness brings you home to the only moment you ever have for sure, which is right ... *now*.

> *You can experience this for yourself by trying a simple experiment. Choose an internal sensation to focus on—something you're experiencing in your body right now. Let's say, for example, that your eyes are squinting. Or that your hand is holding this book in a relaxed fashion. Or that your toe feels a little bit squished. Notice what the sensation is and describe it briefly: squinty eyes, relaxed hand, squished toe.*
>
> *Now change your position so that the sensation goes away. I was sitting on my foot, so I just moved my leg and wiggled my toes.*
>
> *When you do this, notice that once you adjust your position, <u>you can no longer feel that same sensation</u>. You may feel the residual effects of it—instead of feeling pressure, my toe is now a little tingly. Using conceptual self-awareness, you can think about how your toe or hand or eyes felt a moment ago. But you can't actually <u>feel</u> the same squished sensation unless you sit on your foot again.*
>
> *In other words, you can only <u>experience</u> any given sensation in the present moment.*

While this may sound obvious, it's actually quite profound. The implication is that your moment-to-moment sensations are a powerful and always-available means to bring you present. And when you are more present—when you can *feel* yourself more—all manner of benefits accrue. In upcoming chapters we'll explore just what those benefits are and how embodied practice gives rise to them.

Recall that we are biologically designed to filter out a great deal of sensory input, and nowhere more so than with those smaller, slower interoceptive nerves. In fact, interoception only reaches conscious awareness when it crosses a certain threshold of emotional significance. Before that, it simply drives your actions without your conscious involvement—you'll "scratch that itch" without even realizing what you're doing.

But as you become more aware of your sensations, you introduce the possibility of *choosing* your response. Which is why strengthening your capacity for embodied self-awareness is a first step toward developing more courage, compassion, composure, and all manner of personal qualities that support your success and satisfaction. These may be bold claims, but they're rooted directly in our biology.

Embodied Learning and Change: The Power of Neuroplasticity

If you want to develop those qualities, your best bet is to follow the original process of biobehavioral learning. And that process is, as we now know, inherently embodied.

Although we automatically tune out much of our sensory experience—especially our interoceptive experience—it is absolutely possible to train the body and brain to make those signals stronger. The science of neuroplasticity reveals the hopeful news that it's far more possible to change your brain than biologists once believed. As little as two or three decades ago, many doctors still thought the brain changed very little in adulthood, if at all. With the advent of new technologies that let us peer inside the living brain, we now know that's not true. While the pace of change slows as we age, our bodies are always in a state of becoming.[37]

We tend to think of the body as solid, fixed, and immutable, but nothing could be further from the truth. Our bodies undergo constant change from the day we're born until the day we die... and beyond. We've all heard stories of people who have made radical changes to their level of health, fitness, and weight. And every few years all of the cells in your body are replaced with completely new materials as cells die off and are replaced.[38]

With all this change, we ought to think of the body more like a river than a rock. Like a river, the body is constantly exchanging new for old, renewing and replenishing tissues and cells. This is why wounds heal. It's also how the food you eat becomes your flesh and bone.

Given this, our capacity for change is often vastly underestimated. With enough practice, stroke victims have been able to regain the use of their semi-paralyzed limbs.[39] By training their attention, people suffering from obsessive-compulsive disorder have rewired their brains... and vastly reduced their symptoms.[40] With the right kinds of interventions, we can change our brains—as well as those stubborn neuromuscular patterns that have created biobehavioral blind spots.

Several elements of neuroplasticity play a central role in psychobiological learning both early in life and later on.

- **Relationship**: Experience-dependent brain development occurs embedded in social environments. Our emotional brain—including the distributed part of our brain that reacts to intensely emotional moments with a blush, a shudder, or a sigh—takes shape in relationship with important others, including caregivers, teachers, coaches, and peers. As Lewis et al. put it in *A General Theory of Love*, "It takes a limbic system to rewire a limbic system."[41] When you want to develop new actions and habits, you need close relationships with others— clergy, counselors, coaches, friends, or a learning community— to support that change.

- **Emotional Engagement**: Learning only happens, says neuroscientist Michael Merzenich, when the behavior is important to the organism.[42] Strong emotions support the neurobiological conditions for learning. Joy, anger, and fear release certain neu-rotransmitters—dopamine, norepinephrine, and more—that play a key role in learning and memory formation by strength-ening neural connections.[43]

- **Attention**: Experienced meditators have a thicker prefrontal cortex than non-meditators.[44] And I've already mentioned how stroke patients and OCD patients have changed their brains. In another experiment, participants wore blindfolds for a week. Within a few days the brain had already linked hearing to the visual cortex, associating certain sounds with previously famil-iar sights.[45] Our brains take shape based on where we repeatedly rest our attention. So you would be wise to pay attention to, well... what you're doing with your attention.

- **Practice**: When your brain learns, neurons throughout your entire distributed nervous system undergo structural and chemical changes that make them more likely to fire.[46] This learning happens through intensely emotional events as well as through repetition over time.[47] Whatever language you were immersed in while growing up, your brain wired your speech and hearing to match its native sounds. If your brother sits on your left at the dinner table and strikes you most evenings, you may wire in a left-sided tension that's easily triggered by future mealtime disagreements.

- **Movement**: The cerebellum, a part of the brain involved in physical balance, is tightly tied to the emotional brain.[48] This may explain why habitual movements that become part of our physical structure can influence how we see the world. (Recall that your body is both a lens of perception and an instrument of action.) Right-handers tend to associate a rightward direc-tion with "goodness," whereas lefties usually see the opposite. But they both agree that up is good and down, bad. This and many similar studies show that how you habitually move, sit, and stand affects your perspective on the world.[49]

These five elements of neuroplasticity contribute to our learning early in life, but for new learning in adulthood you need more thing:

- **Disruption**: I've talked about de-armoring—the disruptive process of unlearning that is so necessary to adult development. This deliberate interruption of tightly wired behavioral patterns that have been on autopilot for years—sometimes decades—is what Brian achieved when he beat the bolster. But de-armoring is rarely so dramatic. It's possible to disrupt long-held patterns through certain forms of emotionally engaged bodywork, for example—a quieter process, by far. Although it's less common, it's also possible to disrupt armoring through conversations that reveal incontrovertible disconfirming evidence of old beliefs and assumptions.[50] Often, when we berate ourselves for being unable to change, it's because we haven't done the necessary embodied unlearning. Disruption is a vital part of learning and change in adulthood.[51]

The bottom line: Psychobiological learning is an inherently *experiential* process. Your best shot at gaining the many benefits of increased embodied self-awareness is to follow this original process of biobehavioral learning.

What Becomes Possible

Because of the way our sensory perception is tied to the emotional and social parts of our brain, strengthening embodied self-awareness has a wide range of benefits. Training to increase embodied self-awareness can help you align with a sense of purpose and meaning, make a bigger contribution, experience more satisfying connections with others, find the courage and composure to face down challenges, and step into more powerful and authentic leadership. In short, you can come to embody the kind of social and emotional intelligence that is critical for success in life and leadership.

Thanks to Daniel Goleman's groundbreaking work popularizing emotional intelligence, it is now common knowledge that your EQ has a far greater impact on your success in professional and personal life than your IQ.[52] And that's good news, because your EQ—which encompasses both emotional and social intelligence—can absolutely be developed. That's what the rest of this book is all about.

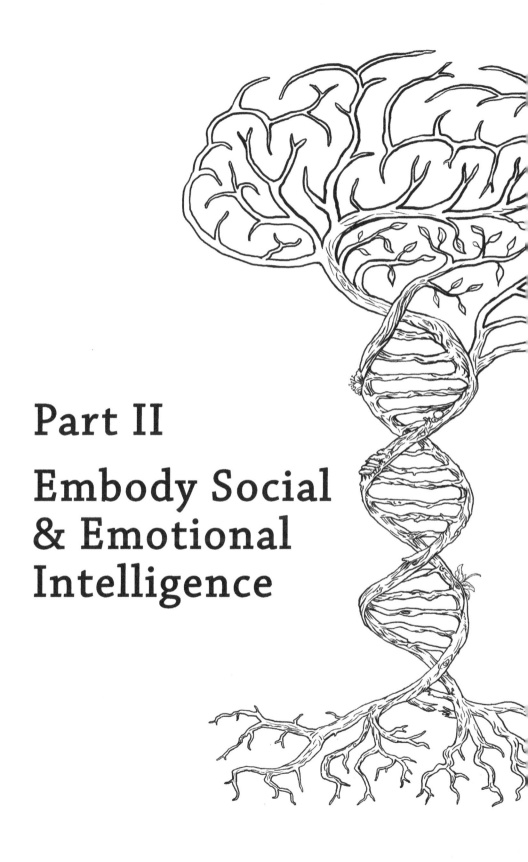

Part II

Embody Social & Emotional Intelligence

SECTION

1

Find Purpose

All acts of leadership—whether personal, professional, organizational, or societal—begin with a clear sense of purpose. But sometimes that sense of purpose is murky or elusive, buried under countless distractions. And even when your vision is clear, it can be challenging to take sustained action toward your desired future.

So how do you build the clarity and commitment you need to pursue a meaningful life and make a contribution that matters? In this section, we'll hear stories from a handful of individuals who have done just that.

Chapter 4, "Care," tells the story of Peter Maynard, a preoccupied banking executive who learned how to reconnect with his family, his heart, and a meaningful vision. In Chapter 5, "Choose," I'll tell you how I conquered chronic indecision as I tried valiantly to chart a course through life in early adulthood. Then in Chapter 6, "Commit," we'll hear from Jennifer and Helena, two women who both struggled to take action on what they cared about—and one of whom succeeded. And in Chapter 7, "Contribute," we'll return to Peter's story to discover how making choices and commitments from his felt sense of care affected not only his own life, but also the lives of dozens of employees, as well as the health of the planet.

These stories were not chosen randomly. They fit into a framework that we'll be exploring throughout Part II: a model for how you can come to embody greater social and emotional intelligence. Throughout Part II we'll take a tour through the elements of the following chart, exploring in detail how your capacity to *sense, center, get present,* and *galvanize from care* affects your day-to-day actions, success, and satisfaction.

Over the past few decades it's become increasingly common knowledge that emotional intelligence has an enormous impact on both success and satisfaction in life. But many people are still somewhat murky on what emotional intelligence actually *is,* and even less certain about how to develop it.

Fundamentally, emotional intelligence is the ability to be aware of and manage your own moods, and to take action on your own behalf. Social intelligence relies on those same skills of awareness and action, as applied to others. It's the ability to accurately pick up on others' emotions and to rely on that understanding in order to skillfully take action as a coordinated group. And somatic intelligence—the ability to discern subtle nuances between different bodily states, moods, and thought patterns and to respond effectively to those nuances—is the underpinning of both social and emotional intelligence. As we progress through Part II, we'll tour each of these dimensions of social and emotional intelligence as we explore how to develop self-awareness, self-mastery, empathy, and social dexterity through embodied practice.

Embody Emotional and Social Intelligence

	AWARENESS	ACTION
Emotional Intelligence – **SELF**	**FIND PURPOSE** *align w. yourself + the mystery* core skill: *self-awareness* somatic competency: SENSE Care Choose Commit Contribute	**BUILD RESILIENCE** *settle + strengthen yourself* core skill: *self-mastery* somatic competency: CENTER Courage Composure Confidence Credibility
Social Intelligence – **OTHERS**	**DEEPEN EMPATHY** *listen deeply...* *w. all of your senses* core skill: *empathy* somatic competency: PRESENCE Connection Compassion	**INSPIRE OTHERS** *act from centered care...* *for self + others* core skill: *social dexterity* somatic competency: GALVANIZE Communicate Collaborate Conflict to Consensus

Adapted from Daniel Goleman and others

Collectively, the stories in this section reveal a path to purposeful action: Connect with your felt sense of care, make wise choices, and commit to making a contribution that is rooted in what you care about. The core skill that supports this process is self-awareness. And self-awareness is undergirded by an essential somatic competency: the capacity to *sense* yourself. This means becoming aware of all of your sensations and emotions, at a finer and finer level of detail, until you are self-aware not just in a *conceptual* way, but in an embodied way, too.

That requires building your capacity for interoception and pro-prioception—not just for their own sake, or to perform some athletic task—but rather to accurately inform you about what you care about and what move to make next. The somatic competency of sensing is about becoming more acutely aware of your postures, gestures, movements, and subtle internal sensations. This capacity forms the foundation for all of the other competencies and qualities I talk about in this book, so we begin here.

Self-awareness, as we've already seen, involves both embodied and conceptual elements. In fact, researchers at the University of Iowa have discovered that people with damage to the neural networks involved in embodied self-awareness have measurably reduced emotional intelligence.[1] With a lower capacity for emotional awareness, these folks make poorer decisions and struggle with important life outcomes. (More on this topic in Chapter 5.)

On the flip side, expanding embodied self-awareness connects you to your felt sense of care and supports a commitment to making the contributions you choose. This is not just a work-related pursuit; it is a life pursuit. It affects you as a citizen, parent, spouse, friend, and volunteer. It is about knowing what matters to you in a deep, holistic, felt-sense way, and consistently aligning your actions with that care. Doing that requires both conceptual and embodied self-awareness. In the next few chapters we'll see how.

Practices to help you sense more can be found in
Appendix A and at yourbodyisyourbrain.com.

4

Care

Peter: The Heart of a Banker

Peter Maynard raked his hands through his dark brown hair, shaking his head as his boss lodged the career dagger a little farther into his heart. "We're not going to use this model, Peter." All around the conference table his colleagues shifted uncomfortably in their seats. Visibly agitated, Peter lodged a weak protest. "But..." He had worked hard on this project. He knew he was a good statistician. And he was proud of his creation.

"I don't want you to just go *build* a model, Peter," his manager interrupted. "I want you to take a step back. Look at the big picture and tell me what kind of model you think we need, and why. And show me you've got other people's buy-in on your idea." As the meeting drew to a close, the bankers gathered their papers and took to the corridors, heading back to their offices in twos and threes.

Peter Maynard is a tall, lanky economist, a self-described introvert who curls to his numbers, long thin fingers flying over the computer keyboard like a concert pianist. His superb statistical skills earned him two promotions in two years, and by 2004 he had risen to the director level at Capital One, one of the nation's largest banks. It was when he moved to the newly created Collections Division that his meteoric rise began to stutter.

"It was devastating," Peter says of this particular encounter. "Complete rejection."

Peter's job had shifted from statistical modeling, which he excelled at, to influencing others. "I was smart," Peter told me, "but so what? That didn't amount to much. I had been promoted to a leadership role, but I really had no idea how to lead."

Over the winter holiday, he stole time from family and festivities to cook up a new approach to his model in response to the tough feedback he'd received. Back in the office come January, he shopped his reconfigured idea around amongst the business leaders in Collections. They provided valuable feedback and suggested some important refinements. "I really should have *started* by talking to people," he said. "But that honestly never occurred to me. I finally got there, but I definitely took the long road."

This kind of collaboration didn't come naturally to Peter. He didn't oppose it; he just wasn't accustomed to it. During his childhood, Peter's mother often teased him for getting lost in thought midsentence. His ideas would captivate him like so many errant butterflies, and before he knew it, he'd hear her saying, "Earth to Peter..."

Thoughtful and studious, Peter often kept to himself as a child, wandering for hours in the world of his imagination. This approach to life—deeply embodied after decades—worked well for him all the way through graduate school and beyond. But once he was promoted to a leadership role, Peter realized he had a lot to learn. "I didn't know what I didn't know," he told me. "There was a whole world around me that I wasn't even aware of."

Keen to rise to the challenge of his new role, most weeks Peter spent sixty or seventy hours at the office. But he didn't let the sense of overwhelm curb his ambitions. While he burned the candle at both ends, his pregnant wife stayed home with their two young children. They were expecting twins. "With two kids, I could kind of get away with working myself to death," Peter said. "But we were about to double that. With four, there was no way I wasn't helping out at home."

It was against this backdrop of increasing intensity that Peter Maynard first encountered Peter Luzmore. Capital One enlisted Luzmore's company, Synthesis, to help Peter's team merge with another.

Peter anticipated the two-day meeting with Synthesis with about as much enthusiasm as a visit to the dentist. He rolled into the parking lot at the lush Kingsmill Resort and tromped toward the richly appointed grounds expecting a long dull day of PowerPoint parades and droning speeches.

Instead, Luzmore kicked off the morning by asking the dozen or so attendees to pull their chairs into a circle. "I want you to have a conversation about what you care about," Luzmore began. "What do you value? What makes you who you are?"

Peter raised his eyebrows. He hadn't expected this.

One by one, the participants shared their personal and professional hopes. They spoke candidly about why they had chosen—or in some cases, stumbled upon—their careers. They talked about how they spent their free time, and why. They spoke about their families, their hobbies, and the causes they believed in.

Although many of them worked together daily, these were new conversations. Luzmore encouraged an openness that gave rise to closer relationships. By the end of the morning, the bankers were laughing more and listening more. They felt more like a team.

In the afternoon, a representative from their customer base joined them to speak about *his* cares and concerns. When he left, the members of the new team turned their attention to generating ideas for the future. How could they pool their strengths and interests to create something really worthwhile for the customers they served? They spent the remainder of the two days crafting a vision for their new unit and mapping out a plan for getting there. Looking at what it would take to bring that vision to life, Peter's excitement grew.

"I left that offsite feeling totally refreshed," Peter says. "It was amazing." Previously, meetings like this one had always been draining. But Luzmore did things differently, and Peter found himself energized by the unfamiliar approach. He wondered if Luzmore might know of something that would help him tame the perfect storm of growing responsibilities ahead. Peter asked how he could learn more.

Conversations about values are frequently viewed as stealing time from the work at hand. We all have more than enough to get done each day, and making time for conversations such as these often seems like a luxury. In a business setting, it falls resoundingly on the side of the "soft stuff" that can be maddeningly tricky to measure and tie to results. So it's easy to put it off for later, or sometimes, never.

And yet, anyone with a vision needs to paint a compelling picture of the future—preferably with the input of those who will have a hand in building it. The most successful undertakings "start with why," as Simon Sinek points out in his popular book of the same name. The first act of leadership is to envision a new future and to declare it will be so. Clarity about shared purpose is critical to engaging others and to enlisting resources. So conversations about purpose, meaning, and values are hardly idle chatter. Finding and harnessing the shared meaning at the heart of any endeavor is a central act of leadership.

Meaning is also one of the core pillars of positive psychology, alongside positive emotion and deep engagement.[1] The relatively new field of positive psychology was established in 1998 to study mental health and thriving, rather than mental disturbance and disease. Since that time, researchers have conducted thousands of studies that affirm the rather common sense news that connecting to a sense of purpose larger than ourselves is critical to thriving. When people do work that matters to them, they give their best efforts and go home happier at the end of the day.[2]

Perhaps that sounds like a self-centered pursuit, and it certainly can become so. But research shows that our own state of mind affects others up to three degrees of separation away. Nicholas Christakis and James Fowler, in their groundbreaking investigations of the power of social networks, have measured emotional contagion across widespread networks of relationships. Like the common cold, emotions spread through groups and create a ripple effect: Happier people breed more happy people, including your friend's friend's friend. And happiness depends, in large part, on cultivating meaning.[3]

So finding a meaningful path through life is an enormous gift not only to yourself, but also to the rest of us as well. Whether you derive that meaning from relationships with family and friends, through work or sports or art, through spiritual pursuits or social activism—it *matters*. Failing to factor in meaning can lead to lives of quiet desperation, in which we inadvertently (and often, resentfully) spend time and energy building a world that nobody particularly wants to live in.

The importance of infusing your life with meaning can hardly be overstated. And discovering a sense of meaning, as you may have already begun to suspect, is best done by involving your body.

Luzmore responded to Peter's question by inviting him to join a week-long workshop known as the School of Embodied Leadership.[†] A rigorous dawn-to-dusk program of intense physical and mental training, the school was designed to help leaders improve their performance on a number of measures, including the ability to build trust with others, fight for what they cared about, and perhaps most importantly, know what that was.

Peter was again surprised. The two dozen participants talked about values here too... and then went well beyond that. Each day began with sit-ups, push-ups, and running. That might have been followed by a meaty philosophical conversation about the true nature of power. Or

---

† The School of Embodied Leadership emerged out of Richard Strozzi-Heckler's work with the Army Special Forces, which I described briefly in the Introduction.

perhaps a unique kind of arm-wrestling match designed to test determination more than physical strength. Or maybe they'd engage in a slow, tai-chi-like series of movements choreographed to foster connection. Everyone's leadership ability was tested real-time in small teams that rotated leaders and community chores daily. Each person was assessed, directly and publicly, on his leadership capability, and received suggestions for improvement from both coaches and peers.

When I asked Luzmore how the program affected Peter, he laughed. "He grew by about three inches!" he said with a grin.

Like many tall men, Peter had a habit of stooping, caving in his chest and dropping his head. But this unconscious attempt not to overwhelm others came at a cost. During the program, fellow participants told him that while he seemed very capable, he also came across as distant and inaccessible. This was a biobehavioral blind spot for Peter—the invisible thing that tripped him up without his even realizing it. Although they'd only known him a few days, these participants were already echoing the message Peter had received when his boss demanded he get other people's buy-in on his plans.

Responding to this feedback and using some of the centering practices he had learned, Peter began to unfurl. Although it felt unfamiliar at first—even a little uncomfortable—he practiced straightening up to inhabit his full length. He became more present, Luzmore told me, and easier to connect with. He looked more dignified. There was a different light in his eyes.

Ten years later, Peter still speaks of his experience with a quiet reverence. "This somatic work is so powerful," Peter told me. "It's like... it connects you to your *soul*."

We both sat silent as that statement rang in the air. "How so?" I finally asked. "And what was that *like*?"

The quiet stretched out between us. "That's a really, really good question." Peter fell silent again. After a moment, he said, "I guess what happened was, I straightened up. I opened up my chest. And I really *felt* my heart."

As Peter made more space to feel the sensations in his chest, he opened the door to a world of internal information that had long been hidden in plain sight, much as color had been invisible to Brian. He found a wealth of wisdom inside that he had neither suspected nor imagined, much less had any idea how to access.

Your heart is one of the essential organs of your distributed brain. It has its own intrinsic nervous system: Small clusters of nerve cells known as neural ganglia monitor blood chemistry and heart rate, sending nine messages to the brain for every one sent the other direction.[4]

These messages travel by way of the vagus nerve. One of twelve pairs of cranial nerves that bypass the spinal cord and plug directly into the brain, the vagus nerve provides a communication highway between brain and viscera. Most vagal nerve cells—between 80 and 90 percent—send interoceptive signals from the trunk to the head.[5] In other words, your heart is constantly talking to your brain. This anatomy makes the vagus nerve and the organs it's connected to—particularly the heart and the gut—key players in the social and emotional sense organ that is your body.

The heart communicates with the brain in other ways, too. It is the rhythmic leader of the entire body: Breathing, brainwaves, and even blink rate are all affected by the pace set by your heart.[6] The startle of a near-miss car accident and the subsequent heart-pounding recovery sends rhythmic and electrochemical signals to the brain, sounding the severe-threat alarm. In nanoseconds your brain has already coordinated a complete physical response.[7] As I mentioned in Chapter 3, a small cluster of cells inside the amygdala fire six to eight milliseconds *after* each heartbeat. In other words, in addition to taking its cues from the surrounding world, oftentimes your brain takes cues about safety and danger directly from the pace of your heart.[8]

So if your heart is beating slowly or expanding with tenderness, your brain gets that message, too. Love is far more than a reflexive hormonal response, but even so, just thinking about someone you love can invoke the heart's production of oxytocin—a hormone that supports pair bonding.[9] Your heart speaks the silent physiological language of connection on a daily basis.

Poets have sung about this for centuries, of course, and every one of us has felt it: the way the heart blooms open like a flower in the presence of great love. Most of us were taught to envision the heart like a mechanical pump, its four chambers shunting blood from one end of the body to the other. This conception is accurate, insofar as it goes, but for centuries doctors have been perplexed by the unique shape of this muscle, unlike any other in the body. After decades of careful dissection, the Spanish scientist Dr. Francisco Torrent-Guasp discovered that the heart is shaped more like a double helix than a mechanical pump. When your heart feels squeezed, the muscle twists in on itself like a wrung-out towel. When it expands, it does, in fact, unfurl.[10] This sense of expansion and contraction in the chest can tell us a great deal about who and what we love, long for, and care about, should we choose to listen.

There is even some evidence that the heart holds implicit emotional memories. Earlier I mentioned that the heart contains a few cells that resemble hippocampal cells—specialized cells in the brain that play a critical role in long-term memory storage.[11] This, coupled with the process of armoring, may provide an explanation for some of the strange stories reported by heart transplant patients. In one case, a middle-aged woman began craving hot dogs and beer after receiving a new heart from a motorcycle-riding young man who loved both.[12] In several other cases heart transplant recipients have taken on similar kinds of characteristics typical of their donors, even when the donor's identity is unknown to them.[13]

Of course, your heart doesn't remember where you left your keys or the answer to three plus seven. But perhaps the heart's memory explains why a certain movie scene can trigger the tears of a long-ago lost love, or why your heart softens and lifts when your thoughts wander to quiet moments snuggling with your toddler. While the evidence on the heart's memory is far from complete, we do know that implicit memory and emotional armoring can affect physical structures long after the original learning took place. The heart is a muscle, and there's no reason to imagine it would be exempt from this process.

So the heart holds a vast store of wisdom, if we know how to listen. It offers a direct assessment of danger. It affects your sense of connection. It expands in joy and contracts in fear. It holds some of your most touching, tender memories.

Tapping the heart's wisdom and sensing your deep care often requires literally making more room for the heart. Which is just what Peter did when he stood up straight, opened his chest, and began to listen more keenly to those quiet messages from within.

Back at the leadership retreat, Peter stood facing his partner, whose outstretched palm rested gently on Peter's chest. They were surrounded by pairs in a similar stance; the room was hushed. As he took in the kindness of the gesture, Peter felt himself lengthen up along his spine and expand across his shoulders. His partner asked him to speak aloud. "Peter, what do you care about?" he asked. "Who do you love? What really matters to you?"

Peter could feel his heart softening and opening in response to the question. Tears stung behind his eyes. "We're here for a limited time," he realized aloud. "And I really, really want to make the most of it." He spoke about his deep love for his wife and children. To his mild astonishment, he also found words pouring forth about his love for the earth.

Something about the long grass undulating on the hills outside the window brought his hometown of South Kingstown, Rhode Island, to mind. He flashed on a fragment of a memory, walking the land with his sister. As a child, his most direct path to school was through an idyllic New England farm long since fallen into disuse. Tefft Hill—the highest point in South Kingstown—was home to sacred native sites that few can locate and none will reveal.

Peter and his sister romped there in the afternoons, playing capture the flag with their friends after school. The two of them made an ongoing adventure of looking for the highest point, and he remembers the day they found it. Cresting a gentle rise, they turned to see all of Narragansett Bay to the east and the full sweep of the Atlantic Ocean to the south. Peter's heart swelled with joy.

Although he had always been a passionate man, for the most part Peter kept feelings like these to himself. He did his job diligently and well, and looked forward to curling up on the couch in quiet conversation with his wife at the end of each day. He was so busy parenting and pursuing career success that it had hardly occurred to him to devote attention to his interests outside of work or home.

But as he came to sense his care more and more, Peter began to give his connection to the land more weight. He vowed he would be more present for the environment. For him, that statement wasn't just about the earth. It included his family, as well. More than anything, Peter wanted to show up fully for the people and places he cared about most.

Try this: make a list of the people, places, activities, and causes that matter to you.

Now really *feel* your care for them.

For some of us—perhaps for you—this can be surprisingly challenging. It's not that you don't care, of course. It's that you don't necessarily know what to *do* in order to *sense* your care. We normally think of love as a capricious creature that comes and goes of its own accord. But it is entirely possible to cultivate the capacity to deliberately shift gears so that you can feel more of it, more of the time.[†]

"Look, I'm a numbers guy," says Peter. "My work is all about data, analytics, being in your head. Feeling is a lot harder for me. It was

---

† If you want to learn how to do this, Appendix A contains practices that will help.

really foreign at first. But if I can grasp this stuff, learn from it, and be a better person because of it, well... a *lot* of people can."

It may seem obvious to say so, but it's important to bear in mind that care is a *feeling*. Purpose is *palpable*. Listing your loves is an entirely different experience from feeling your love. And in fact it relies on entirely different parts of your brain. The list emerges out of conceptual self-awareness, which draws primarily on the speech and language centers. But it's embodied self-awareness that lets you genuinely *sense* your care.

Consider what Peter did:

- He stood up straight. This changed the position of his body in space and the proprioceptive inputs to his brain. It also literally made more space for his heart, amplifying the sensations in his chest rather than stifling them through the unconscious contraction of his habitual stoop.

- With the help of his friend's hand, he directed his attention to his heart. He felt inside, listening to the quiet whispers of his interoceptive sensations: an ache, a fluttering, an expansive sense of longing. And subtly, the hint of a memory...

- ... A memory fleshed out by his exteroceptive senses as he took in the grasses on the hills outside and flashed on his childhood explorations of Tefft Hill.

Recall that all of these aspects of embodied self-awareness affect your lens of perception. Peter always *knew* he cared about the earth, but until he returned to his *sense* of care, he'd more or less been ignoring it. And without really intending to, he'd been ignoring his family a bit, too, getting wrapped up in his work at the office and remaining distracted and preoccupied at home.

Peter's return to care had a significant impact on his life, as well as the lives of many others at Capital One and beyond. His story continues to unfold in Chapter 7, where we get to watch him make a large and unexpected contribution to his company and society. But first, we need to learn about some of the other elements that go into making such a contribution. Because your felt sense of care only gets you into the starting blocks.

5

Choose

Mandy: Axing Indecision

When I was in my early twenties, I brought my boyfriend along on one of our regular family ski trips. I have a large extended family—more than twenty-five relatives on my mother's side. As we stood at the top of the chairlift waiting for everyone to arrive, we got into what I thought was a perfectly ordinary, completely normal extended conversation about which run we would take.

My boyfriend was nonplussed. "Why are you guys debating this as if your lives depended on it?" he asked, shaking his head. "Why don't you each just pick whatever run you want and meet at the bottom?"

As insignificant as it sounds, this comment was pivotal for me. Having been raised in a family that was overly committed to group decision-making, it had literally never occurred to me to choose my own path down the mountain... or anywhere else in life. Growing up, one of the hallmark features of my family is that we all did everything together, all the time.

If there was a family event scheduled and you had a conflict, you were expected—and pressured—to move heaven and earth so you could be there. Absurdly, my grandmother once asked my mother to change the date of her employer's quarterly earnings announcement in order to make a family event run a little more smoothly. The unspoken rule: your individual needs are considerably less important than the needs of the group.

The strength of this approach is that it tied us together with a beautiful bond. We were a big, boisterous family that enjoyed an overflow of affection and good times. The weakness—for me at least—is that I never properly learned how to sense my own preferences. I spent so much of my life adapting to everyone around me, from such an early age, that I literally never learned how to carve my own line.

This makes me great in communities. I'm often told that I am the glue that bonds groups of friends together. I love this about my life, and it's a strength I treasure. But it's also served as a significant biobehavioral blind spot that has tripped me up again and again.

By the time I was a young adult, this biobehavioral blind spot was deeply embodied. Facing important choices about career, relationships, and life path aroused a palpable sense of dread and panic. I remember the feeling well. I would get tense and still, and in a shallow breath whisper a plaintive wail. "I don't *knooooow*," became the mournful anthem of my twenties.

Well-meaning mentors advised me to follow my heart, and I longed to heed this call. But I honestly couldn't understand what they were talking about. It was an interesting concept, but how would one actually *do that*? What did they *mean* follow your heart? How was I supposed to know what my heart felt? I had no idea. I couldn't perceive my own desires clearly, and I literally *could not imagine* that there could be another way. As it goes with most biobehavioral blind spots, I simply didn't know what I didn't know.

All my life I had been praised and rewarded for academic excellence. So naturally my default strategy was to think through big decisions as carefully as I could. As my college graduation drew near, I was lucky to have two really wonderful job opportunities: my dream job as an educator at a residential high school set on a working farm, and another exciting opportunity to work with executives leading wilderness-based leadership programs. One would take me far from home; the other was right on my university campus. One paid considerably more than the other. One was more comfortable given my skills, the other was more of a stretch. One was an idea I'd had in mind all along. The other was a brand-new opportunity I'd never even considered.

I remember sitting in a dark corner of the library, constructing a list of pros and cons about each option. I can still feel the pitted surface of the old wooden desk, the cramped quarters, the dimly lit corner. Above all I remember the sense of frustration that arose when I stared at that list and had no idea how to choose.

Ultimately, of course, I had to decide. Although I was strongly drawn to the executive education job, I wound up traveling across the country to work for the innovative high school that had flattered me with an unexpected job offer. For reasons I probably couldn't have foreseen, I was miserable there. I don't know that I would have been any happier in the other job, and I'm grateful for the year I spent among the truly exceptional faculty, staff, and students. But it turns out that the work I do now is quite a bit closer to the job I didn't take than to the one I did.

This story of indecision played out over and over again throughout my twenties. If I had an important choice to make about a job, a relationship, or where to live, I would call my friends and ask what *they* thought I should do, rather than consult with myself. Even making choices off a dinner menu could leave me sweating bullets. Looking inside for answers was something I had just never learned how to do. I took my friends' advice seriously, and I often followed it. I continued to make spreadsheets to analyze even the simplest of decisions. And I struggled mightily to find joy and satisfaction with my life.

Imagine you're a participant in a research study. You walk into the room and sit down in front of four decks of cards. The experimenter hooks you up to a skin conductance monitor that tracks your nervous system arousal. She then explains your task. You are to pull cards from each deck. Every now and then you'll pull a card that has a payout— say ten dollars, or maybe one hundred. Every now and then you'll pull a card that requires you to give money back. Your goal is to maximize your profit. Go.

You begin drawing cards randomly. Occasionally the researcher stops you to ask whether there's any rhyme or reason to why you're choosing from each deck. At first your answer is no, but gradually you might start to get a hunch that something's up. It seems like you have better luck in some decks than others.

And indeed you do. Unbeknownst to you, the decks are stacked. Two decks have more cards with a higher payout, but they also contain much bigger losses. If you were to pull from only those decks, you'd lose the game. The other two decks are stacked in the reverse: smaller payouts, but more of them, and fewer losses.

If you have a healthy brain, you'll gradually start to play profitably, pulling more often from the decks that are more likely to give you a small win. In fact, you'll start pulling from the more profitable decks before you even develop a hunch about what's going on, and well before you figure the game out, if you ever do. Fully one-third of participants never catch on that the game is rigged, and yet they *still* play advantageously, thanks to subtle sensory cues sent by their bodies. Because as it turns out, your body learns quickly which decks are more favorable. Your nervous system registers an anticipatory response to the big-loss decks long before the dim dawning of your hunch takes hold. And those subtle interoceptive signals buried below your conscious awareness sway your choice of cards.

But there's a twist. The tables turn when the game is played by people who have damage to their ventromedial prefrontal cortex (VMPFC). This area of the brain right behind your forehead helps you make meaning out of sensation and stores associations between prior experience and a given bioregulatory state. People who don't have full access to this part of their brain play very differently from those who do.

VMPFC-compromised participants begin the same way healthy participants do, by sampling cards from all the decks. But gradually, they begin to play disavantageously, pulling more and more from the decks with big wins and even bigger losses. Often they will continue playing this way until they lose, *even after they've figured out the game—* which about half of them do. Notably, their skin conductance graphs stay quiet. They show no anticipatory nervous system response when pulling from the disadvantageous decks, or from any deck at all.

The bottom line here is that people with VMPFC damage have limited capacity to *sense* their preferences, and hence they do not have the benefit of an embodied guidance system that quickly learns from prior experience and prompts future behavior. This decreases decision quality. Simply having knowledge of the best decision is insufficient, the researchers conclude. Quality decisions inherently rely upon subtle sensory guidance.[1]

Along with the VMPFC, several other areas of the brain, notably the orbitofrontal cortex, the anterior cingulate cortex, and the insula, are recruited for both embodied self-awareness and decision-making.[2] Anatomically speaking, your capacity to feel your sensations is inseparable from your ability to choose a wise course of action. In order to make good decisions, you must be able to *sense* your preferences.

This gives people with healthy brains and bodies an advantage: Their bodies subtly signal choices consistent with past experience and their behavior is biased accordingly. Learning happens throughout the whole body. Which is exactly how our biobehavioral blind spots form.

I used to heat my house with wood. This quaint way of life meant I spent a lot of time wielding an axe. At the time, I was working with a coach to explore some changes I wanted to make in my career. But what kept coming up again and again was my ambivalence about the on-again, off-again relationship I was in. So when he interrupted my repeated complaints to ask whether there was anywhere in my life I felt decisive, I had a ready answer: chopping wood.

We had an illuminating conversation about how it felt to chop wood and how ambivalence felt different. After that, my daily wood chopping chore expanded into a way to practice being decisive. And it worked. With a picture of neatly split and stacked wood on my refrigerator as a reminder and the familiar feeling of swift finality in my bones, I finally put an end to that unhealthy relationship. Inflated with my newfound sense of decisiveness, I also quit the job that I had previously enjoyed up until a new manager had been installed a few months prior. It was a true victory for decisiveness. And it led to one of the darkest, most painful periods of my life.

What was going on here? Swinging the axe is a decisive move. I thought more of that was what I needed. And something seemed to be working, because I was definitely swinging the axe pretty decisively in my life. It was abundantly clear that it was past time to leave both the relationship and the job. So why was I now worrying and second-guessing and fretting my way through a protracted period of heartbreak and loss?

No doubt some of it *was* a simple response to loss. But these were hardly the biggest losses I had experienced in my life. Something else was going on.

Here's what I now believe: While I had successfully trained my body to take more decisive action, a crucial piece was missing. I still hadn't learned how to *sense* my preferences. I knew what the "right" decisions were, and I put an end to my vacillating and enacted them. But those decisions were still missing a fundamental base of support from inside of me. Instead of fretting in ambivalence *before* the decision, I second-guessed and worried *after* it. It was the same discomfort of uncertainty; it just came at a different point in the process.

Make no mistake—these were unquestionably the right decisions for my life. I don't regret them, not for a moment. But the absence of my feeling-self from the process meant there was a lot less of me standing behind the decision. And I continued to suffer from the pain of ambivalence as a result.

Today, my sweetheart and I had a good laugh about this topic. He asked me what I was writing about, and I started to explain. "Well, I'm working on this section that used to have four chapters, but then I decided that it should only have three. But then I changed my mind and decided that I should split up one chapter into two, so today I'm working on two chapters called 'Choose' and 'Commit.' But I'm not really sure this is the best way to organize it, because..." I went on.

In his wry, understated way, he gave me a sideways look and pointed out:

"Well, you could just... *choose*."

Touché.

My partner sees me at close range, and he is well aware that I'll never be remembered for decisiveness as my greatest strength. But still, he's a beneficiary of the work I've done in this part of my life. Before I met him—an event that fortuitously happened to coincide with another more successful attempt to improve my ability to choose —I was fairly commitment phobic. Long after my peers had settled into careers, bought homes, and started having families, I was still on the hunt for the person, the place, and the line of work that suited me. Afraid to land on a particular choice lest it turn out to be the wrong one, I continued to vacillate in all of my important decisions. Ambivalence remained a familiar—if uncomfortable—home for me.

It was in this shaky and self-judgmental space that I one day finally heard that "whisper" that everyone else seemed to understand. At this point I had been studying embodied leadership for about six months. On a daily basis I was practicing a much gentler but still decisive series of martial arts movements. My practice included stating aloud what I cared about, then paying close attention to the feeling of my internal sensations and the quality of my movement as I went through the series of moves.

Because I had been practicing paying such close attention to my movement and sensations, I was able to "hear" that quiet whisper when one day an unfamiliar and yet totally unmistakable sense of *rightness* descended over me. I was sitting on the floor in a training program, practicing a simple breathing exercise alongside another student. And suddenly, I just knew that this was what I was here to do. I didn't know what that meant or how I would do it. I just knew that this whole embodied leadership thing was my path.

This wasn't an idea and it wasn't a voice or a vision, though for some people intuitive hits can arrive that way. Instead, it was a simple felt-sense of *knowing*. That certainty was conveyed through a deep sense of peaceful stillness infused with open-hearted love and supported by unshakable ground. It was a physical, embodied sense of conviction. Right then and there I made a choice to pursue this path of learning, wherever that might lead me. I've now been on that journey for a solid decade, and it's clear I've only just begun.

About a year after this incident, I met the man I now share my life with. To tell you the truth, all my habits of ambivalence came roaring back. There were clear positive signs early on—hints of that same sense of knowing that I felt about my work. But choosing wisely is not just about being able to *feel* your sensations. It's also a matter of trusting them.

Trust is built over time. It may be weeks or months or maybe even years before you feel comfortable enough to tell your new coworker that actually, you can't stand your job. Or to reveal to a new friend that you're afraid your son might be an alcoholic. Feeling comfortable enough to share these kinds of secrets of the heart generally doesn't happen overnight.

The maxim "trust takes time" is no less true when the person you are building trust with is yourself. In my case, I had never before been so decisive as when I was swinging that axe. But I also hadn't built the basis of trust to feel confident in my choices.

I needed help learning to trust those early whispers about my partner. So I enlisted my friend, relationship expert and fellow somatic coach Paula Love, to help me uproot the blind spots around my habitual ambivalence. Over the course of several months, our work together helped me deepen my capacity to clearly sense what's important to me in an intimate partnership and align my actions and choices with that. Bringing those quiet messages into conscious awareness and learning to trust them is a skill, and it's one that's learned gradually over time, not in one fell swoop of the axe.

The more deeply I learned to feel my preferences, the more I was able to combine head knowledge with heartfelt sense to make the best possible choices for my life. As I learned to do this, I found my way into a life that includes far more meaning, contribution, intimacy, and love. I'm happier now than I've ever been—and it was a deep exploration of my embodied intelligence that got me here.

Consider the big choices you've made in your life. Have you ever made an important decision that was backed by your full intelligence, with all the clarity and settled sense of rightness that comes along with that?

Whether yes or no, it's worth taking a look at how you typically arrive at the choices you make. Perhaps you have a tendency to rely heavily on either your conceptual or your embodied self-awareness, making decisions either exclusively from rational analysis or solely from your gut. Both of these patterns can create biobehavioral blind spots. Either way, when you emphasize one aspect of your intelligence at the expense of the other, you miss out on important information that can help guide your choices.

Studies have repeatedly shown that emotional intelligence holds more sway than IQ in life and leadership success.[3] One reason is that people with higher EQ tend to make better decisions—decisions are rooted in their *full* intelligence rather than just one narrow part of it. And of course better decisions lead to better outcomes.

If I told you that to get better results in your life you ought to stand up straighter, feel your heart more, and listen carefully to the whispers of interoceptive sensation, you might think I was crazy. But in actual fact that is *exactly* how you create better outcomes—by inhabiting your body more completely so you can harness your full intelligence. Something not working in your life? Learn to *sense* your preferences, and combine that knowing with your ample intellect before you make your next move. Happier days are ahead.

6

Commit

Helena: Embodying Enoughness

Peter Maynard connected to what he cared about, and that opened up a whole new set of possibilities for him. But an experience like that becomes nothing but a nice memory unless and until you can mobilize your care into action—until you can make clear choices and sustain heartfelt commitments. This principle is perhaps best illustrated in the breach.

Single mom Jennifer† came to me asking for help with work/life balance. As a highly sought-after Silicon Valley consultant and the mother of a ten-year-old, she was overwhelmed by the many daily demands she faced. She knew her son Ryan wasn't going to be young forever, and she was afraid if she didn't learn how to put boundaries on her client relationships she'd miss his childhood, shortchanging both him and herself.

---

† Name and identifying details changed.

Because she worked at home, and because of the 24/7 nature of the technology business, she found it exceedingly difficult to turn off her electronic tethers and go shoot some hoops or do a puzzle with her son. She always *meant* to make quality time for him, but most days ended with a sense of disappointment that once again, she had devoted herself to client demands over the life of her family.

Jennifer's clients loved her work, and one of the things they appreciated most was how responsive and available she was. They regularly praised her reliable delivery and quick turnaround times, and she was proud of that. In the past she'd timidly tried to put boundaries around her work life, but before her clients even had time to object she'd be seized by fears that the money would dry up, and back to the computer she'd run.

My instinct was to help Jennifer articulate why it was so important for her to spend time with Ryan. While it may seem self-evident that a parent would want to show up for her child, there are as many reasons for this as there are parents. Jennifer found it helpful to reflect on her reasons, and as she became more clear about why she cared about making this change, she left our early sessions with a strong sense of motivation.

But as time went on, she still struggled to put the computer away. Clarity about her reasons wasn't enough. So next we explored what happened for her when a client called or an email came in. What would she do? What did she say to herself? What were the underlying beliefs about work, money, and parenting that drove her compulsion to respond immediately?

As we talked about these questions, Jennifer started to make progress here and there. She realized that she automatically assumed her clients needed to hear back from her right away; it had never really occurred to her to ask when they needed a reply. She also discovered that some of her sense of self-worth was entangled with being an ultra-responsive consultant. These insights led to the occasional win: she made it to her son's soccer game this time, or they watched a movie together. We started to codify some of the changes she was making—always turn off the computer by six p.m. Let good enough be your end point, rather than perfection. Renegotiate some of your deadlines with clients. Let them know you won't be answering emails on the weekend.

Jennifer found it helpful to lay out these sorts of plans, and she had considerable enthusiasm for implementing them. But when the rubber hit the road, she continued to struggle to put her good ideas into action. Despite her clarity and her ample desire to change, she continued to get stuck. As our coaching engagement came to a close, Jennifer expressed her gratitude, but I felt like more was possible for her and I suspect she did, too. She was spending more time with her son, but not as consistently or as much as her ideal. And the changes she made were still more of a struggle than either of us would have liked to see.

Why was it so difficult for Jennifer to make the changes she sought? While her intention was strong and her motivation high, Jennifer's commitment to action was sorely lacking. At the time, I was mystified by this. She was clear about what she wanted, and she knew what she needed to do; so why wasn't it happening? As her coach I felt frustrated.

Knowing what I know now, I can go easier on both of us. I worked with Jennifer early on in my coaching career, before I was exposed to the experiential approaches that I explore in this book. Her story clearly illustrates the limitations of conceptual self-awareness as the sole point of intervention for creating change. What was missing is an *experiential* awareness of her moments of driven compulsion along with a felt sense of her longing to be more present with Ryan.

Without this experiential awareness—a tangible, in-the-moment, felt-sense awareness of the sensations, postures, gestures and moods that accompanied her compulsion—she really didn't have any direct point of intervention. All she could do was repeatedly tell herself, "I should really stop doing this," which is a setup for failure, self-blame, and shame. Deeply engrained embodied habits can be extremely difficult to change, even when you know exactly what you want to do differently and you know how.

I definitely did some things right with Jennifer, and one was to help her articulate her cares. We had quite a few clarifying conversations that were genuinely useful for her. But what I wasn't aware of at the time is that talking about what you care about is not the same as *sensing* your care. I don't recall doing anything to help her connect to her felt sense of care—the suffusion of joy, appreciation, warmth, openness, and expansion that her love for her son might evoke. We certainly explored this idea, but our exploration tapped only one aspect of her intelligence—her conceptual self-awareness.

As far as I'm aware, Jennifer had nothing wrong with the brain and body networks that would have helped support the choices she wanted to make. But just like you and me, she lives in a culture that has historically dismissed the wisdom of the body and its related emotions, hunches, and "gut feelings" as irrelevant at best and hysterical at worst. For most of us, Jennifer included, listening to these subtle sensations is hard. And the vast majority of the time, we don't even realize it might be worth doing.

Now I wonder about what sensations Jennifer might have experienced when she turned to her computer instead of her son. Were there any patterns in the way she would sit or stand or walk? Anywhere she felt cool or hot or jumpy or more calm? How was that different from—or similar to—how she felt when she was with Ryan? Answers to questions like these would have given us more leverage to help her deliberately shift from one to the other. It would have given us a different point of intervention that I've come to believe would have helped her far more.

The more we build our interoceptive and proprioceptive embodied self-awareness, the better we can become at making decisions and choices for our lives. Recall that interoception happens mostly outside of conscious awareness, and interoceptive discomfort drives our knee-jerk reactions. But when you deliberately pay attention to your sensations, you get the chance to make a more conscious choice about how you respond to the discomfort of fear, sadness, anxiety, or any other emotion.

I've come to believe that this was the missing link for Jennifer. She had very good *intentions*, but she was hard-pressed to put those intentions into action. Years later I had the opportunity to test this idea with a similar case.

Helena Solomon[†] is a bright, thoughtful woman in her early 60s. Like Jennifer, she faced challenges balancing her work and family life. When I met her she was three years into a relatively new relationship, and with Craig she felt she was finally getting it right. But there was one persistent bone of contention—a conflict that had plagued her previous relationships as well. Craig was anxious for her to slow down and just *be* with him, without any agenda or activity. Unfortunately, Helena found this impossibly difficult. As a self-employed strategy consultant to foreign aid organizations, her to-do list was never-ending. And like Jennifer, she had a compulsive addiction to her list. She felt "wired and tired"—an ultra-responsible professional who was completely exhausted but could never fully rest.

When I first spoke to Helena, she was upfront about having tried many avenues to ease the persistent anxiety that prevented her from slowing down. She had already done a great deal of personal growth work with psychotherapists, coaches, and even somatic practitioners. All of this had been helpful in various ways, but even so, the remaining anxiety she experienced was disheartening.

"I've just never found a practice I could tolerate," Helena said. She had tried both medication and meditation to soothe her constant anxiety. The pills had side effects she didn't like, and they hardly helped, anyway. Meditation, on the other hand, actually made her *more* anxious.[††]

Given all that she had already tried, I wasn't entirely sure I'd be able to help Helena, and I said so. But when I explained how I would approach her challenge, she said she wanted to give it a shot.

[†] Not her real name.

[††] It's not uncommon for trauma survivors to find themselves overwhelmed by uncomfortable sensations when they slow down their activities. The body holds on to unprocessed trauma and sometimes the only thing that keeps discomfort at bay is to stay in constant motion. If you like constant motion, that doesn't necessarily mean you're a trauma survivor—some people are just high energy! But for some people meditative practices can be temporarily contraindicated until they've de-armored from trauma.

As I had with Jennifer, I worked with Helena to help her clearly articulate the change she was longing for: a release from the grip of persistent anxiety and the capacity to slow down and be more present with her husband. But instead of immediately jumping into how she could make that happen, we began by looking carefully at how she experienced her anxiety. I encouraged her to bring details of her experience into the foreground by noticing and naming them. She discovered that her anxiety was accompanied by penetrating "eagle eyes" rather than a more diffuse attention. She realized she had several different "flavors" of anxiety, which she named Push Through, Flurry, and Watch Out. Each was accompanied by a different physiological signature: tension in her neck and shoulders, say, or a restless, agitated movement in all her limbs. Especially when there was no obvious point of completion—small talk at a cocktail party, say, or relaxing on the couch—she would get a panicky, prickly sensation in her esophagus and all through her core. "I had no idea these were all so different!" Helena exclaimed as she felt her way into these discoveries.

A few sessions in, I asked whether there was anyplace in her life where she already had an experience of slowing down. "Well, actually, yes," she replied with some surprise. She spoke about walking with her dogs, spending time with a close friend on a trip out of town, and giving her clients her undivided attention. The problem, it seemed, wasn't so much that she couldn't *do* what she wanted; it was that she didn't know how to *access* it. Sure, she could slow down and be more present at times, but it wasn't really something she deliberately chose. It felt more like something that happened *to* her.

When I asked Helena to describe these experiences of presence and ease, she drew a blank. Sputtering, she spoke only of what was absent. "Well, I don't have that feeling of anxiety," she said. "There's less tension. I don't feel as restless and jittery as I normally do." When I pointed out that she was describing this state of ease with far less detail and nuance than her state of anxiety, she was taken aback. "You're right," she nodded. "I guess I don't really have much of a sense of what it's like to be relaxed and present."

Over the next few weeks, Helena watched intently for signs of ease in her life. As she got more familiar with this state, she got better at describing it in terms of what was actually going on, rather than what was missing. She realized that when she was walking her dogs she felt wider between her shoulders, and that her chest, upper back, and neck were more relaxed. She looked up at the world around her, taking in the trees. Her jaw was relaxed, her teeth apart. Instead of those laser-focused eagle eyes she was accustomed to, she had more diffuse attention. A similar kind of relaxed and open-hearted stance was often present when she was working with her clients.

At our next session, we looked for what I sometimes call a "keystone"—one physical habit that holds the entire constellation together. Helena described it as a snag in a sweater: the piece that, when you pull on it, everything else comes along.

For Helena, this was her shoulders. We experimented with ways she could shift her shoulders from tension to ease regularly throughout the day. First she tried leaning back in her chair, lifting her eyes from her desk to get a wider view. As we explored this and other options, a memory came to mind of a bodyworker who used to put a hand on her chest while she was lying on the table. "I always found that very comforting," she said.

Experimenting, she leaned back in her chair, dropped her shoulders, and put her hands on her chest. "Is there something you can say to yourself that will support this state of ease?" I asked.

After a pause, "I am enough," Helena replied simply. "I do enough."

Tears welled up as she breathed a huge sigh of relief. "This feels *amazing*." She went quiet for a bit. Then, "Wow, I actually can't get tense in this position!" she exclaimed with astonishment.

This simple movement opened up a whole new perspective for Helena. (Recall that the body is an instrument of perception as well as an instrument of action.) "What does your to-do list look like from this vantage point?" I asked. She laughed. "I can see what's important," she said. "And not all of it is."

While this session was an important turning point, it was only a beginning. Helena decided she would lean back in her chair, place her hands on her heart, and tell herself "I am enough" five times a day. She set an alarm on her phone to remind her. But she arrived at our next session frustrated that she wasn't yet noticing a difference. I encouraged her to stay with it. "Musicians spend 80 to 90 percent of their time practicing," I pointed out. "Your body is still learning how to relax and be at ease. Just keep playing those scales. And don't be afraid to hit a few wrong notes."

By the next session, she was pleased to report that her body was automatically responding to the sound of the bell. This was an encouraging indication that she was starting to build the muscle memory for a sense of ease. A few weeks later, a dear friend of hers broke five bones in a cycling accident. Helena volunteered to take on much of his care. In the midst of the rush and intensity of this unfortunate event, Helena surprised herself by stopping spontaneously to widen across her chest and lift her gaze. "I am enough," she reminded herself. "This time, it's *not* all going to get done... *and that's okay.*"

These were significant wins for Helena, and they bolstered her commitment to practice. In the sessions that followed she reported that the practice was becoming integrated into her life. In fact, it wasn't long before she reached a point where she couldn't go through a day without stopping several times to relax and remind herself that she is already enough.

This embodied emotional practice didn't make Helena's discomfort with slowing down disappear overnight. What it did was gradually engrain the *felt sense* that wherever she was, whatever she was doing, she could lean back into a sense of relaxation and ease. This started to teach her overreactive, agitated, and anxious physiology that slowing down was safe, acceptable, and could even feel good. As she began to embody this deep sense of sufficiency through repeated psychophysiological practice, her capacity to set aside her compulsion and anxiety grew. At first gradually, and then more often, she was able to make time, space, and attention available to relax with her husband. She and Craig were both pleased.

In our last session, I asked Helena what she wanted to celebrate. "I stayed really committed," she said with satisfaction and pride.

A year after our coaching engagement came to a close, I had the chance to catch up with Helena. I was thrilled to hear that she was still regularly practicing leaning back, slowing down, and experiencing a sense of being enough. It had become a touchstone for her—a way to continually remind herself that her worth lies more in her presence than her productivity.

Jennifer had good intentions, great ideas, and high motivation. But she was unable to consistently galvanize her ideas into action. Good intentions, it turned out, were not nearly enough. Because the body is so deeply involved in making choices and decisions, and because all action involves the body, including her body in our coaching might have made all the difference.

The difference between my work with Jennifer and my work with Helena is that I had a way to offer Helena something to *do*. Jennifer had actions to take, too—she renegotiated some agreements with clients, stopped working by a certain time, and so on. What she didn't have was a way to *be and feel differently while doing those things*. She could renegotiate deadlines until she was blue in the face. But until she had a regular, repeatable experience of what it *felt like* to take action on her cares, she was operating with only half her intelligence. And what she most wanted remained just out of reach.

I've since come to believe that evoking sustained commitment requires a strong synthesis of conceptual and embodied self-awareness. It's vital to know where you're headed and why: to articulate a clear vision of the future and its importance. It's equally vital to connect to your felt sense of care, and then to consistently mobilize that care into action. This movement into action—and it is a physical *movement*, not an intellectual idea—is precisely what distinguishes true commitment from otherwise flimsy intentions.

	what it is	**where it arises from**
Clarity	ability to articulate your cares	conceptual self-awareness
Care	felt sense of care	embodied self-awareness: interoception, emotion
Choice	decision, volition, conviction	conceptual self-awareness embodied self-awareness: interoception
Commitment	movement, action	embodied self-awareness: proprioception

Lasting change requires clarity + care + a choice + commitment

Clarity, care, the capacity to wisely choose, and conviction about your chosen direction are each essential components of sustained commitment. Helena had all of these. And she regularly engaged in an embodied practice that built the change she sought into her whole nervous system, musculature, and worldview. This holistic approach made it easier for her to take action on her commitment in her everyday life. This is entirely different from having good intentions.

Co-activating the neural networks for embodied and conceptual self-awareness means more of you is involved in making a commitment. This makes it easier to align your actions with your cares and to sustain action over time. When challenges arise, more of you is literally "standing behind" your commitment. The challenges may not be any less difficult, but your commitment to overcoming them goes deeper. When you come to embody a powerful, sustained commitment to what you truly value, you can become an unstoppable force of love in action.

7

Contribute

Peter: Building the Environmental Council

Leaders throughout history—both the silent and the celebrated—operate from a powerful commitment to construct a future that is qualitatively different from the past. As Peter Maynard returned from the embodied leadership workshop, a commitment of this sort began to emerge.

Working with Luzmore, Peter took on a daily practice of connecting to his cares. Each morning, he spoke aloud his commitment to be present for the environment. He took ten minutes to sit still and pay attention to his sensations, which strengthened his interoceptive sense and over time made it easier to feel those previously invisible visceral messages. To connect with his family outside the distractions of meals and electronics, he took daily walks with his wife and children. As the children grew older, their walks turned into jogs. Now the six of them run together every day. Neighbors affectionately call them "the running family."

He also started to change some of his habits at home. Feedback from Luzmore and his peers helped him see how he disconnected from others when he got lost in thought. As he paid more attention to his in-the-moment sensations, he started experiencing deeper and more meaningful connections. One day his eighteen-month-old daughter made a tiny gesture in his direction—one he swears the old lost-in-thought Peter would have missed. He followed her up the stairs, where she climbed onto the kiddie toilet to solemnly demonstrate what she had taught herself by watching her older brother. It was a proud moment for both of them as their newfound skills created a sweet sense of connection.

Peter and his wife were both heartened by these changes, and Peter felt better equipped to be more present at home when the twins arrived. But it was Capital One that had paid for his training, and naturally the bank expected a return on its investment.

After the workshop, Peter returned to all the same challenges that he had faced before. His new role still required collaboration and leadership skills he was only just beginning to develop. He continued meeting regularly with Luzmore to sharpen these skills. Meanwhile, an idea started taking shape in the back of his mind.

A few years earlier, his childhood treasure Tefft Hill had been under threat from developers. Peter's father had joined the town water council so he could fight to protect this special place. The developers won a few rounds, but thanks to the council's efforts, alongside the new houses an undeveloped parcel of land remains permanently protected. Watching his father stand up for this precious place had been an inspiration to Peter. Now he saw an opportunity to do something similar in his own sphere of influence.

Peter wanted to find a way to make Capital One a better environmental steward. His day job granted him the organizational authority to lead, and he clearly had the technical skills, if not yet the people skills, to back that up. But his idea for an environmental council fell well outside the scope of his everyday responsibilities. And he wasn't even an environmental expert—he was just an ordinary guy who cared about the earth.

Recall how I'm defining leadership in this book:

a leader cares deeply.
he or she focuses on creating a new future, and
she or he has the skills to collaborate well with others.

Peter had reconnected to his sense of care, and—working with Luzmore—he was strengthening his capacity to collaborate. Together, they began to sketch out an approach to Peter's vague vision. His first move would clearly require him to engage others in bringing his nascent idea to life, putting his newly developing collaboration skills to the test.

A colleague of Peter's had recently moved to a position in another division. Their jobs no longer overlapped, but during a casual conversation one day, Peter mentioned his idea. "You should talk to my boss," his colleague replied.

Peter requested a meeting with Dorothy Broadman, the vice president of corporate reputation and governance. He and Luzmore had already discussed the need to answer the unspoken question "What's in it for me?" Peter had prepared a pitch he hoped would inspire Dorothy to action. Walking to her office, Peter reminded himself of his commitment to be present for the environment. He placed his hand on his heart, took a few deep breaths, and straightened himself to his full height. That wasn't yet his habitual stance, but it was gradually becoming more comfortable and familiar.

Bolstered by this move, Peter walked into Dorothy's office. After a few preliminaries, he got straight to the point. "We don't look at emissions, recycling, paper usage," he pointed out. "All of this affects the environment in negative ways ... and it affects public perception, too." The year was 2004, and environmental groups had recently vilified Victoria's Secret for its catalogue-mailing practices. At the time, Capital One was the fourth-largest customer of the US Postal Service. It didn't take long for Peter to make the case that as social conditions changed, Capital One would would face increasing pressure to build a stronger environmental record. "We can—and should—do better," Peter insisted.

To Peter's delight, Dorothy readily agreed. Together, they started asking questions: What kind of organizational support would they need to move ahead? How would they involve others? What should they tackle as their first project? Which senior leaders would be most likely to grant support?

Today the public expects companies to pay attention to their environmental track record. But in 2004, with Al Gore's film *An Inconvenient Truth* still two years in the future and hurricanes Katrina and Sandy still off in the distance, that was hardly the case. While millions of Americans shared Peter's concerns for the earth, in the wake of 9/11, climate change and other environmental concerns barely registered as issues of widespread public concern.

Dorothy and Peter weren't sure where the land mines were. They knew this could be a politically charged issue in any company, and perhaps even more so in the conservative banking industry. They felt it was imperative to get senior-level backing right away.

They started with Dorothy's boss, the chief legal counsel. Once she got on board, they went to Gregor Baylor, the CIO. Both were happy to get behind the effort. Emboldened by their early success, Dorothy and Peter started mapping out a process whereby each business leader would nominate representatives from his or her division to join a company-wide environmental council.

From concept to kickoff, it took Peter and Dorothy nine months to launch the council. They decided to tackle paper use as their first project. But when they went to the procurement department with their proposal, the cracks started to appear. As a company reliant on direct mail, changes to programs that were working could spell disaster for their business. Their early conversations with procurement encountered some concerned resistance.

All this time Peter had kept up with his daily practices. Every day he would rise, remind himself of his commitment, and connect to his heartfelt sense of care. This became so automatic that when resistance arose in the conversations with procurement, he automatically straightened his spine and reminded himself of his commitment to be present for the environment. All the sensations that accompanied frustration and disappointment were still there—the furrowed brow, the heavy heart, the collapsed shoulders of his old stooped posture. But instead of collapsing in defeat he straightened up, reconnected to his felt sense of care, and forged ahead. Returning to his overarching objective, he looked for ways to navigate around the challenges until success was again in his sights. It was a major step forward in his leadership.

Peter and Dorothy quickly changed tactics, reassuring procurement that they had no desire to disrupt the business. They simply wanted to do business in a better way. They shifted their focus from paper to the use of fake "credit cards" that were regularly included in credit offers sent to people's homes. These credit cards weren't functional, so the toxic PVC-based plastic wound up in the landfill regardless of whether customers took advantage of the offer.

When Peter pointed this out, the folks in procurement agreed they could probably find a way to reduce this unnecessary use of plastic. After much research and discussion, they wound up replacing the PVC cards with a thick paper "credit card." After this success, the resistance in procurement abated. They went on to increase the recycled content in the millions of mailings done each year; now over 70 percent of the bank's paper is either post-consumer waste or certified by the Forest Stewardship Council.[1]

Since then the environmental council has sponsored projects to reduce energy use on the Capital One campus, offer home electronics recycling to employees, and set up charging stations for electric cars, among many other projects. The council has become an independent cross-functional department inside the company, sponsoring and executing multiple projects annually. In 2010, Capital One was proud to make Newsweek's Top 100 Green Companies list.

Depending on your point of view, you might view these successes as modest or enormous. However you look at it, they might never have happened at all if it were not for one person who turned inward and felt his deep care—and then developed the courage, commitment, and skills to act upon it.

"It's what taught me how to lead," Peter says of the environmental council. As he made his way through the confusing and unpredictable process of proposing a brand-new initiative inside a large organization, Peter developed the skills he needed to succeed in his everyday job. "I knew how to do well at work," he said. "I knew how to make money. But this was the first time at work that it wasn't about me and my career. It was about something bigger than me, bigger than the company, and more important than both."

That meaning is what gave Peter the motivation to learn how to enlist others in a collaborative effort and persist in the face of obstacles. By connecting with what we care about and sustaining a commitment to mobilize that care into action, we are called forth to be the best version of ourselves we can be, and to truly make a difference. This lesson held Peter in good stead through the 2008 financial crisis.

Just prior to the economic downturn, Peter was leading a team of forty people. Like many companies at that time, Capital One faced the need for layoffs. Peter's team was slated to shrink to fifteen. Twenty-five men and women under his leadership could soon be out of a job.

While building the environmental council, Peter learned how to build trust and enroll others into his visions and goals. Employing those same skills now, Peter reached out to other business leaders, looking for internal positions for team members who were slated to lose their jobs. He's proud that in the midst of this incredibly challenging time he managed to find a home for every single one of his employees who wanted to remain at Capital One.

It's now been over a decade since Peter's first meeting with Luzmore, and his desire to do good work is now just a part of his everyday outlook. "For me, it's about making a difference. I can get a paycheck from a lot of places—it's not about that. For me it's really about how do I give to something that's larger than me. I had always done that as a father and a husband, but establishing the environmental council was the first time I had ever mobilized people to do that. It was an act of looking at something beyond myself and creating and mobilizing the resources to get that accomplished."

As much as possible, Peter aims to infuse his everyday work with this attitude. Now the Senior Vice President of Enterprise Analytics at the credit reporting giant Equifax, he has proposed a project to derail the alarmingly common crime of foster parents stealing their foster children's identity. As a board member with the Credit Builders Alliance, he's helped nonprofit lenders build a credit history for their customers. But in his view, perhaps his most meaningful contribution has been the opportunity to develop, care for, and build lasting relationships with his colleagues and staff.

"That's what this work did for me," Peter said about his experience of embodied leadership training. "It made me wake up. It made my life stand for something."

Until he moved to Equifax, a few times a year Peter and his family would take a walk on the wooded Capital One campus. "My work is really heady and complex. It's hard to explain to a child," he told me. "It's just really hard for them to relate to the work I do."

On one of those campus walks, the Maynard family visited a butterfly garden created by Capital One's environmental council. It was full of native plants and small signposts that explained the history and importance of each one. Peter turned to his kids. "See this?" he said, pointing out the beauty all around. Tears welled up and threatened to spill over. "*This* is what Daddy does."

SECTION

2

Build Resilience

By connecting to his sense of care, Peter initiated and then built the internal organization now charged with continually improving Capital One's environmental impact. But his success required far more than just a felt sense of care. He also needed to develop the skills to enroll others in his vision, to effectively handle stressful setbacks, and to negotiate inevitable differences of opinion.

Even when you're clear about your vision and deeply committed to bringing it to life, doing so depends on the personal and interpersonal qualities effective leaders share. This is true in your personal life just as much as your professional life. Once you know where you want to go, you need the courage to take the first step, and then to continue stepping out. You need the composure to handle inevitable rough waters without calling it quits. And you need the confidence and credibility to successfully engage others and enlist support. In other words, you need to build the personal qualities that support purposeful action.

The chapters in this section tell stories of people who've done just that. From a human-rights lawyer facing a pressure-cooker environment in war-torn Afghanistan (Chapter 8, "Courage"), to a returning vet reclaiming his life (Chapter 9, "Composure"), to handling more everyday stressors such as high-stakes presentations (Chapter 9 again), uncomfortable networking events (Chapter 10, "Confidence"), and important performance reviews (Chapter 11, "Credibility"), each person featured in the upcoming chapters learned to embody a centered approach to the difficult tasks he or she faced.

Embody Emotional and Social Intelligence

	AWARENESS	*ACTION*
Emotional Intelligence – SELF	**FIND PURPOSE** *align w. yourself + the mystery* core skill: *self-awareness* somatic competency: SENSE Care Choose Commit Contribute	**BUILD RESILIENCE** *settle + strengthen yourself* core skill: *self-mastery* somatic competency: CENTER Courage Composure Confidence Credibility
Social Intelligence – OTHERS	**DEEPEN EMPATHY** *listen deeply...* *w. all of your senses* core skill: *empathy* somatic competency: PRESENCE Connection Compassion	**INSPIRE OTHERS** *act from centered care...* *for self + others* core skill: *social dexterity* somatic competency: GALVANIZE Communicate Collaborate Conflict to Consensus

Self-mastery is the core skill that supports the inner qualities we'll explore in these chapters. Sometimes called self-regulation or emotional regulation, this skill is what enables you to face challenges with resilience, equanimity, and authority. It is the "action" part of emotional intelligence, and it is essential to navigating just about any difficult terrain.

The basic somatic competency that undergirds resilience, emotional regulation, and self-mastery is the capacity to center yourself. Centering is about building your capacity to tolerate strong sensations without having to automatically act to make the discomfort disappear. It's about actively returning yourself to a state of psychophysiological coherence when you are frazzled. It's about adjusting and aligning your posture so that the maximum amount of breath and energy can reach every nook and cranny of your body, so you are well positioned to *use* all of that energy to your advantage. And as you'll come to see, it's about far, far more than taking a deep breath and counting to ten.

Like self-awareness, self-mastery involves both embodied and conceptual elements. It's well known that stress is a physiological experience. If that's so, then it must also be true that resilience—the capacity to recover quickly from stressful difficulties—is also physiological. In these chapters, we'll see how training the body to build resilience can change your life in ways both subtle and dramatic.

Practices to help you center can be found in
Appendix A and at yourbodyisyourbrain.com.

8

Courage

Mandy: A Bully Named Bob
Marianne: Harrowing Moments in Human Rights Law

I looked up from my work as the phone rang, and stood to answer it. On the other end of the line was a familiar voice. I sighed and shook my head, readying myself for the inevitable invectives.

A few months earlier, I had been hired by a management consulting company to lead the launch of a new product line. The first of the slated products was a reprint of an obscure but seminal book that had been out of print for over a decade. The CEO handed me the project with an accompanying apology. "The author is not the easiest guy to get along with," he told me. "No one else in the company can stand working with him. But if anyone can do it, you can."

I was flattered by his faith. We had worked together at a previous company, so he knew my working style. I trusted him. I figured I'd be fine.

My confidence took a hit the first time I went to visit the author at his home office. I knocked, and heard a gruff "come in." Entering the mini library, I scooted down the narrow aisle between the overflowing stacks to an untidy desk at the back, where I was greeted with immediate mistrust. A bitter man nearing the end of his career sat behind the desk. "Your company has really screwed this up so far," Bob told me right off the bat. "I hope you're going to be able to do a better job." Abashed, I assured him I'd do everything in my power to make sure he was happy with the project.

That pattern repeated itself for several months. He shouted his disappointment at every turn, often in unprofessionally foul language. I soothed ruffled feathers while complaining bitterly after hours, sometimes to the point of frustrated tears.

The day of this particular phone call was typical. Bob lit into me as soon as I answered. He was angry about an error the printer had made in the galley copies, and he blamed me. As he hurled abusive insults, attacking both my competence and my character, I walked out onto the deck of my small cabin home. I could barely get a word in edgewise.

My jaw clenched in anger; I could feel my heart racing. I shook my head. I really shouldn't have to put up with this. Even so, I sensed that I was once again about to apologize profusely for something I had absolutely nothing to do with.

Stress is fundamentally a physiological event. Under pressure or perceived threat, the body is flooded with adrenaline, cortisol, and other hormones. The sympathetic branch of the nervous system kicks in automatically, increasing heart rate and breathing, slowing digestion, and shunting blood to muscles, readying us for fight or flight.

All of this is well known, but it's hardly the whole story. Dr. Stephen Porges, professor of psychiatry at the University of North Carolina and previously director of the Body-Brain Center at the University of Illinois, has conducted a wealth of research on visceral and behavioral responses to threat. These responses begin with a process he calls neuroception—a perceptual process that distinguishes between safety and danger by combining exteroceptive perception of the environment with interoceptive perception of one's visceral state.[1] Porges' studies of anatomy have revealed the illuminating and previously unrecognized fact that our threat response has three distinct neurobiological pathways that result in very different behaviors. He calls this the polyvagal theory.[2]

The oldest part of our neuroceptive biology, evolutionarily speaking, is the dorsal vagal complex, a part of the vagus nerve that signals the body to freeze under threat, just as lizards do when startled. Opossums feign death, which is a similar response. In human behavioral terms, this can show up as passive avoidance: steering clear of answering the uncomfortable email or phone call, or ignoring the elephant in the room.

This freeze response can also be expressed as an actual deer-in-the-headlights physical freeze, or on some occasions what psychologists call dissociation: mentally checking out of present-moment experience as a self-protective measure. This often happens when the threat is overwhelming and escape is impossible, such as in situations of combat or abuse. Immobilization is a common response in terrifying situations of extreme, life-threatening danger.

Because the fight/flight response gets so much airtime, the freeze response is not as well recognized as a biologically adaptive reaction to threat. This misunderstanding has very real consequences, such as when victims of rape or domestic violence are revictimized by a justice system that relentlessly challenges their actions: Why didn't you run? Why didn't you fight back? But the truth is, immobilization is one of our most ancient and reliable responses to being attacked. Oftentimes not aggravating an aggressor is the smartest way to stay safe.

Distinct from the freeze response of the dorsal vagal complex, the fight/flight response involves the amygdala, the sympathetic nervous system, and the hypothalamic-pituitary-adrenal (HPA) axis. In this case, your body is flooded with cortisol and adrenaline. You feel jacked up. Your heart races, you sweat, your muscles pepare for action. Rather than freeze, you're ready to *mobilize* in response to threat—to jump into the fray, to argue, fight, or run. Whether you're shouting or storming off, fight/flight reactions are invariably active and energetic.[3]

The part of the polyvagal system that evolved most recently is known as the ventral vagal complex. This portion of the vagus nerve links to the cranial nerves that innervate the facial muscles used in communication. In other words, *our biological systems of threat detection tie directly to our biological systems of communication.*[4] In situations of relative safety, high-pressure interactions can immediately and involuntarily affect what we do and say. In situations of perceived (or actual) threat, you may find yourself automatically appeasing your adversary and soothing ruffled feathers. Which is exactly what happened to me every time I tried to reassure Bob.

For months, I didn't see that I had any choice whatsoever in dealing with him. He yelled, I apologized—it was as predictable as the sun rising each morning. But I knew my apologies were unnecessary, and I had no question his vitriol was out of line. I desperately wanted to stand up for myself, and I felt justified in doing so, but somehow I hadn't ever managed to bring myself to actually do it.

———

Back on the deck, phone in hand, I felt the automatic urge to appease building up inside me. By now it was a familiar feeling: a rising ball of fear fluttering in my chest, accompanied by rounded-up shoulders and a deeply furrowed brow. I momentarily pulled the phone away from my ear, turning down the volume on his rant. Shifting my attention to what was happening inside my own skin, I felt my heart pounding with anger and apprehension. I became aware of my bare feet on the wooden deck, of the warm sun on my skin, of the slight breeze moving through the pines.

By this point, I had been studying embodied leadership for several months. Over and over I had practiced calling up a felt sense of dignity and self-respect by changing my stance. My practice paid off now as muscle memory kicked in. I straightened my spine, got my hips underneath me, and planted my feet. With no time to plan or rehearse, I brought the phone back to my ear and interrupted him midstream. "Bob," I said firmly, "the way you're speaking to me right now does *not* make me want to partner with you." I paused.

"We need each other for this project to work," I went on. "If you want this project to succeed—and I know you do—then I'm going to have to insist that you treat me with more respect."

My heart wanted to jump out of my chest. I was breathless with alarm. I had poked the bear, and I had no idea how he would respond. Past experience led me to believe it would be bad—very bad. I was genuinely afraid.

Bob's response floored me. Quieter now, he said, "You're right. I was out of line." He paused.

"I'm sorry."

I was stunned. In that moment, I realized the true power of body-oriented behavioral practice. When I picked up the call just a few minutes earlier I had no idea it was him on the line, no idea I was in for a stream of abuse, and once it began, no idea how to respond. Simply by standing in a more dignified manner, I managed to find the words I needed to break a patterned interaction that had caused me untold amounts of stress.

I wish I could tell you that Bob was a gem to work with from that point on. Regrettably, he was not. But after that point, I was no longer so afraid to stand up to him. If he got out of line, I would call him on it, and postpone the conversation until he could settle down and speak rationally. It never became an easy working relationship, but it did become more manageable.

And it all began when I learned how to take a stand.

Over and over I've heard this from clients: When they really learn how to center themselves, the words they need seem to miraculously appear. While this seems obvious to me now, back when I had that pivotal conversation with Bob I found it quite astonishing. I was furious and frightened, but somehow once I shifted my posture, the right words just seemed to speak themselves. Even in the face of my fear I was able to be clear, firm, respectful, and powerful. And it had an unexpectedly persuasive effect. I had never experienced anything remotely like it.

Any artist can tell you that posture communicates mood. A drawing of a man slumped on a bench tells a sad story of someone grappling with life's challenges. A woman standing with her chin lifted, spine erect, eyes gazing toward the horizon comes off as a stalwart adventurer. Writers, visual artists, and actors all use this knowledge to enhance their craft.

But it may surprise you to learn that posture actually *generates* mood. I first learned this through my own experience. As I watched myself and my clients become happier and more courageous by changing our posture, I became avidly curious about why it works this way.

Dr. Amy Cuddy's research provided one early answer. You may already be familiar with Cuddy's research—she delivered one of the most-watched TED talks of all time. In it, she explains how simple postural changes affect real-life outcomes, like whether you get the job, the date, or the raise.

Cuddy's flagship experiment demonstrated that sitting or standing in a powerful posture for as little as one minute generates measurable changes in physiology, psychology, and behavior. Experimenters asked participants to lean back into the time-honored "boss's office" pose—feet propped up on the desk with hands interlaced behind their head—or to stand with their hands on their hips in a similarly powerful pose. When tested before and after these brief interventions, both men and women showed an increase in testosterone and a decrease in the stress hormone cortisol. Participants' sense of their own efficacy increased. And they became more willing to take calculated risks, such as seeking a potential payoff in a simple gambling task.

The control group spent one minute in each of several closed postures: arms crossed, head dropped, limbs pulled in close. These participants showed the opposite results on all measures.[5]

All that may be interesting from a lab perspective, but what does it have to do with life in the real world? To explore that question further, Cuddy's team had subjects participate in a mock job interview following their time in either an open or closed posture. They then brought in untrained reviewers to watch videos of the interviews. Their task was to predict who would get the job. Consistently, reviewers rated the open-posture participants as more likely to be hired.[6]

Unfortunately, some elements of this research have proven difficult to replicate. The statistical methods that were standard at the time have fallen out of favor and been replaced by more robust approaches, resulting in some debate about the reliability of the results. However, I believe Cuddy and her team stumbled across something important, if elusive. Looking across 55 similar studies, all indications suggest the effects of power posing on one's internal emotions and sense of power are quite strong.[7] This discovery rests on a long-known biological fact: Across many species, open postures both signal and grant access to power and resources, whereas closed postures do the reverse. Not surprisingly, humans are no exception.

However Cuddy's oft-employed phrase "fake it till you become it" may inadvertently reveal why the results have been difficult to reproduce. It's possible that a scant few minutes of "faking it" will momentarily up your game, change your physiology, and increase your sense of power. Or, as some detractors insist, perhaps not. What *is* a sure bet is that practicing new moves repeatedly over time wires new patterns into your neuromusculature. This has the potential to build habits of confidence, courage, and composure that are easier to call up when you need them. So I would say it differently. Instead of faking it till you make it, *practice it until it's embodied.* There's nothing fake about it.

How we repeatedly sit and stand shapes us on the inside, affects how we're perceived, and can change the outcome of life events both large and small. But *how*?

To answer that question, we return to Dr. Porges's lab, circa 1988. Porges's colleague John Cottingham wanted to explore how Rolfing—a method of manually manipulating fascia and other soft tissue—might affect the nervous system. Cottingham was an advanced Rolfing practitioner and a research associate at an Illinois health clinic. He had seen firsthand how Rolfing affected not just people's bodies, but also their lives. He and Porges teamed up with local physical therapist Kent Richmond to explore this phenomenon.

The three researchers recruited thirty-two healthy young men with an anterior pelvic tilt to undergo either a Rolf-based adjustment of pelvic position or a simple massage without an adjustment. Just prior to and immediately following the bodywork, they measured both pelvic angle and vagal tone. Vagal tone is a commonly employed measure used to assess newborn neurological status and ensure surgical patients are given the proper dose of anesthesia, among other things. It is a reliable indicator of parasympathetic nervous system activation—the part of us that's in the driver's seat when we are relaxed and at ease.[8]

Research participants who received the adjustment showed a change in pelvic tilt, which came as no big surprise. The more interesting finding showed they had an increase in vagal tone and parasympathetic activity both immediately following the adjustment *and* when measured again twenty-four hours later. The control group showed no such changes. Translation: the men who received the adjustment shifted into a more relaxed and alert physiological state, and that state was sustained over time.[9]

That's pretty much exactly what happened for me when I confronted Bob. I brought my hips underneath me, which made it easier to straighten my spine into a more dignified and powerful posture. It also gave me better access to my parasympathetic response, counteracting my natural sympathetic nervous system arousal under stress. In this ever-so-slightly more relaxed state, I was better equipped to bring my best to the situation, rather than stuttering and stammering my way through as I'd always done before.

But why on earth should the angle of your pelvic tilt affect your stress response? Several things may contribute to this effect.

First of all, Rolfing works directly on fascia—the connective tissue that sheaths all muscles and allows your organs to slide by one another when you move. Research by Robert Schleip in Germany has revealed that fascia has the highest density of nerve endings of any tissue in the body. Schleip's research has shown that when a bodyworker softens and liquefies dense, dehydrated, contracted fascial tissue, it has a direct impact on the ability of those nerves to carry signals throughout the body and back to the brain.[10]

The pelvic bowl is a particularly potent area of the body to receive bodywork like this, because most of the body's parasympathetic nerves branch off of either cervical or lumbar vertebrae.[11] That means that bodywork on lumbar and pelvic ligaments can free up chronic constrictions that affect your parasympathetic nervous system, allowing you to experience more sustained states of relaxed power.

For several months prior to my pivotal moment with Bob, I had been receiving regular bodywork that helped me increase awareness of my whole body, including my hips and pelvic bowl. And on a daily basis, I had been practicing centering myself by paying attention to my sensations and adjusting my posture to be more open, relaxed, and dignified. When you practice this in your everyday life by getting your hips properly underneath you, you can more readily take a clear, relaxed, firm stand. And because we all unconsciously respond to one another's comportment—think of Cuddy's interview raters—this kind of centering practice can have a direct effect on your biggest opportunities and challenges.[12]

Gathering the courage to stand up to a bully is one thing, but we all face situations that call for daily acts of courage: asking for a raise, say, or firing a difficult employee; extending an invitation to a new friend or taking a stand for your own dignity. But Bob, despite his gruff demeanor, was ultimately harmless. There are far more lethal bullies in the world. What happens when you're faced with one of them?

Picture a mud brick hut in an Afghan village. A few small carpets cover the dirt floor, where a woman and her nine remaining children sit in shocked, vigilant silence. They're not from here—this is her uncle's house. She and her family fled their own village just a few weeks ago, following the murder of her disabled, wheelchair-bound husband and two eldest sons.

In their midst squats a young human rights lawyer from New Zealand. Notebook in hand, Marianne Elliot is there on behalf of the United Nations to capture this family's story and sort out how this particular battle began. She specializes in the rights of women and children in conflict zones, and she is doing her level best to gather accurate information about individual human rights abuses so that justice may be served and the international community motivated to action.

But lately, Marianne has been plagued by the existential futility of her efforts. Her job is to document a seemingly endless parade of human suffering, but it's hard to see how she's making any significant difference. "What are we doing here if we can't even protect these people?" she asks herself daily. Twenty children died in the recent outbreak of violence she's investigating—a fact that keeps her tossing and turning at night. Dozens of families have been displaced. She's now spoken to several such mothers, and universally their concerns are for immediate food, shelter, and clothing. They need a way to provide for their families now that their husbands, sons—and crucially, their homes, farm animals, and saved seeds—have been destroyed. Justice can wait.

It is amidst this background of hopelessness and despair that Marianne conducts her interviews. Her job requires her to gather accurate details about what happened: Was your husband a member of one of the groups battling over political disagreements, or simply a bystander? Was he killed in front of the children, or were they sent outside? As important as these questions are for restoring the rule of law in Afghanistan, they are beginning to feel altogether too intrusive, not to mention fairly useless in the face of the women's more pressing practical needs.

The woman before her looks old, haggard. The deep furrows of poverty and twenty years of motherhood line her face. Marianne is taken aback when she discovers they're the same age: thirty-four. Childless, unmarried, and accustomed to a life of relative safety, good healthcare, and ample sunscreen, she is profoundly affected by the immense chasm between their lives.

With increasing sensitivity and a newfound sense of kinship, Marianne probes into the details of the day of the murder. How did the fighting begin? What exactly had happened to the woman's husband and son? Where were the killers now?

This line of questioning leads to a far more disturbing discovery: The woman's husband had been at the very center of the political maelstrom that led to the outbreak of violence. The men that killed him were hunting for the rest of his family. Right at this very moment, men with powerful weapons were relentlessly seeking this woman and her children, intent on ending their lives in a most violently brutal way. There was no reason to imagine anyone who was with them would be spared.

With this revelation Marianne was instantly gripped by a severe sense of panic. She felt a sudden rush of fear; an overwhelming visceral sensation of *being* prey.

When I spoke to Marianne about this years later, she couldn't remember her sensations in detail. "I'm not gonna lie and tell you I remember exactly what I felt in that moment," Marianne said to me. "It may have been a flush of heat or cold... or maybe my legs turned to jelly. What I do remember feeling was a *huge* surge of energy in my body—a potent visceral, physical desire to flee."

Danger of this magnitude is precisely what our fear circuits are built for. Obviously it's a good idea to mount a strong response when faced with imminent life-threatening danger. Marianne's visceral response reveals the vast intelligence of her biological heritage.

Fear is a crucial protective force, even in everyday life where the tragedies and terrors of war are at a safe distance. The last thing you want to do is ignore or get rid of your fear. When your child steps off the curb into oncoming traffic, fear floods your body with sensation and propels you into immediate action. Similar sensations might arise—perhaps with less magnitude—when you unexpectedly lose your job or stumble onto evidence of an affair. These situations may not hold the same immediate physical threat, but their personal significance can trigger your physiological fear response all the same.

That visceral fear response throws your body into a state of psychophysiological incoherence. When body and emotions are calm, heart rate, blink rate, respiratory rate, and other rhythmic systems of the body show up as smooth, steady, consistent oscillations on a graph, depicting a coherent orderliness on the inside. This is what a centered state of being looks like, physiologically speaking. But in a state of alarm, those graphs go haywire. Your biorhythms become erratic and disordered, rather than regular and synchronized. This is what we mean when we say we are frazzled. Or in Marianne's case, truly panicked.

Sometimes, this neuroceptive response leads to actions that are well matched to the situation at hand, like yanking your child out of the street. In certain situations this kind of automatic reaction is exactly what's called for. But other times, your automatic reaction isn't so helpful. In fact, you may lose it completely in ways that actually make the situation worse. That's because in a state of psychophysiological incoherence, it literally becomes more difficult to think clearly. When your body's systems are unsynchronized and arrhythmic, energy is shunted away from intellectual performance in favor of restoring balance. In fact, research has shown that people in a state of psychophysiological coherence perform better on academic tests and on the job than people experiencing incoherence.[13]

But what about those situations where you want to "feel the fear and do it anyway"? Where you judge what you are doing to be more important than your fear? Maybe you're presenting to a venture cap-italist to get funding for your startup. Or coming out of the closet to your parents. Or making the choice to leave an abusive relationship. Or documenting human-rights abuses. Courage is not the absence of fear. Rather, it is a commitment to something larger and more important than your fear.

If you can return yourself to psychophysiological coherence in these stressful situations you'll have an edge, because you'll have access to more of your intelligence. Whatever the challenge, you'll be better able to contend with it if you've devoted time and training to centering yourself so you can return to a coherent state and call upon your courage when it's most needed.

Marianne wanted nothing more than to get the hell out of that mud hut. But she had another instinct as well, and she followed it. "Fleeing wasn't an appropriate response given my responsibilities. Knowing that I couldn't, I just kept taking these deep breaths. And with each breath I was sending this message as powerfully as I could out into my limbs and down into my belly, like, *Relax. They're not here. The hunters aren't here. They may be out there somewhere, but they're not here right now. Right now, you're here with this woman and these children. In this instant right now, danger is not upon you.*"

Ordinarily, this deep-breathing calm-thinking approach wouldn't have come naturally to her. Marianne had spent much of her previous post in Gaza as many aid workers do—strung out on coffee and cigarettes, with a bit (and sometimes a lot) of wine to take the edge off. When she returned home to New Zealand after that post, one of her primary goals was to get healthy. She joined a gym, took up running, and within months competed in her first 10K. Marianne was an ambitious and aggressive idealist, and that translated to every aspect of her life.

Her gym offered yoga as well, and she gamely tried it out. While she had no patience for the slower, more meditative practices, given the opportunity to push her body on the mat, she would. Gradually she learned to enjoy yoga, though as she packed her bags for her next assignment in Afghanistan, she had no idea how essential her practice would become.

After six months in Kabul, Marianne got a shot at her dream job: working to verify—and hopefully rectify—violations of international human-rights laws. Three months later she was transferred from her Kabul office job to the UN outpost in Herat.

Not long after she arrived, her boss called her into his office with an unexpected request. The entire international staff was overdue for a break. He himself had skipped his last two scheduled leaves, the four-day holiday of Eid was nearly upon them, and most of the staff were scheduled for a break. He asked Marianne if she would head up the office while he went home to Spain for a week.

Marianne squirmed. Although her natural instinct is to help and she's definitely one to rise to a challenge, she didn't like the idea at all. After just nine months in Afghanistan, she was still getting familiar with the extremely complex political and tribal history that fueled modern-day conflicts. And she'd only been in Herat a few weeks. She felt wholly unprepared for the role, and said so.

But her boss looked so forlorn, she eventually relented. "It's only three working days," she told herself. "With the holiday, everything should remain pretty quiet." She drilled her boss for details on everything she needed to know.

But the morning of his departure, she had a sudden crisis of faith. "Are you sure I can do this?" she asked with trepidation.

He shot her a reassuring smile as he boarded the plane. "Don't worry, Marianne. As long as no one kills Amanullah Khan, you'll be fine."

By noon that day, Khan is dead.

The week prior, the murder of a prominent figure in a neighboring Barakzai community had been blamed on Amanullah Khan, a key political player in the region. Khan's assassination was a retaliation for the murder of the Barakzai leader. His death was sure to lead to further revenge killings and a rapid escalation of violence.

Inter-tribal diplomacy was not Marianne's wheelhouse—she was responsible for documenting individual human-rights abuses such as police brutality or illegal detainment. But suddenly, as acting head of the local UN office in Herat, she was thrust into diplomatic negotiations with high-ranking army generals and commanders, seeking any means possible to stabilize the situation. She was out of her depth and scrambling for answers in the midst of an incredibly complex, highly volatile conflict. Meanwhile, her office was stripped down to only the barest level of support. A week later her boss's return flight was canceled, shutting him out of the region indefinitely.

In this pressure-cooker environment Marianne turned in desperation to yoga. She would have preferred to run, but even before Khan's assassination she had been forbidden to walk outside in Herat; all journeys had to be made by armored vehicle. And although there was a treadmill at a nearby facility, she felt awkward about calling a car and driver for such a personal errand. So to relieve the immense pressure and rising sense of panic, she took to running in place and doing yoga in her room.

Following Khan's assassination it took three agonizingly long weeks for Marianne to get clearance to go to Shindad, the village where many of the refugees from the fighting sought shelter. While there she met the woman in the hut, who turned out to be the widow of the brother of the Barakzai man whose murder had sparked the whole skirmish. This haggard and frightened woman was directly at the heart of the conflict, and Marianne was right there with her.

Not long after this unnerving incident, Marianne began to experiment more consistently with yoga. "I hadn't really embedded my practices at that point, but I was starting to get the sense that a lot of my best resources lay in that direction," Marianne says looking back. She began by following along with a recording, but eventually she learned the sequence well enough that she could do it on her own: sun salutations, a few standing poses, and a few seated. Although she continued to steer clear of the more meditative practices at first, it wasn't long before she began regularly adding them to her routine.

When I asked Marianne how her yoga practice contributed to her courage, she had three answers for me. "First," she said, "I became aware that things could arise in my body, and that I could notice them without being completely at their mercy." Working with intense sensations and challenging poses on the mat helped when she had to step out of the car in a dangerous spot. In each case, she could feel the intensity without letting it dictate her actions. If she could hold the uncomfortable pose, well, then she could also handle all the nervous energy in her body as she stood on an exposed ridge to get reception for a vital phone call. This practice of tolerating strong sensations without having to immediately make them go away is part of what allowed Marianne to center herself and draw upon her courage in tense situations.

As well, "A huge, *huge* part for me was discovering the power of breathing—how it could shift the way my body and mind would respond to certain situations. When there was that immediate fear trigger that made everything in my body go into fight/flight, I could actually choose instead. If I knew I didn't need to flee, or it wasn't appropriate to leave, I could use my breath to bring some sense of safety to my body and make it easier to stay." In the next chapter we'll explore how simple breathing practices like the one Marianne used produce a centered state of psychophysiological coherence.

Despite her initial reluctance, it soon became Marianne's custom to end her practice with a seated meditation. Watching her thoughts without responding to them helped her get familiar with the way her mind worked. She discovered that when she gave more attention to her fearful thoughts, they would take her body off in a fearful direction. But as she learned how to unhook from those thoughts and just let them slide by, she got better and better at unhooking from what she calls "the fear train."

This combination of body awareness, breath awareness, and thought awareness helped Marianne throughout her tour of duty.

Over and over her time in Afghanistan would put her in treacherous and uncomfortable circumstances—such as the day she spent squatting in the mud courtyard of a prison surrounded by incarcerated and potentially violent men. Marianne called on the lessons learned in her daily yoga practice: Stay with the discomfort just a little while longer. Breathe. Collect your thoughts. Get present. What is actually happening, *right now?* This ongoing practice allowed her to continue to courageously pursue justice in a country badly in need of it.

Dialing up awareness of body, breath, thoughts, and emotions—*without having to immediately respond*—is one of the best ways to restore psychophisological coherence to the body. Call this the physiology of resilience.

Even if your typical day doesn't require you to find the courage to face down life-threatening danger, courage has a place in your life. Partly for the bullies like Bob, but also for those moments where your life calls you to something new but scary: a move across country, a career change, a second marriage, a first date. Courage can be invoked at any level of fear, and the process is the same. Your body responds with a neuroceptive assessment of safety and danger, and if there is some visceral detection of potential threat, your stress systems will wisely gear up for the challenge.

But if stress is a physiological response, so too is resilience. And so, then, is courage.

The funny thing about courage is that it doesn't usually *feel* courageous. More often than not, it feels exceedingly vulnerable. Courage means taking bold action—or even just staying present—in the face of fear. It's speaking even as your voice shakes, acting even as your hands tremble. It may look courageous from the outside or after the fact. But on the inside, you know something significant is at stake. And you choose to take action anyway.

The word courage derives from the French word *coeur*, meaning "heart." *Have heart,* courage asks of us. *Take action on what really matters.* Courage doesn't offer false reassurances that things are going to turn out okay. It simply supports you in making a bold move despite the risks and potential consequences. We usually invoke it because something larger than our fear is at stake.

So get your hips underneath you. Straighten your spine. Breathe. Tap your body's intelligence and activate your parasympathetic resilience circuits. Take Marianne's lessons and mine, and apply them to your own life. Because whatever is ahead for you, there's no doubt there will be moments that call upon your deepest courage.

9

Composure

Rich: Army Ranger, Meet Groovy Yogi
Nichole: Sharing the Stage with Celebrities

From the time he was a small child, Rich Low had dreamed of becoming a U.S. Navy SEAL. So when he arrived at South Carolina's Clemson University in 1999, he kicked off his military aspirations by enrolling in the Reserve Officers' Training Corps. Rich majored in mechanical engineering, but "from the Army's perspective, I got a minor in leadership."

While enrolled in his university-based ROTC program, Rich also enlisted in the South Carolina National Guard. Hoping to get an edge on his peers, he aimed to augment his leadership skills by also learning what it's like to follow. As an enlisted man, his job was to obey the orders of the Guard officers in his chain of command. As an officer-in-training at Clemson, his job was to learn how to *be* one of the officers giving the orders. He made a point to experience the Army's approach to leadership from all angles.

"There's a lot of psychological training as part of the Army's leadership training," Rich told me. "The first year, it's all about discipline. It's kind of encapsulated by ironing your clothes. You learn that your appearance and how you carry yourself makes a silent impression."

Rich went from learning Army basics in the first year to leading small teams to eventually leading at all levels of a 180-person organization. Throughout his Army career, there was "a desensitization of sorts. They always want you to be that stoic, calm, and cool person." By the time he left college, the ability to keep his cool and control his emotions was becoming second nature.

And it was a good thing, too. After graduating from Clemson, Rich went on to infantry school and then put in for Ranger School—the most demanding leadership training program the Army has on offer. A volunteer-only program, Ranger School is designed to completely drain participants mentally and physically... and then push them to give even more. Weeks of twenty-hour days with heavy packs in hostile weather and treacherous terrain facing unknown "enemies" all around is enough to fray anyone's nerves, even the toughest of the tough. More than half of Ranger School candidates are required to repeat sections of the program in order to meet the Army's high bar; many drop out entirely. No one who makes it through Ranger School is soft. Rich finished "true blue, first time through," one of only nineteen soldiers to do so out of the sixty-five in his starting company.

After Ranger School, Rich moved to Fort Richardson, Alaska, where he joined "America's Arctic Warriors," a self-sufficient fighting group equipped to go anywhere in the world. In 2005, his battalion deployed to Iraq. Rich's platoon was assigned to Al Anbar province, at the time one of the deadliest areas in the country.

"War is 90 percent boredom and 10 percent terror," Rich quoted. "I don't remember where I read that, but it's pretty true, I think." Every six to eight hours, he and his team strapped on their body armor, jacked a round into the chamber, and went on patrol. "You get to a point where you don't even think about what it means, or about what the body armor is meant to do. You don't think about the fact that you could be injured or killed, or cause the same. It becomes almost comforting."

They'd come back to base to eat and sleep, then turn around a few hours later to do it all again.

All that training to be stoic and calm was essential for enduring both the boredom and the terror. "You learn to compartmentalize your emotions," he told me. "The priorities are the mission first, looking out for others second, and last, yourself. Thirty-six people's lives counted on my decisions. You end up looking out for each other more than looking out for yourself, especially as a leader. My platoon sergeant and I would have to remind each other to eat and sleep."

The grueling shifts, the bad food, the horrifying moments you wish you could forget, the nauseating sights and sounds and smells of picking up the pieces after an explosion. It's no accident the Army uses the term "intestinal fortitude" to describe the kind of strength they want to see in their soldiers. "You learn to stomach it," Rich told me, speaking of a particularly gruesome scene. "You swallow all of your emotions. I recognized that I was stifling the emotion in the moment. Everything hinges on 'I gotta get through this. I gotta get through the mission.' Because other people are, and we're gonna do this together. That's how you get through."

After a year of this, the soldiers were over-the-moon excited to get home. Half the unit was already on the way; the other half was packing their bags. Their families had flown to Alaska and were eagerly waiting for them. Then the unit got the news: They would be staying on. Indefinitely.

Rich's team was the first unit extended under the leadership of President George W. Bush and Secretary of Defense Donald Rumsfeld, and they were devastated. The timing couldn't have been worse. The half who had already deployed home gave their families quick hugs and then, to their great and enduring credit, every last one of them made a voluntary about-face and boarded the plane back to Iraq. Despite this strong camaraderie, the decline in morale was difficult to overstate.

Rich was on the lookout for the early warning signs that might indicate potentially suicidal soldiers among some of his team. He made sure there was a bit of time to pour out some of the potent cocktail of frustration, disappointment, and anger. "We'd openly vent for five or ten minutes: *'Yeah, this sucks. It's awful, but we're all in it together. We'll get through it.'* Then we move on. We have a job to do." There were chaplains on staff if anyone needed additional support, but Rich doesn't recall anyone leaning on the clergy. In other words: If life is unbearably hard, spit it out quickly, then bottle it up and move on.

"Vets are just ordinary people in extraordinary circumstances," Rich told me. The military trains its troops to shut down their natural emotional reactions to such extraordinary circumstances. And that's a good thing. No matter what you think about war in general or any given conflict in particular, it's safe to say that if you can't keep your cool in combat, things are likely to get much, much worse.

So disconnecting from your feelings is useful under certain circumstances. So useful, in fact, that we do it automatically in situations of intense physical or emotional trauma. Compartmentalize like this often enough—or even just once in a situation that completely overwhelms you—and your nervous system will quickly learn, wiring it into your whole body like a giant red flashing alarm: Do... Not... Feel. Do... Not... Feel.

It's easy to confuse this shut-down stoicism with a centered state, because outwardly it appears calm and inwardly it may feel numb. But nothing could be further from the truth. Centering rests on sensing *more*, learning to tolerate that intensity, and returning yourself to a state of psychophysiological coherence so you can take effective action.

By contrast, to meet the insistent internal demands of the "Do Not Feel" alarm, you must contract your muscles and move your attention away from uncomfortable sensations and toward something else—anything else. Work, booze, sex, exercise, intellectual pursuits, imagination... whatever distracts you from your discomfort. Tensing your jaw so you don't sob or shout can be both automatic (as with trauma) and trained (as with military drills). As you learn to feel less of your sensations, it becomes a neuromuscular habit—an inside-out armoring. And that neuromuscular armor will shut down your ability to feel across the board, dialing down your ability to experience joy as well as pain.

Now consider for a moment how deeply the lessons of military leadership have influenced our expectations of leaders in corporate, government, and nonprofit arenas. Both deliberately and inadvertently, military leadership has been held up as a model for the very concept of what leadership is. "Leave your emotions out of it" is common human resources counsel, and with good reason. You can't afford to have people falling apart all over the office, either. But we've already seen how subtle sensations and their associated emotions have big consequences for people's choices and commitments. And we know that leadership requires you to connect well with others. As we'll see in upcoming chapters, your body is deeply involved in that, too.

So while the kind of stoic emotional lockdown that Rich learned can be incredibly useful when you're embattled, in everyday life it can actually be a hindrance. Once your body has learned to ward off emotions through automatic contraction, it will do that even when you don't want or need it to. And that's exactly what happened to Rich when he finally got home.

After fifteen and a half months in Iraq, Rich returned to the United States completely numb. "My relationship with my wife became very strained," he told me. "I was just… there. It was difficult to connect with others and have a good time. I extended my survival instinct to my day-to-day life. I just never turned the emotion back on. I never moved back into the life I had before I left."

That's what Rich says now, but at the time, he didn't think he'd been particularly affected by his deployment. He'd spent more than a year shutting down his emotions day after day, and it had become his new normal. But it was clear to his wife that he had come home a different man. And she wasn't happy about it.

One evening she dragged Rich to a stress-management seminar. The workshop leader, an acupuncturist, went around the room asking each participant, "What's the most stressful thing you've ever experienced?" Rich scoffed. "Well, I just did fifteen months in Iraq," he said in a flat voice. It was the first time he had mentioned his deployment to anyone outside of close friends and family.

After the program, the acupuncturist pulled him aside. "You should meet my friend Emma," she told him. At the time, Dr. Emma Seppälä was studying for her PhD at Stanford University. She was busy designing an experiment to study the effects of Sudarshan Kriya yoga—a breathing practice—on post-traumatic stress disorder (PTSD), and she was recruiting veterans to participate. Rich had separated from the Army by then, but he remained involved in a program to help returning vets. Even though he had never been diagnosed with PTSD, the acupuncturist thought he and Emma might be able to help each other.

Seppälä, a psychologist, was concerned that ordinary therapy was failing vets. Many vets resist traditional forms of PTSD treatment, which they often perceive as inducing a victim mentality. Drugs involve side effects, and therapy often requires them to review traumatic events again and again, which can be unpleasant at best and retraumatizing at worst. A lot of vets choose not to go through treatment, and many of those who do drop out. Furthermore, a recent study had shown that, even for those who completed a full course of treatment, only 50 percent saw any measurable improvement. That left a really large group of veterans who weren't being helped.[1] Seppälä was on the hunt for better, more reliable treatment options.

Rich and Emma did meet, and gradually they became friends. The closer she got to starting her program, the more Rich felt compelled to give her the information he had. One day he handed Emma his diary from his deployment. "If you really want to understand stress, read some of these stories," he said. "This is pretty typical of what people go through."

Eventually, Emma persuaded Rich that he'd be a good candidate for the study. He was more than a little skeptical, but he trusted Emma enough to give it a shot. Rich went into the program thinking, "Well, if this helps other people, I'm willing to try it. But this breathing stuff is way too hippie for me. *There is absolutely nothing cool about what I'm about to do.*"

The study participants met for a few hours each evening over the course of a week. A workshop leader kicked off the program with some thought-provoking conversations, but the talking "didn't change anything for me," Rich said. He participated gamely, but the program didn't fully capture his attention until they began the breathing practice.

The leader instructed participants to close their eyes and put their hands on their ribs, so they could sense their breath more easily. Rich found this helped him pay closer attention to his breath from the inside. Following the instructor's guidance, he breathed shallowly at first, and then deeper; faster, then slower. The group moved through a cycle that repeatedly changed the pace, depth, and rhythm of the breath. It was pretty simple, really. Perhaps deceptively so.

Rich was entirely caught off guard by the intensity of his reaction. First his hands started to cramp, then his forearms. His chest and legs were tight. "I could feel tension through almost every part of my body," Rich told me. He flashed back to events in Iraq that he hadn't thought about in some time. Like the moment an Iraqi looked him straight in the eye and told Rich that the bomb that had just killed one soldier and badly mangled another had been meant for him. Or the time when, at his wits' end with a confused driver, he abandoned his planned route... and then wound up being first on the scene reacting to a roadside bomb that had detonated on their original path. "I had so many situations where I came within inches of it being my platoon or me being taken out—it was unreal." There were things that had happened that he didn't realize he felt responsible for; decisions he had made that had cost someone else's life. All of that came flooding back now. By the end of the breathing exercise, Rich was sobbing uncontrollably.

"It was the most intense emotional rush I've ever felt," Rich said. "It wasn't the energy, excitement, strength, and adrenaline of combat. It was all of the repressed emotion—the guilt, the stress—it all just came flooding back in that one session. That's when I started thinking, 'There's something to this.' For somebody who was taught that showing any emotion is a negative thing, it was the most humbling thing I've ever been through."

After the session, Rich went home. By this time, the strain with his wife had taken its toll. He was living alone, divorce proceedings underway. He was grateful for the quiet and the opportunity to reflect on what he'd just experienced. He had no idea where this was all leading. But for the first time in a long time, he slept without dreaming of war.

The next day he went back to the program, and the next. When it was over, Rich continued with the breathing practice on a daily basis, as the instructor had encouraged them to do. Three weeks later, while hunting with his father, his dad said something that surprised him. "I can see the change in you," the elder Low said. "You're you again from five or six years ago."

"That was all he said," Rich told me. "But with that one sentence he acknowledged that I had made a remarkable change, that I had really been different after the war and I hadn't even recognized it. I grew up in a family where crying was not an option. We didn't talk about emotions or feelings. So for him to say that, well, that was a pretty big deal."

Rich continued practicing daily for several months. He began dating again and moved forward with his life. "It taught me a skill and showed me a technique that helps me return and recenter myself," Rich says of the program. He doesn't practice every day anymore, but "Now, when I need it, I can just feel it. It's like being hungry. If I need to do the practice, I just know." Today, Rich's nightmares are gone. He had his last flashback three or four months after the study was completed. He no longer startles as easily, and he doesn't get frustrated as quickly as he did before. And his view of leadership has changed: "The program helped me understand that being a strong leader involves a degree of intelligence about your own emotions."

Rich now sits on the advisory board for Project Welcome Home Troops, an organization bringing this program and others to veterans. "What kept me alive every day overseas is that you're protecting the guy next to you. I'm still doing that now." By way of illustration, Rich told me about what happened when the news picked up Seppälä's research for the first time. A veteran called her before the program was even over. "I contemplated suicide last week," he said. "I want what those guys had."

Breath is tightly tied to mood. Think about it: Laughter has a breath pattern that's very different from crying, which is different yet again from how you'd breathe if you were holding a sleeping baby. Research has shown that just as different postures, gestures, and facial expressions convey different emotions, different breath patterns accompany different moods.[2]

In fact, one of the first ways you'll try to control your emotions is by controlling your breath. That's why the aphorism "take a deep breath and count to ten" works, when it does. (Which is not always; and we'll soon see why that's so.) To stop yourself from crying, you have to swallow the lump in your throat, squeeze your eyes, and hold your breath. To stop yourself from shouting, the process is much the same.

Breath is one of the few bodily functions that is under both conscious and involuntary control, which is why it's such a powerful lever for change.[3] Of course, breath can be constrained by those unconscious neuromuscular habits of armoring. And none of us escape life without any armoring. Imagine the soft and pliable body of an infant. Now imagine the stiff, creaky body of an old man. Armoring is a significant part of what makes up the difference.

It's easy to see the source of armoring when you're talking about military training. But even for those of us who have never been in a combat zone, armoring will set in all the same. We've all held in emotions that are inappropriate to express in the moment, or fended off the unwanted emotional intrusions of others. When we're unable to speak to these concerns, our bodies do it for us, tightening and contracting to keep unwanted emotions either in or out.

Muscle and connective tissue that's been contracted repeatedly for years will slowly harden and become more dense.[4] Over time, this makes it more difficult for waste to exit cells and nutrients to enter. In a very real sense, we slowly "choke" and "starve" the cells in the most armored parts of our bodies.

When you hyper-oxygenate the body as Rich did with the Sudarshan Kriya breathing practices, cells that have been starving for air can finally gasp in relief. Like a drowning person dragged from the water in just the nick of time, the body sputters and shakes as cells pull in long-denied oxygen, nutrients, and nerve communication, and puke out the waste that doesn't belong there. The trembling, sobbing rush of emotional intensity that Rich experienced is an example of this kind of whole-body gasp.

A rapid increase in cell oxygenation can decrease armoring and thereby expand your capacity to feel. Thanks to the breathing practice, Rich no longer had to keep holding his unexpressed grief, regret, fear, and anger at bay. Without a lot of talking or processing, he could directly release those emotions. And once he released them, he was free to live his life without them.

Because emotion regulation is tied to breath, releasing armoring around respiratory muscles can completely change your background mood. Once breath can move more freely, access to greater emotional range becomes available. And indeed, this is what Seppälä's research found. The active group that went through the one-week intervention showed significantly reduced PTSD symptoms, including decreased startle response, fewer nightmares and flashbacks, and more positive emotion. The control group that was waitlisted for the program showed none of these effects.[5]

But Emma's team wasn't sure how far to trust the results. After all, if you went to the gym for a week you might feel better, too. So they checked in with study participants a month later. All their self-reported symptoms remained low. The real test occurred a year later, when they sent questionnaires to both the active and control groups, and were astonished to discover the results remained the same.

They doubted their findings and analyzed the data every way they could think of. But the subjective reports remained solid, and physiological tests of blink rate and startle response correlated strongly with participant reports. The researchers had no choice but to conclude that yes indeed, this simple weeklong breathing intervention had successfully reduced many of the symptoms of PTSD.[6] This finding is great news for vets and other trauma survivors, because rather than depending on a drug or a course of therapy, this practical technique for recentering yourself empowers you to take responsibility for your own healing.

But as anyone who's ever tried to "take a deep breath and count to ten" knows, that doesn't always work to change your mood. If the breath is such a powerful influence on mood, then why does that trick sometimes fail?

Nichole Dunn became President and CEO of the Women's Fund of Central Ohio at just thirty-three years old. Reporting to a board of twenty-five powerful and influential community members, she was both proud to be heading up the organization and daunted by the role. The first year, she was sick to her stomach for six months straight. She joined the organization barely two weeks after her second child was born, and quickly dropped to fifteen pounds below her prepregnancy weight. "I've never had such a strong physical reaction to circumstances for such a prolonged period of time," Nichole says of that first year. "I remembered the person I was before... but where did she go? My true sense of self was being eaten away."

You don't usually get to a position of such leadership and responsibility without merit, and Nichole had that in spades. Raised by a prominent Minneapolis family, Nichole held herself to high standards in all areas of life—first in school and later in her career. Growing up, achievement was valued and high expectations were the norm. Nichole was driven, ambitious, and most of all, *caring*. She wanted to make a difference and she worked relentlessly to do so.

After her first year on the job, Nichole engaged leadership coach Suzanne Roberts. Exhausted by the daily pressures and yet eager to continue her work, Nichole knew she needed support. Working with Suzanne, Nichole uncovered her conditioned response to stress: Bear down, grit her teeth, and just get through it. If this sounds like an echo of Rich's Army training, that's because it is, but not for the same reasons. Thanks to her upbringing and her high expectations of herself, Nichole embodied the habit of shouldering more responsibility than was necessary. Faced with the pressure of a difficult job worth doing, Nichole soldiered on without rest.

With Suzanne's help, Nichole discovered more about her neuromuscular biobehavioral habits. Her gut was exquisitely sensitive to stress, but her reaction didn't stop there. Under pressure she'd drop her chin, narrowing her view to the immediate issue at hand and losing sight of the bigger picture. Consistent with feedback she'd received about a tendency to hold back and hesitate to lead, she also had a tendency to lean back physically. Valiantly futile attempts to keep everyone happy resulted in a freeze-and-appease reaction to virtually every issue and request.

In Suzanne's office and at her women's leadership program, Nichole learned how to physically center herself while connecting to what she cared about. She brought herself forward and squared herself over her hips. She lifted her chin and looked to the horizon, toward her vision for the future of the Women's Fund. She learned practices that helped her shift from a gut-churning physiological stress response into the more coordinated internal rhythms of psychophysiological coherence. As her tension declined, her capacity to take stronger leadership grew. But when it came time for the annual fundraiser, with celebrity guests on stage and thousands of attendees waiting to hear from her, Nichole needed to find a whole new level of composure.

Taking a deep breath may calm you, but typically that only works when the situation is relatively low-stakes, familiar, and more or less under your control. Nichole's days were so demanding and action-packed that the proverbial "deep breath and count to ten" barely registered. When the stakes get higher, you need more powerful tools.

In the last chapter we saw that how you stand impacts courage: The psoas muscles that control pelvic tilt also affect your capacity to relax and stay calm, cool, and collected. Because these muscles attach on the same vertebra as the diaphragm, they also affect how you breathe. And the muscles you use to breathe are the same muscles you use to stay upright. With every breath, you subtly challenge your balance and postural stability.

It may surprise you to learn that in addition to your respiratory diaphragm, your pelvic floor and thoracic inlet also play a role in both breathing and structural stability. In other words, you have not one diaphragm, but three. And they all act in unison to fill the body with breath. Watch a baby breathe and you'll see the belly rhythmically rise and fall. Infants breathe using their whole torso.

According to research by Massery, Hagins, and Hodges, these three diaphragms function like interlocking gears.[7] They contract automatically to stabilize the body during movement, which means how you move can affect how you breathe, either to your benefit or to your detriment. Dysfunction in one diaphragm affects each of the others, creating a loss of function and power in the extremities, spine, and—germane to our purposes here—respiration.[8] This can affect not only mood, but also cognition, digestion, sleep, pain, and more.

Physical therapist Matthew Taylor has pointed out that such dysfunction can arise not only through physical injury, but also through the slings and arrows of everyday life: spiritless work, long-held resentments, marriage troubles, or—as in Nichole's case—chronic stress.[9] Tough situations such as these can cause chronic muscular contraction that can affect any muscle in the body, including the psoas and any of the three diaphragms. See if you can sense the muscles involved in "biting your tongue," for instance, or "being a tightass." Metaphors like these are often less metaphorical and quite a bit more literal than we typically realize.

By the time we're adults, most of us—both men and women—have been "sucking it in" for years, in a decades-long attempt to meet society's flat-bellied standards of beauty. Unless you pause to consciously make it so, you probably no longer engage your entire torso on a breath-by-breath basis. Unconsciously breathing from the neck and upper chest places an ongoing burden on your body, subtly activating the sympathetic branch of the nervous system and keeping you in a perpetual state of low-level fight or flight. Because shallow breathing is associated with emotions such as fear and surprise, this habitual breath pattern propagates a persistent message of mild anxiety throughout your entire system.

You breathe at least nine hundred times an hour. That's over 21,000 times a day and more than 150,000 times a week. Only your heart muscle moves more.[10] So you have ample opportunity to develop the muscle memory that makes a particular breath pattern automatic. And because the way you breathe is tightly linked to the way you move, how you habitually stand is going to affect your breath.

If you typically move in a driven way (chin down, jaw clenched, eyes focused, leaning forward) or in a hesitant way (leaning back, brow furrowed, gut churning in response to stress), that background mood will be repeatedly evoked by your breath. This can limit your ability to breathe in a way that calms you down. If your body's structure interferes with the full range of motion of your breath, that "deep breath and count to ten" trick will have invisible constraints that you're almost certainly not even aware of.

Centering yourself—claiming or regaining composure—means aligning yourself physically in such a way that the maximum amount of breath and metabolic energy can move through your body and nourish you. As little as possible is constricted, blocked off, or closed. Nichole released some of the long-held armoring that affected her posture, her breath, and her composure by engaging in regular body-work with Suzanne. As she changed her stance in subtle ways—a lifted chin, a more erect spine, wider shoulders and a wider, more powerful stance—Nichole brought her three diaphragms into a more effective working relationship. By practicing to make this new way of standing, walking, and moving her new normal, she was able to access more of a sense of calm, clarity, and focus with every breath. This change greatly enhanced her ability to lead.

The Women's Fund annual gala is the biggest fundraising event of the year, and a lot rides on its success. The event is held in a beautiful historic landmark theatre with over 2,500 guests in attendance. Celebrity guest speakers such as Whoopi Goldberg and Vanessa Williams take the stage. The pressure on the organization and in particular on its CEO swells to an annual all-time high. "Are you kidding me?" Nichole asks rhetorically. "I'm just this one little 5'6" woman." As is common for leaders who battle impostor syndrome—particularly women—unspoken words seem to hang in the air: *Do I really deserve to lead this powerfully?*

Each year, Nichole calls Suzanne the moment the date is set to book an appointment for the morning of the event. When the big day arrives, she heads to Suzanne's office first thing, climbing the stairs to the familiar quiet space overlooking the vibrant green of the Ohio springtime. They begin with bodywork, releasing unconscious blocks that constrict Nichole's posture or breath. As Nichole lies down on the table, Suzanne gently cradles her head. Placing both hands under Nichole's upper back, she waits for Nichole to exhale and then stretches her scapula away from her spine. She does a diaphragm release and then nods with satisfaction as Nichole spontaneously takes a deep breath. Suzanne continues like this, finding different points of contact that support release and relaxation, for about an hour.

When Nichole stands up, Suzanne asks her what feels different. "I feel taller," Nichole says. She has more room inside for her breath. Her chin is level with the floor, and she feels more solid over her hips. She feels rooted like a tree.

"What's the opportunity today, Nichole?" asks Suzanne. "What's your vision for social change? And how do you want to lead the community into this vision?" Nichole replies, but her voice sounds hesitant, wavering. She's leaning back ever so slightly. Suzanne reminds her to connect to her vision and bring all of herself forward. This time, Nichole sounds more self-assured. "I am a stand for safety for girls," she says earnestly. As her voice fills with breath, it becomes more resonant. "I am a stand for women to own their voice and their power."

This process of aligning breath and body, care and commitment, voice and vision is one way of centering—of settling yourself and strengthening yourself for the task ahead. Nichole doesn't speak about this in the terms I use in the book, but essentially she enlisted Suzanne's help with de-armoring, feeling her sensations more acutely, connecting to her care, and organizing her psychophysiology for greater coherence. This is what allows her to show up in the high-pressure environment of the annual fundraiser—as well as day to day—with equanimity and enthusiasm rather than stress and anxiety.

Later that day, Suzanne and Nichole meet again backstage for another tune-up. Nichole has been out circulating in the large crowd, greeting donors warmly and soaking in their excitement. Now she's got about an hour to prepare for her talk. Recalling how it felt to speak powerfully on behalf of her vision earlier that morning, Nichole aligns her body, breath, and voice to do so again.

Suzanne stands beside her and places her hand on Nichole's back. "Name the people who have your back," she says. "Who stands with you in support?" Leveling her chin and feeling her feet, Nichole speaks the names of the friends and fans who are rooting for her success and the success of the Women's Fund. While she may stand alone on stage, she knows she's backed by dozens, hundreds, even thousands of supporters in their community. Suzanne's hand at her back gives her a physical experience of this ample support, so that it becomes more than just an abstract concept. As she rests into Suzanne's hand, Nichole's whole body gently relaxes.

Suzanne invites Nichole to amplify the power of her words by speaking her commitment aloud as she steps forward and extends her arms outstretched, as if inviting others to join her. With a resonant voice and a relaxed body, sensing the support of her backers and committed to her vision, Nichole feels increasingly aligned with her mission and ready to head on stage.

Still, like any adrenaline rush before a big event, strong sensations come flooding in and butterflies do a number on her stomach as she walks out to greet the crowd. What's different now from her first year on the job is that Nichole has a more effective way to contend with those intense sensations. In working with Suzanne, she's learned how to ground that powerful energy through her posture and her breath, channeling it into her message so she can better engage the community in the mission of the Women's Fund.

After several years of this kind of annual event preparation as well as ongoing work with Suzanne, Nichole now rocks these speeches every year. She's developed a magnetic, compelling presence, and she shows up as powerful, engaged, and connected with the audience, even when she's silent. Both the event and the organization have grown substantially under Nichole's leadership, and the pressure she faces now is considerably greater than it was during her first year on the job. But by training her body for greater resilience, Nichole has built both the inner fortitude and the leadership capacity to handle that pressure with grace and composure. People who are typically critical about presentations have called Suzanne to ask "What have you done with Nichole?" Her growing leadership is changing Ohio for the better. And all indications suggest the best is yet to come.

Composure is not about getting rid of the nerves. Nice as that may sound, sometimes it's not possible. Rather, like courage, composure is about being able to *tolerate* all the strong sensations that go along with making a big, important move. It's about consciously feeling all of the intensity and physical discomfort while aligning yourself in such a way that those sensations can move through you without getting stuck in a swirling whirlpool of anxiety. It's about using your breath as best you can and choosing to take action from your commitment rather than your fear. This is what courage and composure *really* feel like. It's not always comfortable. In fact, it rarely is. And yet it's often the one thing that makes all the difference in meeting challenging circumstances.

Even if you don't deliver speeches alongside celebrities or face life-and-death decisions in a combat zone, your life surely makes demands on your composure. Moving to a new town and reaching out to make new friends, or stepping up into an exciting-but-challenging new job, or supporting a loved one through a major illness, or facing any number of other ordinary life challenges will test your composure and your capacity to meet the pressures of your life with a calm, collected presence.

We know that stress is a physiological response to pressure. And if stress is physiological, then your capacity to recover from stress must be, too. You can't always talk yourself out of anxiety. And actually, that's fantastic news. Because just as you can build bigger biceps or stronger abs, you can build the muscle memory that makes composure and resilience easier to access.

Just as Nichole and Rich have done, you can de-armor chronic contractions, learn to tolerate intense sensations, get your hips underneath you, and open your belly and chest to more breath. All of this allows you to regulate wild emotions and face the slings and arrows of life with a more relaxed and settled stance, cultivating a psychophysiological coherence that not only improves your mood, but also improves your performance.

With practice you can make these ways of inhabiting your body second nature, so that reaching for courage and composure becomes as easy and automatic as getting a spoon to your mouth. And therein lies the magic. Because when you embody composure, you can contend with a whole host of things that previously seemed difficult or impossible. And that brings success more easily within reach.

10

Confidence

Anthony: Befriending Networking

Am I going to graduate? Are we gonna win this game? Will I get into college? Will I get into a good college? Will I find a girlfriend? What if I don't make friends? Will I pass the test? Am I smart enough? Will I get into graduate school? What if I don't do well in graduate school?

Terrors like these plagued Anthony Attan throughout his youth and early adulthood. Common ones, to be sure, but for this sports-oriented high achiever, the concerns could at times be debilitating. ("Terror" is his word, not mine.) He suffered from migraines, neck tension, back aches. Perhaps worst of all, by the time he got to Michigan State—his top-choice school—he could hardly eat. His stomach was constantly tied in knots, but the multiple specialists he visited didn't offer any clear answers. Although one rather unhelpfully warned, "You have the gallbladder of a fifty-five-year-old woman."

Anthony's ever-present concern about being good enough was like an eight-cylinder engine without an off switch. It drove him to high achievement, which was great, but it also drove him straight to the doctor's office. The constant self-induced pressure was taking a toll on his body.

Everyone knows that the highly sensitive gut is extremely responsive to stress. This connection shows up in our everyday language. You get "butterflies in your stomach" when you're excited or nervous; you "feel like you're gonna puke" when you're furiously upset. What's up with this?

Back in Chapter 3 I touched on a few of the fascinating facts about the enteric nervous system, which functions a bit like a second brain in your gut. This "gut brain" operates largely without input from the brain in your head, and it both influences and is heavily affected by mood.

Across the animal kingdom, the gut also plays an important role in relationships and social dominance. The alpha dog usually eats first; the underdog typically defers. Next time you go out to eat, watch the diners at the restaurant. It won't be long before you see it—as with other species, we subtly do the same.

For Anthony, the constantly upset state of his stomach reflected his anxieties about performing well and being liked and accepted. But he couldn't easily see another way of handling his life. This was his biobehavioral blind spot. Left unattended, it could easily undermine all the success he was trying to achieve.

In college, Anthony decided to go into psychology, thinking he'd learn to help others. At the time, it didn't really occur to him that his choice of major might benefit him as well. He tackled the topic with his customary academic rigor and drive, and he did well. After earning both a BA and a master's degree, he entered the PhD program at Capella University, where he focused on industrial and organizational psychology. But his interests remained wholly academic.

In graduate school, he stumbled across research about how facial expression and body posture affect psychological state. Intrigued, he reached out to Dr. Ginny Whitelaw, whom he had met a few years earlier through a mutual friend. Ginny was developing a new leadership-assessment tool grounded in the link between body and behavior. Anthony wanted to learn more.

Ginny, a biophysicist, Zen priest, and executive coach, had noticed something that bothered her. As a senior manager at NASA, she had experienced a lot of leadership training "from the neck up." But as a fifth-degree black belt aikido practitioner, she had seen again and again how her students changed their lives as they trained their bodies, becoming more able to roll with the punches, for example, or to take quick, decisive action. She felt that when leadership training ignored the body, it was missing something vital. And she wanted to help fill that void.

Some years earlier, Ginny had crossed paths with Betsy Wetzig, a celebrated dance teacher who had taken an interest in how patterned movement showed up in her dancers' personalities. Ballet dancers were as precise and orderly in their lives as they were on the stage, arriving promptly on time and keeping their dance gear tidy. Whereas jazz dancers seemed to have more drive, and swing dancers were often more playful. She noticed similar patterns in other artists too: poets, painters, potters. She had been observing and experimenting with these patterns herself for some time when a colleague introduced her to some kinesiology research from the nineteen-thirties, forties, and fifties that pointed to the same patterns and showed that each had a distinguishably unique neuromuscular signature.[1]

As Betsy explored the research, word of her work started to get around. The Lincoln Center in New York City invited her to develop movement pieces to go along with a series of paintings. She decided to mimic each painter's walk based on the shape of the colors on canvas —a tall order given that she didn't know any of the artists. After her performance, friends of the artists were astonished by the accuracy of her portrayals. Without knowing a thing about the painters beyond their expression on canvas, she had nailed each artist's walk, down to the tilt of their head and their habitual gestures.

Eventually, news of her work on these patterns landed on the desk of one Dr. Alex Lotas in Detroit. Lotas found Betsy's number and rang. After a few preliminaries, he got straight to the point. "Where did you learn about Jung's archetypes?" he asked her. "Your patterns describe the Jungian archetypes perfectly." Betsy furrowed her brow. "I don't really know much about Jung," she asked. "What do you mean?"

Their conversation affirmed her hunch that the neuromuscular patterns she was playing with might have a significant tie to psychology. She ended that phone call shaking her head in astonishment and reimagining what the patterns were really about. She and Ginny went on to explore that tie with respect to leadership development. And it was thanks to this exploration that Anthony's understanding of psychology finally became more than academic—and far more useful to him.

Understanding the patterns remained an intellectual curiosity for Anthony until he had the chance to experience them himself. Anthony's preferred pattern is what Ginny calls the "Organizer," that ballet-like perfectionist driven to get things just so. His secondary pattern preference was for Driver. This combination of striving for perfection and driving for achievement had contributed to his success, but it was also the source of the ailments and anxieties that drove him to the doctor's office. Feeling driven to perfect performance— and worried about achieving it—is a hallmark characteristic of the Organizer-Driver energy.

When Ginny asked Anthony to get into the physical movements characteristic of Driver and Organizer, he felt right at home. But when he started moving in what Ginny has termed the Collaborator and Visionary energies—a more swinging, drifting, free-floating sort of movement—Anthony *hated* it. The movements felt altogether unfamiliar and they made him deeply uncomfortable. Nauseated, even.

As he continued his exploration, Ginny became an important mentor to Anthony. Eventually, she hired him to do validation studies on the leadership assessment tool that she had developed. During a strategy meeting one day, Anthony complained about his frustrations with networking. He was connected to plenty of professors and students, but he knew he was going to need more professional contacts for his career. Networking events seemed like a necessary evil. They brought up all kinds of worries about how he would be perceived, but nevertheless he attended one after another, trying with all his might to "win" at networking. But the results he was hoping for were never really forthcoming, even though he was giving it his all. Before each event, he would do sit-ups and push-ups to heavy-metal music, setting his jaw in determination and walking through the door intent on handing out more business cards than anyone else. He had written a giant note on his whiteboard to boost his success: "I am going to make WAR on networking!"

Ginny just smiled when he told her all this. "Perhaps your approach is part of the problem," she gently prodded. She helped Anthony redesign his pre-networking ritual, teaching him how to leverage the swinging, back-and-forth movements of Collaborator energy instead. She had him lie down on the floor and say "blaaaaahhhh," loosening up his diaphragm and making room for deeper breathing. She had him swing from side to side, loosening up his hips and lower back. She had him shake his whole body, ridding himself of any residual tension.

This loosey-goosey way of moving was still mightily uncomfortable for Anthony, but all his academic research told him that if he practiced enough, it would become easier. So he ditched the pre-networking sit-ups and push-ups and switched to more lyrical, lilting music. He spent time loosening up before these events. And he changed the note on his whiteboard to read "I'm making *friends* with networking."

This combination of words, music, and movement helped Anthony center himself around a different set of priorities and settle into a different way of being. He found a way to strengthen himself for the task ahead by practicing movements that put him into a state of mind more conducive to meeting people and making connections.

Now, he not only enjoys going to networking events, he actually looks forward to it. He relishes the opportunity to connect with like-minded colleagues and to make new friends. He's less about handing out business cards and more about curiosity; less about "killing it" and more about kindness. And the business results are unmistakable. Only eighteen months after moving to Baltimore, Anthony had gathered more professional contacts than he had ever had before.

As Anthony started to build this loosened-up way of moving into his life more and more, other things started to change, too. Instead of starting his day "ice skating uphill" by checking email before his feet even hit the floor, he now eases into his day with a bit more leeway. Even in the midst of a really stressful time at work, he can go out to dinner, relax, and talk about other things—a welcome change his wife regularly comments on. He no longer worries about whether he'll measure up academically, professionally, or otherwise; he just confidently offers whatever he can that will help others. And perhaps most importantly, his health has improved. The neck pain, back pain, and GI upset that he experienced in his more pressured and driven state have all faded to the background. And it all started by changing the habitual way he moves.

When you walk up a flight of stairs, which do you use more: your quads or your hamstrings? It may surprise you to learn that not everybody does it the same way. It may surprise you even more to learn that how you do it reveals a great deal about you. For someone who knows how to look, your heavy footfall, delicate steps, or dancing walk speaks volumes.

Thanks to Betsy, Ginny, and Anthony's work, we now know that these movement patterns do indeed have clear positive correlations with several personality-typing assessments. The FEBI assessment tool that Ginny developed has been validated against the better-known Myers-Briggs, DISC, and NEO personality testing tools, and it correlates strongly with each one. So the data is in: How you move does indeed reveal a lot about who you are.

Whether you're walking up a flight of stairs, readying a golf club for a swing, or raising a glass for a toast, moving your body relies upon a tight communication loop between your somatosensory cortex— the bit of brain that runs from the crown of your head down to your ears—and the skeletal muscles of your arms, legs, and torso. This link between your nerve cells and your muscle cells is what allows you to walk, sit, stand, and move.

We are as different on the inside as we are on the outside, so everyone's pattern of neuromuscular firing is unique. But as Josephine Rathbone discovered in the 1930s and Valerie Hunt later explored, there are four distinct neuromuscular patterns. And most of us start preferentially relying on one or two of them as early as infancy and toddlerhood.[2] To understand how these patterns work, and how they are tied to action, behavior, and personality, you need to know a bit about muscular anatomy.

Skeletal muscles work in pairs. Flexor muscles, which close the angle of a joint (helping you bend your knees, for example) are paired with extensor muscles that open the angle and help you bend back. Muscles can only exert a pulling force, so without these pairings you'd be in big trouble: once you bent your leg you'd never be able to straighten it again.

But these muscles don't work in the simple one-to-one fashion you might expect—bicep to bend, tricep to straighten. Instead, distinct patterns call on both muscles at once. Some people tighten up their extensor right before flexing, resulting in a swift, powerful movement. Others use both bicep and tricep in equal measure, creating a ballet-like precision. Some swing between both in alternating sequence. Still others rely mostly on the flexor muscles, which creates more of a slow drift. These are the movement patterns that Betsy observed, and they reveal much more about you than what's visible on the surface.

Barring significant illness or injury, all of us have the neurological and muscular capacity to use any of the patterns. And we do, drawing upon each in different sets of circumstances. But like anything in life, we all have our preferences. The good news is that because you already have access to each movement pattern, you can call on underutilized capacities—or dial back overused strengths—simply by practicing a different style of movement. So, like Anthony, you can come to embody confidence (or any number of other qualities) by changing how you move. Whether it's networking or presenting, competing or performing, planning or executing, you can improve your results by moving in a style that supports the activity ahead.

Got a results-oriented meeting this afternoon? Schedule a kick-boxing class for lunch. Need to counteract your scatter-brained tendencies? Stand with good posture and take careful, composed steps before you sit down to clean up your desk. Need to take a look at the big picture? Lean back and gaze at the horizon for a bit. Practice and you'll find what Anthony discovered: calling up the energy you need for the task at hand is far more than an academic exercise.

11

Credibility

Denise: Standing Tall, Striving Less

Years ago I was working at a large company when a new general manager was hired to lead our group. On his first day, Dan assembled the entire three-hundred-person division for a mandatory meeting. He started off by saying, "Over the next several months, I'll get to know each of you. But as of today, your job is to follow my directives. And you don't know me from a hole in the wall. That doesn't seem fair."

He went on to tell us about the personal and professional journey that brought him to this place and time. Within days I forgot many of the details, but more than fifteen years later one thing stands out in my mind: he didn't stop at sharing his successes.

Earlier in his career, he had founded a business that turned out to be, according to his colorful account, "a spectacular failure." He talked about how he leveraged the learning from that experience to help him become a better leader. He spoke with honesty, humility, and humor.

Of the many impressive accomplishments he shared, this was the one that humanized him, that made him easy to relate to, and that made me confident the right person had been hired for the job.

Contrast this with another leader hired by the same company a few years later. Sharon (not her real name) also held a mandatory meeting somewhere near the beginning of her stint. When we arrived, a woman we didn't recognize stood up and started talking about the financials from last quarter, the plans for the next quarter, and what was expected of us—even going so far as to attempt to pull a tepid cheer from the crowd. I guess she assumed we knew who she was. By the end of the meeting, many of us still didn't.

Unfortunately, this leader's many fine qualities were buried under the mistrust created by her initial gaffe. She lost credibility with us. And she never quite earned it back.

Credibility requires many things: A track record of trustworthiness. The skills and experience to deliver whatever it is you've promised. And, notably, the capacity to be appropriately vulnerable—to share your humanity in a way that makes you relatable without undermining others' trust in you.

Trust is one of those things that you can't see or touch or count or point to, and yet its absence creates all kinds of mischief. Without it, nothing gets done. But when trust is strong, great things can be accomplished.

And authenticity is the currency of trust.

The people who are real with us are always the most credible and trustworthy, because we know we can count on them. What you see is what you get. That's why Dan's vulnerability was so disarming—and so galvanizing. From day one, we knew he would own up to his mistakes, hold us accountable for our own, and tell us the truth. And that went a long way toward building the trust that was necessary for him to get the job done.

But conveying this kind of authenticity is easier said than done. Typically it requires considerable courage to be real, because often "getting real" involves some degree of vulnerability. And when you're in a leadership role where the pressure to perform is immense, this kind of vulnerability can feel like an incredibly risky move.

The courage, composure, and confidence that we've been exploring throughout this section create a stable foundation for credibility. Because it's rarely comfortable to reveal the foibles that make you most relatable. But doing so in a way that establishes both your confidence and your competence is precisely what's required to build trust.

Denise Rundle is known as a high achiever, and she likes it that way. For more than two decades, she has dedicated herself to high performance and achievement at Microsoft. In appreciation of her good work as a senior director, she was offered some coaching as a development opportunity. True to form, she aimed to be John McConnell's number-one star coaching client, the one he beamed with pride about. "I wasted the entire first year of coaching trying to impress my coach," Denise says with a wry smile.

This striving for an A+ affected every area of her life, from her appearance (impeccably stylish at all times), to her work (stellar and worthy of much praise), to her relationship with her sister (where she played the role of responsible rescuer, always bailing her sister out of jams). At work, her unspoken wish was for the Microsoft executive team to think "What on earth would we do without Denise Rundle?"

But this constant striving to impress had its downsides. She was doing well in her role, but she had plateaued. She was incredibly driven, always working hard to look totally together. And usually she nailed it—her high performance was no act. But in striving to appear perfect, she wasn't being particularly authentic or transparent. Her colleagues trusted her, but only so far. She didn't have the executive presence required to move to the next level.

One day, her coach invited her to meet him at the rock-climbing gym for their session. She agreed, even though she thought it would be a waste of time. "What are we going to do at the gym?" she wondered, rolling her eyes on her way there. But she was into efficiency, and she figured she'd kill two birds with one stone. "At least I'll get my workout in," she thought.

She was battling a knee injury, which she had mentioned to John before agreeing to this absurd plan. She assumed she wouldn't be able to climb at all. But as she roped up and tried one route after another, she kept exceeding what she thought she was capable of. She surprised herself, and she was immensely pleased. But as she tried harder and harder routes, eventually she came to one where she couldn't go any further. "Okay, I'm done," she said. She asked John to lower her.

"Sure, no problem," John replied. "But before I do... have you considered asking for help?"

Startled, Denise realized that the thought hadn't even once crossed her mind. But as soon as he asked the question, she also realized that John had a different perspective from the ground, not to mention considerably more experience climbing. He offered a few suggestions, and she made it to the top. For the rest of the session, she kept pushing past her perceived limits by climbing as high as she could on her own, then asking John for help. Toward the end of their time, they sat down to talk it over.

"The way you do one thing is the way you do everything," John said. "Where else are you putting limits on what you're capable of before you've even tried? Where else are you not asking for help?"

A skilled observer can set up exercises and experiments—as John did with the climbing—that reveal your embodied habits so you can see them, too. Working with your body is a particularly evocative way to discover your blind spots, because the habits and ways of being you embody typically lie outside your conscious awareness. After all, one reason embodied patterns develop in the first place is so you can put them on autopilot and enact them without having to think about it.

Once those invisible habits become visible, all of a sudden you have options you couldn't even see before.

As she climbed, Denise discovered that a strong fear of failure drove her to appear polished in every way—and put a lid on her potential in the process. "There was before climbing, and there was after climbing," John says of Denise. "She was like a different person after that."

After the climbing session, Denise started to rely on the coaching relationship in a different way. She brought her concerns and, yes, even her frailties into their conversations. John continued to use physical practices to reveal her longstanding habits and invisible blind spots. Together, they engaged in exercises to help Denise build her composure—something she was sorely in need of throughout a protracted and contentious divorce. But most of all, she learned to soften her striving.

Not long after the day at the climbing gym, Microsoft's midyear review was held. This meeting intimidates. Tables and chairs form a square in a large hotel ballroom. At one end sit a dozen or so of the company's top executives. Division heads sit along the sides, where they await their turn to stand at the front and speak to recent achievements and challenges.

In the past, Denise had always gone into these meetings eager to please. "The executives could withstand a lot of conflict in order to come to the best outcome," she told me. But that kind of friction made her palms sweat and her heart race. She avoided going toe-to-toe and instead spent her few minutes in the spotlight highlighting accomplishments and hoping for high marks and praise.

After her climbing epiphany, Denise took a different approach. She realized that by striving for an A+, she was wasting an opportunity to seek another valuable perspective, to get the other smart minds in the room to think about the challenges she faced. So instead of her usual spiel, she spent a scant minute or so highlighting her team's wins. They had exceeded many of their goals, but she didn't belabor the point.

Instead, she shifted into discussing the challenges and opportunities ahead. She spoke about the most common frustrations that customers reported in her division, and she championed finding solutions. Not just workable solutions, but *outstanding* solutions. Behind the scenes there was a lack of coordination among service teams. "This is unacceptable," she asserted. "I'm embarrassed that we have to take calls like these. I want us to have outstanding products. I want to be proud of what we're creating." Her powerful call to action successfully enlisted other senior managers to join her in making substantial changes to the way they delivered service at Microsoft.

"She's talking this way to the top ten executives in the company," John told me later, "and they're ready to roll up their sleeves and get going."

Brené Brown's research on the complex intersection of shame, perfectionism, vulnerability, and authenticity reveals how common the impulse to perform and appear polished is, particularly among women. It also points the way toward a more effective approach. Brown has found that the more forthcoming you are about your challenges (within appropriate boundaries, of course), the more trust and connection flourishes.[1]

Asking for help is an act of authenticity. Done well, it builds credibility. Done poorly, it can erode it. Working with John, Denise had been practicing standing, breathing, and moving in ways that made the unfamiliar act of asking for help come more naturally to her, so that she could reveal her challenges to the executive team while maintaining her dignity, confidence, and composure. Saying you don't know and revealing you can't do it alone has a much different impact when you come from a foundation of centered strength rather than simpering fear. It is this kind of courageous authenticity that builds trust and cements credibility.

We pick up on this authenticity not only through someone's words, but also through how they carry themselves. Are they fidgety or settled? Restless or relaxed? Making eye contact or scrutinizing their shoes? When your body and your words convey a settled, calm, relaxed state of being, others can trust in the truth of what you say. Naturally your credibility must be grounded in solid knowledge and strong skills in the relevant domain. Assuming that's a given, your credibility also rests upon your capacity to center yourself and embody the confidence, courage, and composure you need to be powerfully authentic.

This kind of authenticity isn't just a professional thing. Centered-yet-vulnerable truth-telling is also the glue that sustains many a deep friendship and happy marriage. It's the unspoken safety net that allows a recalcitrant teenager to open up to a parent when most in need of guidance. It's the satisfaction and relief that comes from being real; from not having to hide your uncertainties, your frailties, your failures, and your humanity. And because we all have our own all-too-human stories, authenticity can be deeply connecting. Which is what we're about to explore next: how embodied self-awareness supports meaningful connections and deeper empathy.

SECTION

3

Deepen Empathy

Once you have built the somatic competencies of sensing more and centering yourself, you'll be well on your way toward embodying the kinds of emotional intelligence skills that are so vital for success and satisfaction. But while the place to begin is your relationship with yourself, that really only gets you in the starting blocks.

We live embedded in a sea of relationships. It can be challenging to build relationships and to foster connection while navigating the daily nuances of power, intimacy, leadership, conflict, and kindness, but if you have dreams and desires you want to bring to life, you must learn to do so. And at this point it should come as no surprise that your body is intimately involved in that process.

In Chapter 12, "Connection," we'll see how a single mom and busy executive Laila Tarraf developed a deeper capacity for connection by strengthening her embodied self-awareness. Then we'll explore how physical therapists in a rehab center leveraged embodied learning to connect more deeply with their patients, and how that affected patient outcomes. Chapter 13, "Compassion," explores Claus Wieser's journey from unintentionally steamrolling his Microsoft peers to standing up for his team with greater empathy.

Embody Emotional and Social Intelligence

	AWARENESS	*ACTION*
Emotional Intelligence – *SELF*	**FIND PURPOSE** *align w. yourself + the mystery* core skill: *self-awareness* somatic competency: SENSE Care Choose Commit Contribute	**BUILD RESILIENCE** *settle + strengthen yourself* core skill: *self-mastery* somatic competency: CENTER Courage Composure Confidence Credibility
Social Intelligence – *OTHERS*	**DEEPEN EMPATHY** *listen deeply...* *w. all of your senses* core skill: *empathy* somatic competency: PRESENCE Connection Compassion	**INSPIRE OTHERS** *act from centered care...* *for self + others* core skill: *social dexterity* somatic competency: GALVANIZE Communicate Collaborate Conflict to Consensus

In these chapters we turn our attention to social intelligence: the capacity to be aware of others' emotions and to rely on that understanding to take more effective collective action. We'll begin by focusing on empathy, and we'll soon come to see how embodied self-awareness provides a critical neurobiological foundation for this core social intelligence skill.

In addition to feeling your own sensations, empathy also requires the ability to listen deeply with all of your senses to what another is saying... and to what he or she is *not* saying. It's about building the ability to pick up messages on all channels; to read the nonverbal "vibes" in a situation and to genuinely acknowledge and legitimize what others may be feeling.

The somatic competency that underlies empathy is presence. I define presence as the capacity to have your attention simultaneously on yourself and another (or others). Deep presence requires feeling all of your own sensations while also actively "tuning in" to the people around you. This is distinct from focusing all of your attention on someone else while abandoning your own values, vision, and needs. It's also different from focusing all of your attention on yourself at someone else's expense. Presence is a both/and sort of thing.

Recall the last time you experienced someone being fully present with you. Now think about the last time someone was definitely *not* present. Odds are there was a palpable difference. That's because our bodies are open systems. All day long we engage in a silent neurobiological dance with those around us, affecting one another's physiology through space and time. Your heart rate, brain waves, and other physiological markers both affect and are affected by the quality of your own and others' presence—or lack thereof. And as we'll come to see, our capacity for presence and empathy has a tangible, measurable effect on health, happiness, and even financial results. Let's find out how.

> Practices to help you get present can be found in
> Appendix A and at yourbodyisyourbrain.com.

12

Connection

Laila: I've Got Your Back
Courage Center: The Humanity at the Heart of Healthcare

You may recall from earlier chapters that connection is one of three essential nutrients that shape the nervous system. We all have unique biobehavioral patterns with respect to connection: Some of us crave more of it; others push it away. Some seem to be naturally given to the sort of social graces that help them connect; others stumble and falter.

However you feel about connection, you can't escape the fact that we're social creatures who live embedded in a sea of relationships. Even if you turn away from many of those relationships, you cannot avoid taking some stance with respect to connection. No matter what, you have some way of being in a relationship that is specific to you. And the way you connect has far-reaching implications for your satisfaction and success in life.

But most of us live in a sea of disconnection. Technologically, we are more connected than ever, and naturally this digital network has many benefits. I, for one, relish my relationships with friends and clients around the globe. But our ubiquitous virtual connection comes at a cost. When you're distracted by devices and you've packed your schedule to bursting, genuine in-the-moment connection takes a hit.

Picture a carpool of teenage boys, each playing a different video game on his own separate device. Or a parent, dejected kid in tow, frantically texting someone at the office. Or imagine racing from work to soccer practice to church to a packed-itinerary vacation and then back to work again. These are everyday experiences, and each one of them compromises our ability to slow down, get present, and connect. Culturally, we're in a growing habit of disconnection. And sadly this erodes one of the core aspects of our humanity.

When I first began working with her, Laila was vice president of human resources at Peet's Coffee. Like many executives, she spent her days on the run, with little room to slow down and relax. She hired me to help her find an alternative to the impatience and anger that automatically gripped her whenever she felt overwhelmed. Recently she had begun doing yoga, and it made her anxiously eager to "get back into my body," as she put it.

Laila and I had already had several phone sessions by the time I visited her beautiful San Francisco home. After lugging my massage table up the steep steps, I was admitted into a spacious kitchen, dining, and living area by a lithe woman with long chestnut brown hair. Laila buzzed about the kitchen bar, chattering away as she enthusiastically offered up an extensive list of beverage options. I settled on water, and we moved to the couch.

Laila propped her elbows on her knees, leaning in to discuss her hopes for the day's session. A widowed single mother, she had been the primary caregiver for a husband that struggled with depression, as well as for their small child. At work, she found it difficult to rely on her team despite their ample competence. She had great staff, but even so she always felt like she had to hold everything and everyone together all by herself. She was tired, and frustrated, and hurting. And she longed to change things.

We tend to think disconnection is all about wanting more friendships or an intimate partner. And yes, Laila wanted more of that in her life, too. But disconnection doesn't always show up in such an obvious way. Sometimes it sounds like this: "I feel unsupported. It's all up to me. I have to go it alone."

I found myself nearly breathless under Laila's intense gaze and ceaseless chatter. I noticed she was nearly breathless, too. When she paused, I suggested an experiment. "I wonder what would happen if you leaned back and let your back touch the couch?" I asked. She did so, and almost immediately she started to squirm. "Oh! I *never* sit like this!" she exclaimed. "It's really uncomfortable. I get a little antsy, like I want to get up and rush around." Even a moment's rest made her yearn for the familiar constant motion of distraction and disconnection. Her body couldn't handle the support of so much as a couch cushion. No wonder she felt unsupported!

That gave me all the information I needed for us to move to the table. Fully clothed, Laila lay down on her back and took a few deep breaths. I stood quietly by her side, paying close attention to my own sensations of warmth and coolness, tension and relaxation. Without yet touching her, I was also paying close attention to Laila, noticing the pace of her breath, the expression on her face, and a subtle tension that ran through her whole body like a tightly strung wire.

I asked her to count how many places she could feel her body making contact with the table. She mentioned her head, seat, and heels, but notably absent was any mention of her back. Finally, I reached to touch her. I made a few simple moves to help her continue to relax, and I reminded her to keep breathing. Then I gently slid my hands under her upper and lower back. Holding very still and listening with all of my senses, I asked, "What's got your attention now?"

"It's weird... I know your hands are there, but..." Laila wiggled a little bit. She was perplexed. Although she had a vague sense of my touch, it was as if her back was numb, frozen. Each time I asked about the sensations in her back, she couldn't quite describe them. Instead she launched into another chattering monologue about her daughter, her work, her family.

Unsurprised, I kept my hands where they were, gently present, motionless. "When in your life have you felt supported?" I asked. Laila shared stories of her upbringing in a "family of five individuals" who were never all that connected to one another. Her parents fought constantly and the kids didn't band together. The oldest child, Laila often took on adult responsibilities before she felt fully prepared to. "I've always had to hold it together in my life," she told me. "I've always had to be the responsible one. I grew up taking care of my parents. With my husband, I handled everything. At work, the buck stops with me. To be honest with you, I can't really think of a time when I've felt supported."

"If you could make more contact with my hands, what might you have to let go of to do that?" I asked. Suddenly, she hit upon a memory that brought tears to her eyes. Keeping my hands where they were, I encouraged her tears. Weeping for the losses she had experienced as a young girl and a young mother, she cried tears of longing for connection and support. Gradually, she quieted down. As her tears subsided and her breath slowed, she took a big gulp of air, and on the exhale her whole body softened. And then suddenly, "I can feel your hands!" Laila exclaimed. She looked at me with astonishment. "In fact, I can feel my whole back touching the table!"

From her breathless chattering monologue to her discomfort relaxing into the couch to the unconscious tension that kept her from fully contacting the table, it was evident to me that Laila was absent from some part of herself. In working with her, my primary goal was simply to slow down and be present, and through my presence, invite her own.

Of course I could have made an observation: "You really don't seem very present right now." Or I might have issued an invitation: "Can you bring yourself more present?" But presence isn't an idea; it's an experience. A state of being, not an activity. You know it when you feel it, but how do you actually cultivate it? Words can only take you so far toward that fundamentally nonverbal experience. Typically, that's not far enough.

So what did I actually *do* to get more present as a way of inviting Laila to do the same?

There's a deceptively simple trick to presence: Feel your own sensations. This works because sensations happen only in the present moment. You know how when you've been sick, you can remember that you felt awful, but you can't quite call up the awful feeling itself? That's because the sensations of illness are no longer occurring. Pay attention to the sensations you're feeling *right now* and you'll automatically become more present. Your ability to observe your own sensations without immediately reacting to them is precisely what makes presence possible.

Of course, paying attention to sensation while you're alone in a room with your eyes closed is one thing. It's quite another when you're busy interacting with someone else. That's why dialing up your capacity for embodied self-awareness is so important. If you wish to tap the benefits in your daily life, you need to be able to call upon your embodied self-awareness while you're engaged with others. Put another way, you need to pay full attention to both yourself *and* others at the same time. When Laila was on the table, I held my attention simultaneously on my own sensations and also fully on her, as if my attention was a giant invisible bubble surrounding us both. That may sound relatively straightforward, but it's often easier said than done.

The result of this deceptively simple way of paying attention is attunement, or what Dr. Daniel Siegel calls "feeling felt."[1] When others sense that they have your full attention from a place of deep listening and non-reactivity—a place you get to, incidentally, by being attentive to and non-reactive to your own sensations—they feel fundamentally seen, heard, and received. This kind of felt-sense attunement is one of the truest, deepest experiences of connection we can have. And it happens entirely without words.

But still, how could my presence silently invite Laila to be more present as well? Doesn't it seem odd that she had such a significant personal breakthrough thanks only to my motionless touch and a few simple questions?[2] This works in part because our bodies and brains wordlessly respond to one another's internal physiological state. The term limbic resonance describes the neural process whereby two people's internal emotional states converge—the unconscious syncing up of brainwaves and bodily rhythms that underlie the felt sense of attunement. This means that the more deeply attentive I am to my own embodied self-awareness, the more access Laila can have to hers.

Touch is a particularly powerful way to be present and to invite presence, because our skin is so tightly tied to emotion. Without any effort, you can probably tell the difference between aggressive touch and kind touch. That's because when someone touches you, they're reaching straight into your emotional brain. We have several different kinds of touch receptors in our nervous system. Most communicate with the sensory-motor part of the brain, helping you move, grasp objects, and kick tires. But some of them, the C tactile afferent cells, have a direct link to the emotional brain, where they tie straight into the limbic system and communicate emotion just as clearly as a shout or a smile.[3]

That's why you don't need someone to explain whether their touch carries an intention of care. That's something the nervous system determines directly with zero conceptual input. In research out of Dacher Keltner's lab at UC Berkeley, people were able to accurately identify the emotional tone of a one-second touch from a stranger nearly 60 percent of the time, when the odds of guessing the right emotion by chance were only 8 percent. In fact people can often differentiate between different kinds of touch more accurately than they can read the emotional tone of facial expressions or vocal communication.[4] Just as we can misinterpret someone's words, we may be more or less accurate at understanding people's intentions through touch. Nevertheless, we come equipped with a neurobiological touch-radar that allows us to send and receive important emotional messages without the use of words at all. Of course, we all know this from our own life experience. A warm hug feels entirely different from a cold shoulder. Loving touch involves someone's full presence.

When researchers watched nurses soothing young children at a midwestern hospital, they discovered that when caregivers tried to pacify children using words alone, saying things like "there there," or "it'll be all right," only 17 percent of children could calm themselves down and manage their distress. But when nurses touched the children in some way, maybe by rubbing their backs or holding their hands, 88 percent of kids were able to calm down in the same five-minute observation period.[5] Touch can stimulate the vagus nerve, release oxytocin, and calm cardiovascular stress.[6] Young children whose sensory-motor brain is more developed than the linguistic part of their brain may be especially sensitive to messages communicated through touch.

Touch is a vital connecting force for humans. In infancy, it's how we figure out what's "me" and "not me," and thus it plays an important role in your sense of self straight from the get-go.[7] It's also our most primal sense—the earliest to develop and the only one we can't ever switch off. You can cover your eyes, put in earplugs, or hold your nose, but you can't turn off your sense of touch. In fact if you dial down any of your other senses, you'll use your sense of touch to substitute. Put on a blindfold and you'll quickly "see" what I mean.[8]

Of course, you can be "touched" by things that don't touch your skin at all: a beautiful sunset, say, or a meaningful piece of music. Or someone's full attention when you really need to be heard. When we are touched in this way, we tend to sit up and take notice, as our attention is drawn to our own fullest feeling in the moment. This is how Laila came home to more of herself.

Laila never felt like anyone "had her back," so it makes sense that she was "holding her own." Metaphors like these occur in our language because we experience the world in an inherently physical way. These phrases are far more than metaphor; they actually reflect a deeply accurate picture of our day-to-day embodied experience.

No amount of insight about support was going to sink in for Laila until she could allow herself to relax into the support of the couch—or the massage table, or my hands—without tensing, squirming, and pulling away. She had learned so long and so well to have her own back that her automatic neuromuscular pattern unconsciously held a tension and numbness that she wasn't even aware of. This physical armoring was neurobiologically linked to a behavioral pattern of holding it all together, all by herself. When her body finally relaxed, it felt like she sank two inches, gently nestling into the soft, firm support of the table at last.

You can approximate this yourself: Lie on the bed or the floor and deliberately tense up. Aim to make as little of you as possible contact the surface you're resting on. Then, with a deep exhale, relax. Let yourself sink into the support that is already there. The difference between what you've just done and what Laila did is primarily a matter of awareness. You were deliberate about your tension; she was not. Unconscious tension functions largely the same way conscious tension does; the difference is that you're not aware of it and you can't relax it at will.

And unfortunately, unconscious tension interferes with presence. If presence is predicated on feeling sensations, then presence becomes next to impossible when chronic tension or prolonged absence of attention makes you numb to sensation. And I guarantee you're holding unconscious tension. We all do. To relax it, you first need to become aware of it. And there is no better way to do this than with the direct connection of touch.

That moment of feeling her back was pivotal for Laila. It woke her up to something that had been missing in her life, but invisible to her up until that point. As we continued working together, we developed practices to help her sense her back more and more: leaning into her office chair, standing against a wall, lying in her bed before falling asleep. The more she learned to sense her back, further inhabiting this once-vacant part of her, the more she softened the armored defenses that had long stood guard against letting anyone really truly help.

Over time, Laila built more and more of an internal willingness to receive support. She found herself asking for help more often from her team, her nanny, even her seven-year-old daughter. Her growing ability to rest into support counteracted the irritability and sense of being overwhelmed that originally brought her to me. And in the process, she started to feel less alone, more connected, and more alive.

A year or two later, Laila had an unprecedented exchange with her mother. Laila's father had passed away, and following the memorial service she went to stay with her mother for a few days. Laila had never felt very supported by either of her parents. In fact, when her own husband died, Laila's mother didn't even attend the memorial service. And so even though she had just lost her father, Laila went into this visit expecting to be her mother's rock, just as she had always been.

And indeed her mother understandably looked to Laila to console her grief. But one afternoon, as they sat together in the kitchen, Laila made a point to pay attention to her own sensations as she sat listening to her mother. She kept sensing her back against the chair, aiming to let her body feel as supported and fully present as possible as she listened intently to her mother speak. And then suddenly her mother turned with a start and realized aloud, "Oh, you lost your husband, too! You've been through this as well."

The conversation shifted from a one-sided monologue to a mutual exchange—a sharing of stories and emotions and lessons and grief between a mother and a daughter who had each lost a husband. In that moment, a newfound mutual support blossomed between them. Laila's presence silently invited her mother's presence, and it opened up a rare and treasured moment of genuine connection between them.

"I don't think you can actually love in your head," says Laila now. "The *idea* of love is in your head. But the act of loving is physical and energetic. It's a quality that you have to embody. Until you feel it, you can't really describe it. But there is nothing more gratifying and fulfilling than this. It connects you to people in such a meaningful way."

Later Laila made some initial forays at bringing her learning about embodied emotional intelligence to the crew at Peet's Coffee and Tea. She told me she only gave them "2 percent" of what she herself had learned, and she was delighted that some participants reported the sessions were life-changing. Laila left Peet's before she got to see her efforts fully bear fruit. But fortunately other organizations have explored similar territory, and even measured how increased presence and connection can affect the bottom line.

On a dark Friday night just outside of Minneapolis, Minnesota, a couple of dozen employees of the Courage Center streamed in from the blistering cold and shook off their coats. As they gathered in the large open room, they chatted curiously about the weekend program they were about to embark upon.

At the front of the room were two men named Matthew. Matt Taylor, a physical therapist and yoga-rehab specialist, had come all the way from the heat of Arizona to work with them. The other, Matthew Sanford, had been a rehab patient himself years ago, following a car accident at age thirteen. A paraplegic and a yoga teacher, he ran a popular adaptive yoga class at the center. And that was the reason for this weekend's program.

The Courage Center faced major challenges. As a rehab center supporting stroke victims, spinal cord injury patients, and people with central nervous system impairments such as MS and cerebral palsy, its mission was to empower people with physical disabilities to reach for their full potential in every aspect of life. But patients regularly missed appointments, staff morale was low, burnout was high, and turnover was alarmingly common. Rehab is a tough road for patient and caregiver alike.

Meanwhile, Matthew Sanford's yoga class was oversubscribed. He was having success with patients that the caregivers, managers, and executives on the weekend program wanted to emulate. So they planned a training session and set up a research program to monitor the results. Because it was designed as a collaborative inquiry, Taylor and Sanford approached the weekend as members of a group with a shared problem they were working together to solve, rather than as experts and consultants with all the answers. They kicked off the evening by sharing their own stories.

Sanford spoke about his experiences as a patient, and his passion to redesign the way rehabilitation services are delivered. Taylor spoke about his frustrations as a rehab provider trying to work in a more holistic way. Then they asked participants to lie back and sense what it was about their work that made them uncomfortable, frustrated, sad. And conversely, what inspired them? Why had they gone into rehab in the first place? After this, participants paired up to tell their own stories: What led them into the profession, what they were grateful for and disappointed by, what they were longing for now. The evening wrapped up with some guided imagery to help them drop their assumptions and open up to the learning ahead.

The next morning began with a data download about the efficacy of mind-body practices. All day Sanford and Taylor alternated medical evidence with direct practice and experimentation, helping these healthcare professionals explore new breathing practices, postures, movements, and ways of aligning the body. They did an alternate nostril breathing practice, followed by a discussion of the shifts in heart rate and blood pressure it can produce—a shift that the participants experienced themselves as they practiced. They did some traditional yoga poses, and then played around with inventing their own, getting a feel for how they might adapt postures to help their patients. Throughout the day they continued to tell their stories... to express their longings, their frustrations, and their care.

On Sunday afternoon, after a long session of yoga poses and another guided visualization, Taylor and Sanford brought in a few patients. Their goal was to give providers a chance to explore how they might apply what they were learning to their practice. They got to see, for instance, how a cerebral palsy patient would shift her gaze simply by having her chest and upper back supported for a few minutes. They got to experience how much easier it is to teach your patient to breathe differently if you yourself have practiced that way of breathing. And they got to hear directly from patients what they themselves had been saying all weekend: these mind-body practices are making a difference for me.

The short weekend workshop took the Courage Center employees a long way. The link was clear: If I practice feeling more and centering myself, I get more present. When I get more present, how I treat the patient changes. Thanks to limbic resonance, my presence influences the patient's presence. And then the patient's outcome improves. Following the weekend training, the program continued for another seven weeks of practice, storytelling, and learning.

Above all, says Matthew Taylor, "we taught them to slow down, shut up, and *feel*." This skill of feeling, so essential to connection, is something few of us are actually taught how to do. We assume that parents, partners, nurses, or doctors will just "know" how to connect with the people they care for. But medical training emphasizes technical skills over embodying a healing presence. And in our personal lives, the skill of presence is assumed rather than taught. Yet as the work at the Courage Center demonstrates, it is absolutely possible to deliberately cultivate a healing and connecting presence.

The Mind-Body Integration Project made a huge difference for the caregivers themselves, producing significant changes in job satisfaction, quality of life, and reduction of burnout. At the start of the program nearly a third of participants were considering leaving the profession altogether; by the end of it, none were. Commitment to the Courage Center grew as well—the 72 percent that had been considering leaving the center at the start of the program dropped to 25 percent. Given that the cost to the center to hire and train a new staff member approached $100,000, this directly affected not only the emotional health of the organization but also its financial health.

But perhaps the most exciting outcome was the way the caregivers' greater presence and deeper connection improved patient results. Following the program, staff members reported using mind-body techniques in at least two-thirds of their client interactions, oftentimes more. They slowed down their care, focusing more on establishing rapport and paying attention to the relationship over executing a bunch of techniques. They touched more sensitively and listened more deeply. Many found themselves getting better results while doing fewer activities. The connection between patient and caregiver grew. And the no-show rate for afternoon appointments dropped from 43 percent to just 12 percent.[9]

"When the treatment becomes more of a partnership than an intervention I provide to the client," reported one specialist, "we are both more energized and positive about the experience." Clients recognized the benefits, and in addition to more consistent attendance at appointments, they started practicing more on their own between sessions.

Staff members who hadn't been through the training saw these changes and began asking for training themselves. At first therapists taught one another informally, and eventually a second iteration of the program got underway. Phase II went on to train another two dozen staff.

Connection is an essential nutrient for our brains, and thus a powerful healing force for our lives. And presence is a necessary component of genuine connection. When you connect more deeply with yourself, you grow your capacity to connect more deeply with others. As you build your capacity to feel more of your sensations, center yourself under pressure, and engage in embodied self-awareness while interacting with others, your presence naturally deepens. And you can't overestimate the impact that genuine presence and connection can have on your health, happiness, relationships... and even the bottom line. Thank goodness it's a learnable skill.

13

Compassion

Claus: But I Rescue Puppies!

"It's the eyes," Rick Johnson told me when I asked him, years after the fact, what stuck with him about his embodied leadership training. "It used to be that with women, I would just look at their bodies. I never looked directly into someone's eyes. But now, I can look into someone's eyes and I see a happy person, or a sad person, or a kind person. I can just see the person there."

Rick does this with men, too, but he finds it easier with women. Direct eye contact between men is somewhat taboo in the rough-and-tumble mining and road construction industry where Rick works as a transportation manager. But Rick has become something of a softie, and both he and his colleagues appreciate it. On the morning of the day I spoke with him, an employee he'd known for thirty years came into his office, complaining of a conflict with a coworker. He caught the hint of a shine in her eye, like a tear about to fall.

"The only other time I've seen her show emotion is fifteen years ago, when she got cancer," he told me. "But this morning, I just looked in her eyes, and I could see that she was really upset. So I just sat with her, and we talked. I think by the end of the conversation she felt better."

The word compassion derives from the Latin word *compati*, which means to "suffer with." Compassion is rooted in empathy, the ability to wordlessly sense and share someone else's feelings. The capacity for empathy and compassion, like the capacity to connect, begins with your ability to sense yourself. Because as we'll come to see, the neural pathways that make empathy possible are the very same neural pathways involved in embodied self-awareness. Which means that even a tough-as-nails construction boss like Rick, when he learns to feel his sensations more deeply, can discover a compassion he didn't know he had.

As it happens, so can a tough-as-nails Microsoft manager, in this case one named Claus Wieser. Although his story starts with considerably more eye-rolling than eye-connecting.

Claus's boss Jennifer had to talk him into attending the Centered Leadership program at Jempe Center. "Just hear me out," she said as she told him about the program. Claus made a face. First of all, he was doing great in his career. The idea that he might need some sort of help was mildly insulting. Second of all, he'd done some training on emotional intelligence and found it wanting. And last but definitely not least, the program Jennifer was describing sounded "fruity." But she was the best boss he'd ever had. And she was asking him to go as a favor to her. Reluctantly, he agreed.

He wasn't aware of this at the time, but Claus wielded humor like a weapon, laughing as he cut down anyone and anything that stood in his path. Thus it was that he smirked and ridiculed his way through the entire first two days of the Centered Leadership program, using his well-honed biting humor to keep the experience at arm's length. So it wasn't until day three that the program finally made an impact on Claus. And when it did, it hit him hard.

Sitting in a circle of his peers, he listened as one colleague after another told him what it was like to work with him. Instructed to sit in silence and just listen, Claus could feel himself getting flushed, red in the face, and intensely frustrated. Deep down, he knew they were trying to tell him something important. But honestly he just couldn't see it. "They can't all be wrong," he kept thinking as he shook his head in baffled bewilderment. Then his friend Andrew spoke.

"Claus, I love you to pieces. You are the most brutally competent person I know. Seriously, there's nothing you can't do. But you leave dead bodies in your wake, and I don't want to be one of them. So I'm just going to stay the hell away from you."

Whether it was the cumulative effect of everyone's comments or his tremendous respect for Andrew that finally got through to him or both, Claus isn't sure. But in that moment, a light bulb went off. "Whoa, what right do I have to do that to people?" Claus found himself asking inwardly. "I mean seriously, *I rescue puppies in my spare time!*"

Claus shook his head in frustration, a concerned look on his face. "So you're saying that I am hurting people," he said aloud. "That is totally unacceptable," he stated emphatically. *"That is not who I am."*

Prior to this insight, Claus actually took a lot of pride in his bulldozer style of management. "I always got my way," he said. "But I had no appreciation for the collateral damage." A typical incident from a while back came to mind. The meeting was meant to be an hour-long go/no-go decision: a checkpoint to confirm that the support systems for a new product were ready to launch. But the team was disorganized, behind schedule, and nowhere near ready. Claus went into slash-and-burn mode.

He remembers one fellow in particular who was advocating for publishing support documents in multiple languages. That was the standard process, and this guy wanted to follow protocol. Claus turned to him angrily. "What's the impact if we don't do that?" he demanded. "Minimal. You've been overruled. We're not doing it. It's done."

The man stayed silent for the rest of the meeting, which spilled over into two hours, then three. Others in the room were cowed as well. "It was the right decision," Claus still maintains. "But I squashed him like a bug. And there was really no reason to. After that meeting, a lot of people were still scared of me. But I could have gotten the same result so much more gracefully. I lost people that day."

Fun-loving Claus had always thought of himself as a warm and friendly people person, so the realization that he was bulldozing his peers came as a painful shock. With this epiphany, Claus instantly retracted his porcupine quills and dedicated himself to becoming more like a hamster—a nickname his colleagues still use for him to this day. He hired John McConnell of Jempe Center as his coach, and got straight to work de-quilling himself.

To help Claus discover the physical clues that he was about to fly off the handle, John ran different experiments to trigger Claus's startle response. He might shout unexpectedly, for example, or maybe grab his wrist. Even though Claus had readily—even eagerly—agreed to this, and even though he was expecting John's mocked-up "attack," he still felt a whole-body response the moment John raised his voice. After several iterations, he learned to recognize a powerful electric feeling from head to toe as his core tightened up, his own face tensed to shout, and he whipped around ready to square off against his foe. This was his in-the-moment experience of his knee-jerk reaction—an immediate and automatic move into fight mode.[†] Once he became familiar with how it felt, he started to pay attention to how it showed up for him at work, too. Turns out it reared its head on a near-daily basis.

So Claus counteracted this habit the best way he knew: He started taking everything with a smile. Concluding that his hair-trigger fight

---

[†] Incidentally, the same thing happens to those of us who are more inclined to withdraw; it just looks different. Instead of going toe to toe, you might feel your chest get tight or concave. You might close your eyes. You might actually physically draw away or retreat.

mode was too prickly, he tried to erase it from his life. But in the daily political scrum that comprises life inside a large organization, his team was being repeatedly thrown under the bus. Each time his team members were handed work they weren't responsible for, or wrongly accused of not doing their job, or overlooked when others were being praised, Claus just smiled serenely and walked away. In an effort to neutralize his overdeveloped fight mode, Claus shut down all emotion he deemed "negative," inadvertently letting others take advantage of him and his team.

In fact Claus bottled up so much anger that it made him sick. After he had a couple of middle-of-the-night panic attacks, his doctor confirmed he had the dreaded "Microsoft Anxiety Disorder"—a tongue-in-cheek diagnosis for stressed-out managers. He was given two choices: take pills, or change his response to stress. Claus chose to change, and made a beeline straight back to John's office.

He lowered his tall frame into the chair across from John, already unloading about the stress and frustration he was experiencing. After listening patiently for several minutes, John had a ready response. "It sounds like what you really want is access to your full range of emotions," he proposed.

"No, no, of course not!" Claus protested with a wave of his hands. "That's fruity!"

But in the end, it turns out that was *exactly* what he needed.

Why on earth would it be a good idea to have access to the full range of your emotions when A) you're busy trying to crank out results at work, and B) you've determined that your anger turns you into a person you don't want to be? It's a good question. But the fact is, your ability to feel the sensations that underlie your emotions is critical to both connection and compassion. If presence—the ability to pay attention to yourself and another simultaneously—provides the basis for connection, then it must play a role in compassion, too.

And indeed it does. In fact embodied self-awareness is the very basis for empathy and compassion. Thanks to a few Italian monkeys and their intrepid laboratory observers, we now have a growing understanding of the neurobiology of compassion.

In the mid-1990s researchers in a neuroscience lab in Italy were busy mapping the neurons involved in different actions. They had hooked up certain neurons to a machine that made a noise each time the monkey raised its arm. But they were puzzled by random "pings" that rang out even when the monkeys were sitting still. What was going on?

After several failed hypotheses, the eureka moment finally came. It seemed like the monkeys' neurons fired each time one of the researchers raised an arm to drink coffee, eat an apple, or grab a book off the shelf. Further testing supported this hypothesis. Two decades on, we now know that the monkeys were silently mirroring the researchers, without actually making the same movement themselves. They were literally "getting a feel for" the researchers' actions by modeling the behavior in their own bodies.[1]

We now know that humans do this, too. We all have mirror neurons that help us model the behavior of others. But here's the kicker—these mirror neurons don't act in isolation. Situated in the motor cortex, mirror neurons fire when we hear or see someone else move. They also connect to neurons in our emotional brain (specifically the insula, a part of the brain involved in self-awareness) and to motor neurons throughout the body. In other words, *we use our entire bodies to make sense of other people.* Thanks to mirror neurons—and the way they hook into your entire distributed nervous system—when someone picks up a cup, you can instantly sense whether she's about to calmly take a sip or angrily throw it across the room.[2] (Turns out this skill comes in mighty handy around toddlers.)

This nonconceptual modeling process is one of the primary ways you make sense of other people. Mirror neurons tell you about action, emotion, and intention as *expressed* through another's body and *read* through your own felt sense. Essentially, you get insight into others by automatically and unconsciously answering the question "How would it feel to me if I were to make that move?" You perceive others through the very same neural networks that you yourself use to take the same action, employ the same tone of voice, or make the same expression.[3]

But there's a catch. Because we perceive others' actions through the lens of perception that is our body, actions we ourselves cannot take are considerably more difficult, and sometimes impossible, to accurately perceive. When the researchers were testing their hypothesis, they tried waving their arms around randomly. The monkeys' neurons didn't fire. Why not? Because monkeys can't pantomime. They didn't have an internal model for "what it would feel like to do that." And so they literally didn't perceive the arm waving, at least not in any way they could relate to. They didn't—and couldn't—"get it."[4]

So what about us? What happens if your capacity to feel your sensations (interoception) and sense the shape of your own postures, gestures, and facial expressions (proprioception) is underdeveloped? Unfortunately, that's going to limit your capacity for empathy.[5] Because our emotions and actions are so interwoven with sensation and physical expression, when your own sensations are invisible to you, it's that much harder to read others. Where your own range is limited, your capacity to "get it" when others are experiencing something unfamiliar is truncated. It turns out the less you can feel yourself, the less you can "suffer with," or have compassion for, another. Conversely, the more access you have to your own sensations and emotions, the more empathy and compassion you can access. We *feel with* by feeling ourselves.

―――――――

Once Claus learned to recognize the triggers for his anger, John worked with him to help him feel it all without being unnecessarily reactive. Instead of shutting down the powerful rush of sensation that gripped him when he was angry, Claus learned to experience it fully, letting it arise without getting hooked by it. Then he would center himself and allow it to dissipate, until finally he could calmly turn and face John and be fully present. Although it took some time, with practice this came more quickly and easily. As Claus practiced tolerating the flood of sensation without letting it drive his reaction, he developed the capacity to choose his response more wisely.

Claus describes this as getting data on all channels. "All of these emotions are part of my intelligence network—my radar system. Turning any of your emotions off deprives you of a radar station. If one of them is out, you've got a blind spot. You don't know what's coming your way." By shutting down his anger with a smile, Claus deprived himself of some of the important information he needed to determine how to deal with his colleagues. "It took me a while to allow anger to be a listening station," he says. But once he allowed himself to open up that listening post, he could see it as a vital source of input. He could allow himself to feel angry and let that guide his response, rather than succumbing to his old porcupine-like knee-jerk reaction.

When you can feel your strong sensations without compulsively reacting to them, all of a sudden options open up for you. Gaining access to the full range of your sensations and emotions makes connection and compassion more available. When you have strong embodied self-awareness, when you can consistently recover from stress and regulate turbulent emotions, when you are practiced at bringing yourself present, then empathy and compassion naturally arise. It is precisely by feeling yourself that you come to "feel with" another.

As Claus learned to access his emotions across all of his radar channels, he had another encounter at work. A woman in a neighboring department accused his team of failing to deliver on an important project. Claus knew it wasn't true—in fact the reason his team was late was because *her* team had failed to hand off their piece of the work in time. But rather than shooting quills porcupine-style, or smiling and scurrying away hamster-style, this time he did something different. He let himself feel angry. And then—without jumping into fight mode—he used that information to guide his actions.

Claus went to talk to her. Before walking in, he centered himself. Rather than bypassing his anger, he let himself feel it, and allowed it to fuel his commitment to protect his team's solid reputation. He felt ready to be present with her, to really listen to her as well as he could and to connect as genuinely as possible.

In the course of their conversation, he started to pick up on subtle cues he might have missed before. Her tone of voice and body language all conveyed—you guessed it—anger. Once he realized that, all of a sudden Claus could relate on an entirely different level. He could empathize. He found compassion. He could "suffer with."

He started to ask different questions, and it soon became evident that she was passing the buck. A few steps earlier in the chain of action, someone else had done the same thing to her team. They handed off a deliverable late, and then blamed her team for the failure. Her team scrambled to catch up, and in an effort to deflect the blame, she pointed fingers at Claus's team. It was something he himself might have done not so very long before.

But Claus was starting to see the fruits of his efforts to integrate the defensive strength of the porcupine with the genuine sweetness of the hamster. Even in the face of ample anger and a strong sense of injustice, Claus was able to connect with his colleague and feel compassion for her. Rather than succumbing to his emotion or suppressing it, he used it to inform his actions and the conversation. Before, he would have completely overlooked what was going on with her, because he was either too reactive or too shut down. But now that he could feel all of his own emotions, he could sense her frustration, too. Having access to his full range of emotions gave him access to genuine empathy. And because she felt seen and heard, they were able to work out their differences amicably, find a solution, and part as friends.

As he learned to do this in public forums as well as private conversations, "I became a convert," says Claus of his embodied learning experience. "And the conversion is full and irreversible." This conversion has affected many aspects of Claus's life. The handful of panic attacks are in the distant past. His wife is delighted that the things she's been telling him for years finally seem to have sunk in. And his performance reviews at Microsoft took a step up, too.

Claus's reviews typically landed him in the high performer range, but the top ratings and rewards had always eluded him. After he de-quilled himself and expanded his capacity to feel, the art of the polite-but-assertive pushback became his new normal. He learned how to take a strong stand while strengthening relationships. As Claus grew his capacity for centered leadership, he received higher and higher ratings on his performance reviews. This had a tangible impact on both his compensation and his career prospects—a change he welcomed with delight.

Obviously, compassion is a worthy quality to develop in its own right. It can have a tremendous positive effect throughout all aspects of our lives. But it's so easy to think of compassion, or connection, or any of the personal and interpersonal qualities detailed in this book, as squishy soft stuff that doesn't affect the bottom line. But as we've now repeatedly seen, these intangible skills have unmistakably tangible results. They are the fundamentals that provide a firm foundation for taking effective collective action. And that's exactly what we'll take up in the next section as we explore how embodied practice supports clear communication, collaboration, and conflict resolution.

SECTION

4

Inspire Others

As we move into Section 4, it's worth taking a brief look at where we've been so far.

Peter at Capital One showed us how reconnecting with his felt sense of care and committing to a course of action from there can make a powerful contribution. And compulsive workaholic Helena showed us how you can embody a strong commitment once you've clarified where it is you want to go.

Marianne in Afghanistan, Rich coming home from Iraq, and Nichole at the Women's Fund demonstrated how to build the courage and composure to follow through on what's important to you. Then Anthony and Denise showed us how those qualities can be put into action in everyday life and business activities such as networking events and powerful presentations.

Laila's experience learning to feel support at her back and the Courage Center's mind-body integration project both reveal how deepening embodied self-awareness fosters stronger connection. Then Claus at Microsoft showed us how to get present to the signals we receive on all channels, and how doing so can dial up both empathy and compassion.

When you embody the capacity to sense, center, and get present, you will have laid the foundation to take action in concert with others from a place of centered care. That's what these next chapters are all about—how to galvanize others to action by embodying a centered and compelling leadership presence.

We'll hear from Malika Tremont, an educator and entrepreneur who has learned to embody a clarity of words that did not at first come naturally to her (Chapter 14, "Communicate"). In Chapter 15, "Collaborate," stories from two companies—Ropeworks and Human Code—demonstrate how physically coordinated action combined with clear communication can lead to major financial wins for teams. We'll also hear how conflict-resolution specialist Mel Szarek learned to prepare her body for conflict as well as her mind... and the difference it made in an important negotiation (Chapter 16, "Convert Conflict to Consensus").

Embody Emotional and Social Intelligence

	AWARENESS	*ACTION*
Emotional Intelligence – **SELF**	**FIND PURPOSE** *align w. yourself + the mystery* core skill: *self-awareness* somatic competency: SENSE Care Choose Commit Contribute	**BUILD RESILIENCE** *settle + strengthen yourself* core skill: *self-mastery* somatic competency: CENTER Courage Composure Confidence Credibility
Social Intelligence – **OTHERS**	**DEEPEN EMPATHY** *listen deeply...* *w. all of your senses* core skill: *empathy* somatic competency: PRESENCE Connection Compassion	**INSPIRE OTHERS** *act from centered care...* *for self + others* core skill: *social dexterity* somatic competency: GALVANIZE Communicate Collaborate Conflict to Consensus

We turn now to the fourth quadrant of our model: the "action" component of social intelligence. All day long we take action with others ("Please take out the trash," "Why don't you email me about that," "I need you to fix this mistake.") When it's not connected to care, action can become meaningless activity that creates a situation no one actually wanted in the first place. Frenzied action that is not centered in a state of composure often leads to knee-jerk reactions you later regret. And without solid relationships and strong connections, it's hard to collaborate to get things done. But when you embody a centered presence rooted in heartfelt connection to yourself and others, your actions arise from a deeper wisdom and a stronger alignment with love.

This internal alignment naturally inspires others and galvanizes them to action. The core social intelligence skill here is social dexterity—the ability to firmly yet flexibly coordinate well with others. To succeed at this, you must embody the communication skills that are essential to collaboration: the ability to ask for help rather than go it alone, to make clear agreements and say no where appropriate, to delegate clearly and effectively, and to negotiate conflicts and resolve them well.

This section is about training for these relational skills in an embodied way, preparing your body for your interactions with others as well as your mind. Through holistic forms of embodied training that engage not just your mind, not just your body, but *all of you*, you can develop a skill I call *embodied mindfulness in action*—the ability to keep your attention on your own embodied self-awareness while in dynamic interaction with others.

This is a bit like patting your head and rubbing your stomach—a lot easier said than done. It means tracking your subtle interoceptive and proprioceptive sensations while you're moving around: eyes open, in conversation, and taking action.

Embodied Mindfulness in Action

In recent years the benefits of mindfulness have gotten a lot of press. And indeed, there *are* many benefits, from reduced stress to improved immunity and beyond. But in popular culture, mindfulness is too often portrayed as an escape. We run from the pressures of everyday life to sit in peaceful bliss on a cushion, or dash off to a yoga class to be saved from the stress of daily living.

But where mindfulness really serves you best is when your toddler has a screaming meltdown in the midst of a locked-up traffic jam with no escape in sight. Or when you have a high-stakes negotiation with your boss or business partner and you've been up all night preparing. Or when your client is talking about a mission-critical issue and you can't get your mind off of your father's ill health.

How do you remain present and effective in situations like these? How do you keep your composure and draw upon your courage? Access compassion when you're in the depths of impatience? Navigate conflict in ways that build rather than destroy relationships?

Traditional mindfulness practices can be an enormous support in everyday life, but making time for them is difficult for many, and applying them off the cushion or off the mat is even more challenging. If you already have a mindfulness practice, by all means continue. But even if you do—and especially if you don't—you will benefit by incorporating some simple embodied mindfulness practices into your everyday activities.

Embodied mindfulness in action is what makes mindfulness actionable and practical for the everyday householder, leader, parent, educator, or activist.

> *It means when your teenage son drops his dirty socks on the floor yet again, you're aware of the heat rising in you as you raise the issue, but you don't let your discomfort drive the bus. (Interoception)*
>
> *It means when a colleague questions your competence, you feel the supportive solidity of your legs underneath you and you're aware of your back against the chair as you calmly take a stand for yourself and your team. (Proprioception)*
>
> *It means when you're longing for a new direction in your career, you actually take the time to feel the sensations that accompany that longing as you determine your next move. (Interoception, Proprioception, Conceptual, Mood)*

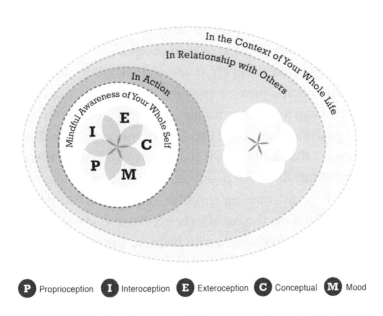

P Proprioception   I Interoception   E Exteroception   C Conceptual   M Mood

Contextualized, embodied, experiential behavioral learning.
This illustration shows two people, but the same process can be used in groups.
P = proprioception; I = interoception; E = exteroception; C = conceptual; M = mood.

Embodied Mindfulness in Action

Embodied mindfulness in action means dispassionately paying attention to the full richness of your internal experience while simultaneously paying attention to others. The capacity to manage your attention this way means you can include yourself and your needs in any conversation without steamrolling another person. This is vital for success in almost any endeavor, from marriage to parenting to leading a team.

It is also the skill that makes ardently principled leadership possible. Think about what celebrated leaders like Nelson Mandela, Gandhi, Mother Teresa, Martin Luther King, and the Dalai Lama have in common. Each of these individuals embody the capacity to ﾠd firmly for their principles while still upholding the humanity of ﾠho rely on more aggressive and brittle forms of power. History shows that this brittle version of power ultimately snaps under strain, whereas the power of embodying strong principles and steadfast kindness holds steady through the most savage storms.

This capacity to mean what you say and say what you mean—to walk your talk and *embody* both clarity and kindness—is vital to your success. So is your ability to step into important conversations rather than let them slide; to foster collaboration within a family, team, or community; and to resolve conflict among the divergent points of view that inevitably arise when people try to accomplish things together. These are incredibly rewarding skills to develop, and through the right kinds of embodied training and a dedication to some simple practices, you can make them second nature.

Let's see how some folks did it.

14

Communicate

Malika: Spinning Out or Staying Sane

Y ears ago, a client came to me with tears in her eyes. "I'm just so overwhelmed," she moaned. "I'm working like crazy, and it won't let up. Help!"

Desperation lay behind her words. Maria Acevedo[†] has a high-stress job with the federal government that keeps her constantly on the run. Her role requires her to be super-responsive... as do her young kids, her aging parents, and her volunteer commitments. She's so busy she barely has space to breathe.

I mean that quite literally. Her normal, everyday breath is a short pant. Her eyes are hyper-focused, vigilant, almost panicked. Her shoulders shrug up around her ears as if she's carrying the weight of the world, making it hard for her to get a full breath. (Try it yourself—lift up your shoulders and see how it affects your breathing.) Inhabiting her body this way affected the way she was responding to the overwhelming pressure.

[†] Name and identifying details changed.

We got straight to work. We stood up and I gave her some brief instructions. I would represent the many requests she hears each day, ranging from "you need to work out a new contract with this vendor," to "Mom, can you help with my homework?" As I walked toward her with a request, she had some choices for how to react. She could join with me and walk in my direction (meaning, "Sure, I can do that"), let me go by ("Not now. Maybe later"), or turn me back in the other direction ("No, I can't help with that. Sorry").

Standing a few feet apart, I walked toward her with the first request. Then I turned around and approached her again with another request. And another. And another. I sped up the pace. I made more requests. I acted like her life.

Under pressure, she spun out. Although she could have stepped aside and let some of my requests go by, or even said no to some of them, she felt compelled to interact with me every time. As the pace increased, she started to back away as I approached. After each request, she would spin around to deal with the next thing—sometimes spinning several times before she moved on.

In this way, her body revealed exactly what she does in her life. Her embodied response to feeling overwhelmed—what she does immediately and automatically, without even thinking about it—is to say yes to every request. She fails to discern what's important to her, and she responds to everything in equal measure, though rarely with her best. In trying to do the impossible and deal with everything that's thrown at her, she panics and spins out, using far more energy than necessary to deal with the onslaught.

As we talked about this, it became clear that she wasn't even aware that she hadn't once said no to me. This was a shocking revelation for her. But as she thought about it further, "I *can't* say no!" she decried. "It's my *job*. Plus, my kids... how can I say no to them? And my parents, who are both ill? There's just no way."

Maria's perception that she couldn't say no was consistent with her embodied response to an onslaught of requests, but it wasn't the truth with a capital T. Nevertheless, it was the only truth she could see. Unravelling this took some work, along with some practice.

I asked her why reducing the relentless pressure was important to her. "Because of my health," she answered. "And my family. I want to feel better, and I want to be able to spend more quality time with my kids and husband." As we explored this further, I helped her get in touch with a felt sense of longing—the ache in her heart and the tears of frustration lying just behind her eyes. This deep longing was the fuel she needed to take on the challenging task of embodying a new communication skill.

Once she felt viscerally connected to what she cared about, I had her experience what it felt like to be relaxed in her body: shoulders dropped, breath dropped, eyes relaxed. As she began to embody a felt sense of relaxed care, we went back to the practice.

I approached her again with requests for her time and attention. Even though I kept up the pace and continued to put the pressure on, this time the entire interaction had a very different feel. Far more present, Maria wasn't spinning out as much as she had before. In the micro-moment between one request and the next she would connect to her desire for better health and more time with her family, drop her shoulders, soften her eyes, and then turn to face the next request head-on. Counterintuitively, by relaxing and slowing down she stayed more in command of the situation.

From this more relaxed and present state Maria was better able to make choices. For the first time, she chose to let a few requests go by. But she still wasn't saying no. To clue her in to this, I asked her to speak her response to each request out loud. This quickly revealed how infrequently she turned down requests. On the few occasions she did, she would hesitate, stammer, and start to spin out again. As I approached her I would nearly bowl her over before she got me turned around and headed back in the other direction.

We stopped to talk about what her body had revealed about her day-to-day experience of saying no. She realized that her assumption that she wasn't free to decline requests wasn't really grounded in a clear-eyed view of the consequences. When she took a closer look at the cost of automatically saying yes compared to the consequences of occasionally saying no, she realized that there were consequences either way... and that the costs of saying no were worth it to her, at least some of the time.

Once she made that choice, we worked on strengthening through her spine and core as she spoke, so that her decline had some solidity to it. I also taught her how to approach me as I made a request rather than backing away, counterintuitively making more space for her own needs by proactively taking the helm. With enough practice, Maria finally got to a place where she could say no clearly and directly, without the wobbly uncertainty that made it so easy for me to push her around before.

And get this: As the person making the requests, I felt better taken care of. Rather than being subject to her panicked, spun-out, frantic energy, I could sense that she was really paying attention. She didn't always give me the response I wanted, but however she responded, she was really there: relaxed, centered, and fully present. And that made the whole experience much more pleasant on my end, too. This is the power of mood contagion: when you show up at your best, others feel it. We'll explore this process of contagion—and its impact on collaboration—in the next chapter.

This kind of practice—and it *is* a practice, not a one-time exercise— works because it harnesses your full intelligence. It combines conceptual self-awareness—*what makes saying no so difficult?*—with embodied self-awareness—*how does saying no feel?*—to build a more complete understanding of the situation at hand. It is this synthesis of conceptual and embodied self-awareness, coupled with relevant embodied practice, that builds the capacity to take a new action.

Integrated Intelligence

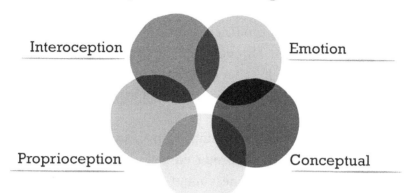

Interoception

Emotion

Proprioception

Conceptual

Exteroception

Working with Maria, I aimed to tap as many elements of her intelligence as possible, helping her build embodied mindfulness in action by paying attention on multiple channels at once.

Interoception: I guided Maria to become acutely aware of her sensations while she said yes and no. Where was there comfort, ease, discomfort? We sought out ways to build more comfort and familiarity with the less practiced skill of saying no.

Proprioception: As Maria practiced saying no, she also changed her physical actions, posture, and position in space. This gave her body a new, never-before-experienced *felt sense* of what it was like to go along with someone automatically versus choosing to say yes, or what it was like to stop me, turn me around in my tracks, or let me go by. This kind of felt-sense insight is a critical prerequisite to embodying a new skill.

Exteroception: In order to interact with me, Maria had to pay attention with all of her senses—listening to my voice, seeing and sensing me approach, and so on. She had to pay attention *outside* herself (exteroception) while simultaneously paying attention *inside* (interoception and proprioception). This capacity to pay attention both internally and externally is a key aspect of building a powerful presence.

Emotion: Saying no produced a lot of anxiety for Maria. This anxiety expressed itself through her chronically raised shoulders and the fluttering she felt in her chest each time I approached. As we worked, we sought to change her emotional experience from one of anxiety to one of ease.

Conceptual: We had revealing conversations about Maria's assumptions and beliefs that produced new insights and helped her develop conceptual self-awareness about saying no. She also practiced unfamiliar language, getting "no" past her lips again and again until she could do so in an increasingly resonant voice.

Notice that we didn't investigate her history of saying no, as a therapist might. We simply explored very directly her regular, everyday experience of accepting and declining requests.

This kind of holistic practice co-activates multiple neural networks, linking intellectual insight with experiential learning in a way that creates powerful, lasting change. As we worked together, Maria's commitment became a living reality. She translated this practice of discernment and choice into her everyday life, pausing to consider her response to the many requests she received each day. She renegotiated some of her commitments at work and at home, and asked for more support from her husband, colleagues, and kids. Ultimately she came to *embody* this new skill of saying no, consistently taking action on it until it became second nature. And as a result, she became far more satisfied with her work and her life.

That's all well and good when you're building the capacity to say the one-word sentence "no." But what about when you're at a total loss for words?

That was Malika Tremont's[†] situation. Malika runs Child's Play, an arts-and-creativity school for kids and families. She came to me early in her entrepreneurial journey, looking for a way to handle certain clients who she felt took advantage of her. Like Maria, Malika had a strongly embodied appease response. She unconsciously nodded her head as we spoke, and she often agreed aloud before she even heard what I was about to say.

Over the course of our work together, Malika struggled to set boundaries with clients, business partners, and employees. Everyone seemed to want special favors: a unique one-off payment plan, a nonstandard work schedule, a change to a previously agreed-upon arrangement. In an effort to accommodate everyone's unique circumstances, Malika was running herself ragged. And as her business grew, this problem grew along with it.

The fundamental question for Malika was: How do I take a stand for my own needs and the needs of my business without compromising my kindness? And most especially, *How on earth do I find the words to do that?*

I worked with Malika to help her embody both clear boundaries and the genuine kindness that she valued so highly. We began with bodywork to release the chronic tension in her neck and shoulders that worsened whenever an unreasonable request came her way. Then we did the same practice I did with Maria, with similar results. Eventually we moved on to experimenting with different ways to sit, stand, and move that either allowed the words she needed to spontaneously arise, or left them stuck in her throat.

I turned the exercise I did with Maria around and had Malika approach me. She walked toward me, hand outstretched as if to shake mine, while saying something like "I need you to adhere to our policies." But when I took her hand to either accept or decline her request, it was slack. All her attention was on me, and none was left for herself. She wasn't quite present inside her own skin. And that made it easy for me to push her around.

---

† Not her real name.

We stopped to work on "filling out" and fully "inhabiting" her whole body. I had her wiggle her fingers and toes so she could really sense herself from the soles of her feet to the top of her head and all the way out to her fingertips. We played with the difference between feeling slack, absent, and collapsed, versus what it felt like to be stiff, rigid, and tense. Then we returned to the practice.

Malika approached me again, this time with a ferocity that the situation didn't call for. After all, these were people that she wanted to continue working with; the last thing she wanted to do was drive them away. But as she approached me with her jaw set, her eyes burning, and her whole body hard with determination, she silently exuded the message "If you're not with me, you're against me." She'd left no room for us to work together, and it was off-putting on the receiving end. Her rigidity was contagious, and I found myself getting stiff and unyielding in response. I immediately pushed back.

We stopped again. I asked her to show me what it was like to have the floppy feeling in her body. Her arms became like a rag doll, easy for me to bend to my will. Then I asked her to show me what it was like to fight for herself and her company. Her jaw set. Her hands balled into fists. Her neck and shoulders hardened. If I tried to so much as move her arm, our bodies immediately locked in combat as we resisted each other.

So we tried a middle way: a firm yet flexible stance that was malleable without too much give. It was important for her to stand firmly for what she cared about, but not at any cost. I showed her how to relax her muscles but extend her attention in such a way that she was *aware* of her whole body at once. This relaxed but alert stance allowed her to be fully awake to everything going on inside of her, with no part of her either left out (floppy rag-doll style) or overemphasized (my-way-or-the-highway style).

At first, this was tricky for Malika. She was so used to letting people push her around and then overcompensating with rigid resistance that this middle way was confoundingly unfamiliar. It might be perplexing for you to read about, too. This kind of felt-sense experience doesn't translate easily to the page. But once you've experienced it, it's unmistakable. And that was the case for Malika. With practice, she got a feel for this middle way. Once she did, we tried again.

Malika approached me with her requests. "We need to negotiate a more equitable use of space," she said, as if I were the business partner she had been having difficulties with. Or, "I'm sorry, but we cannot accommodate late arrivals," as if to a chronically late parent. After a few requests we would stop to fine-tune. Sometimes she was still a bit floppy, other times too fierce. As she practiced building embodied mindfulness in action, she gradually moved closer and closer to that flexibly firm middle way.

As she did, she found new words began to spontaneously arise. The question she had started with—*What do I say to them?*—became a moot point as the answers effortlessly emerged from inside of her. Simply by inhabiting her body differently, she found the words that felt true, powerful, and kind.

"Fear of disappointing others kept me focused on the other person and removed from my own experience," Malika says now. "The body-work we did released some holding patterns that I automatically engaged in when I was unsure of what to do or say in order to avoid disappointing someone. But really what I needed to do was to feel my own feelings in order to get clear, and then sometimes just allow the other person to be disappointed. Once I broke down some of those holding patterns and we practiced some grounded stances, the words came more easily because I was able to be more authentic about my internal state and my need for boundaries."

Over time Malika came to embody this firm-but-flexible approach more and more. Her tone of voice changed—from anxious and accommodating (or more rarely, angry and aggressive)—to steady, quiet, respectful, and clear. She learned to withstand the discomfort that arose when she had to disappoint someone, so that rather than succumbing to her knee-jerk appease reaction, she could speak up on behalf of herself and her business. This allowed her to initiate different kinds of conversations in her life. First she would shift into the feeling state of that middle way, and only then would she make a request of a parent, partner, or employee. She renegotiated the relationship with a demanding colleague and eventually they agreed to part ways. She developed a policy document for parents and made adherence to it a condition of taking on a new student. She created an employee handbook, set performance standards, and started holding employees accountable for meeting them. As she came to embody the capacity to set clear boundaries while remaining kind and connected, her business flourished.

Surely you've had your own version of this experience: the moments that leave you speechless and sputtering because you simply aren't sure how to respond. Stressful conversations can fire up your fight/flight/freeze/appease response just as surely as a startling glimpse of a spider or a snake. When you are surprised or threatened, your body shunts blood, energy, and resources toward your limbic system, brainstem, and muscles, and away from the more newly evolved parts of the brain that play a key role in planning, decision-making, and use of language. That compromises your ability to clearly speak your mind.[1]

But when you embody the capacity to say what you mean, you have a much better shot at finding the words you need. Think about it—when you're relaxed and calm, you don't even have to consider what you're going to say; the right words just flow out of you effortlessly. That's because you have better access to more of the rational and linguistic parts of your brain.[2]

Of course, we don't lose our words just because we're upset. For most of us, certain kinds of communication rile us up on the inside even when the surrounding circumstances are completely calm. Common tripwires include saying no, asking for help, giving feedback, and offering a new product or service. Maybe it's hard to speak up about your secretly treasured dreams or to say hi to an attractive stranger.

When you train your body to be grounded, solid, and clear as you say the things that have historically been hard for you to speak up about, then you have a far better shot not only at finding the words you need, but also at stating them in a powerful way. Put your body in the right state and the words will flow out of you effortlessly. And when the right words arise, you're better equipped to take action on the things that matter to you.

This point is worth dwelling on for a few moments. We do far more with words than simply describe reality—we actually *create* reality with language, just as surely as we create with our hands. In fact, language is one of the primary means by which we take action and bring our ideas to life.

Consider the well-known maxim "Whether you think you can or think you can't, you're right." This phrase points to the indisputable fact that what we *say* to ourselves and others irrevocably affects what we *do*. Asking your spouse to pick up the kids sets in motion a series of events that, had you not taken action with words, would not have otherwise occurred. In this way, we are constantly creating the future with every utterance. As author Chalmers Brothers wisely puts it, language is "a tool we cannot put down."[3]

Of course, we all have biobehavioral blind spots that make it hard for us to say certain kinds of things. Maybe it's hard for you to reveal something vulnerable. Maybe it's hard for you to ask for help. Maybe it's hard for you to give or receive constructive feedback. Stop a moment and think about it—where is it hardest for you to speak up?

Perhaps something comes immediately to mind, but then again, perhaps not. These are often blind spots, after all—by definition they can be difficult or even impossible for us to see without help. Malika was only dimly aware that she even had the option to make requests of her clients. It wasn't until we worked on her embodied approach to the conversation that she found the kind yet clear words she had been searching for.

These blind spots in communication skills can lead to all kinds of crossed wires. You'll probably recognize at least a few of these common communication flubs:

- failing to make expectations, boundaries, and consequences clear
- failing to make clear requests of others, including asking for help
- struggling to insist or demand without damaging relationships
- offering advice so that it's gratefully received, rather than unwelcome
- failing to make a bold statement about the vision you hold
- being diffident when offering to take on a new challenge at work
- failing to make or elicit clear promises and agreements
- confusing opinions with fact

And the list goes on. Of course, you can see how these kinds of skills affect every relationship you're in, as a friend, spouse, parent, partner, employee, employer, volunteer, community organizer, and more.

Have you ever asked someone to do something for you, and even though they said yes, you could tell they didn't mean it? (Parents of teenagers, take note.) How did you pick up on that? Typically it's via a physical cue: something about the tone of their voice, or the way they don't quite meet your eye, or the way their shoulders sag.

When your physical comportment is incongruent with your words, others sense it. Something is palpably "off." This was Malika's challenge—her collapsed and somewhat "floppy" stance was at odds with the clarity and firmness that she wished to communicate. This kind of incongruence between one's body and one's words creates a subtle sense of confusion on the listening end. When it's severe it can even lead to mistrust.

Imagine someone who tells you about his or her most cherished dreams but laughs them off as unimportant. Or imagine receiving some hard-to-hear feedback from a manager who is fidgeting and smiling and nodding. Or imagine yourself having something important to say... and clamming up because you just can't find the words.

When you have a biobehavioral blind spot in communication—such as Maria's discomfort with saying no, or Malika's challenge with setting clear standards—certain important conversations go badly or don't happen at all. And those fumbled and missing conversations limit the future you can create.

On the other hand, when you train your body to be congruent with your intended message, there's less static. Everything comes across more clearly. You find the right words more easily, because you have better access to your higher thinking centers. The congruence you embody builds trust with others and increases your impact and influence, galvanizing others and inspiring their cooperation and collaboration. People can really feel it when you "walk your talk." As a parent, partner, employer, educator, leader—heck, as a human being—when you embody the capacity to hold powerful, clear conversations, you are far better equipped to create the future you intend.

15

Collaborate

Ropeworks & Human Code:
Moving Together in Time

Ropeworks[†] offers work-at-height services for major public-works projects: bridges, dams, wind turbines, even Mount Rushmore. Founded by a rock climber who back in 1994 received an unusual invitation to put his climbing skills to work inspecting bridges after an earthquake near Los Angeles, the company is among the pioneering leaders in this relatively new and now growing industry. Ropeworks provides a more cost-effective way to inspect, repair, maintain, and make safety upgrades to vital infrastructure that we rely on every day.

As a highly professional band of rock climbers, Ropeworks' team members take pride in a company culture that is hip, friendly, and fun. Acutely safety conscious, they will speak up immediately if they see any-

---

[†] Now a division of Mistras.

thing that even approaches a safety policy violation. But outside of that, they found it difficult to give one another performance feedback. Apart from tough inspections in driving wind and rain, for the most part they enjoyed their work and their camaraderie. No one wanted to upset the apple cart by implying someone's not doing his or her job... even when someone wasn't. And without clear performance feedback, team members weren't sure how to grow a career within the company, which many were eager to do.

Once a year, top Ropeworks team members who live scattered around the country come together for a visioning, planning, and training event. Some time ago I was invited in to help address their communication challenges. About forty rope-access professionals gathered in the Reno, Nevada, training center—a cavernous, high-ceilinged warehouse where Ropeworks runs world-renowned training programs teaching engineers and tradesmen and women how to climb. We spent the first morning practicing centering, awakening people to their interoceptive and proprioceptive intelligence. As we went into the afternoon, everyone paired up and we spread out around the room.

I demonstrated the next activity: Standing about ten feet away from my partner, I slowly walked toward him until I was right up in his face. His job was simply to sense his reaction: the normally unnoticed flood of sensations that occur when someone barges into your personal space. After explaining a few ground rules, I turned the group loose to do the same. We tried all kinds of variations: walking up quickly or slowly, meeting eyes or not, adopting different moods, switching partners. The whole goal: Feel all of your reactions. And pay attention how those sensations affect your sense of connection with your partner.

Now, these were guys (and they were mostly guys) who could keep their cool under intense pressure. Or so it seemed. A risky move hundreds of feet in the air didn't faze them. To a person, they could stay calm, focused, and alert during a climbing mishap. They were great at handling intensity and controlling their nerves.

But the kind of "in your face" intimacy we explored in Reno was something entirely different. As we practiced approaching one another, the discomfort in the room was palpable. Finally one man turned to me and exclaimed, "Oh my God, this is how I feel when I have to have a difficult conversation with my wife!" The room burst into nervous laughter, nods of recognition all around.

Mood is contagious. You can sense the chilly atmosphere when you walk into a room where two people have just been fighting, just as surely as you can feel the warmth that emanates from a dear friend. These moments don't simply occur outside of you and around you. Thanks in part to your mirror neurons, they also occur inside of you, subtly changing your own physiological state in response to the world you encounter.[1] We affect one another without words, all the time. Your presence, comportment, and carriage speak volumes. We're often not even aware mood contagion is underway, but it affects us all the same.

All joint projects occur inside the context of a relationship. And the state of the relationship invariably affects the success of the task. If the relationship is one of camaraderie, as relationships typically were at Ropeworks, then you're set up for success. But if you struggle to share information that will improve your team's performance, your success will necessarily be limited. And even if you have a solid relationship built on a great deal of trust, if you're uncomfortable delivering or receiving constructive feedback, your body will convey that and your colleague will feel it. Our bodies are open systems—we affect one another's bodies, brains, and visceral states without even meaning to. What emanates from you affects your conversations, and that in turn impacts your results.

In 2001, researchers at the Yale business school conducted an illustrative study on the effects of mood contagion. They put participants into small groups for a salary-negotiation role play. Each person took on the role of a different department head. In the mocked-up scenario all the participants were responsible for two competing goals. First, they had to argue that one of the top performers in their imaginary department deserved the maximum possible raise. And second, they were responsible for optimizing the financial results for the company as a whole.

But there was a twist. Unbeknownst to them, each team was seated with an actor. As much as possible, he stuck to a script, varying his words as little as possible but radically changing the mood with which he said them. In some groups, the actor was positive and enthusiastic. In others, his voice, body language, and mood all conveyed negativity.

The results were unmistakable. When a team was infected by a positive mood, their ability to cooperate soared. But when they were dragged down by the actor's negativity, conflict increased and grew more heated. Later the researchers repeated the study without an actor. What they discovered is that as people work together, their moods naturally tend to converge.[2]

Other research has shown that when the number of genuinely positive statements on a team outweigh the number of negative statements by three to one, those teams outperform otherwise comparable groups on measures of profitability, customer satisfaction, and 360-degree reviews.[3] This research is consistent with John Gottman's popular research on marriage, in which he has learned to predict divorce with 94 percent accuracy based largely on the ratio of positive to negative interactions.[4]

To be clear, this is not about putting a falsely bright face on things. The positivity has to be genuine. When it is, both relationships and results are strengthened. In other words, mood matters for results. And mood contagion occurs through nonverbal means.

Delivering and receiving performance feedback is one of the most intimate things we do in our professional lives. Power dynamics are typically at play, not to mention issues of financial security and one's pride, self-esteem, and sense of ambition. Conversations about performance can be emotionally triggering on both sides of the equation. Which means how you bring yourself to those conversations matters a great deal.

That's why at Ropeworks we worked on team members' ability to be present before we did anything else. Before we ever got into the question of how to deliver feedback, we practiced paying full attention to yourself and another at the same time. As we continued practicing, staff members got more accustomed to letting the intensity arise as someone approached, staying with it, and centering themselves. After a while we started to add words. They practiced with a framework for delivering feedback that helped them place their observations into the context of what their listener cared about. And I offered the listeners a few words they could repeat silently to themselves to unhook from potential triggers, really hear their partners' words, and deliberately choose their response.

Engaging in embodied mindfulness like this is a far cry from the common "shit sandwich" approach to the same task: first praise, followed by performance feedback, followed by more praise. Not only does this often obscure the key message; it can also feel incredibly disingenuous on the receiving end.

Instead, when the folks at Ropeworks learned to listen deeply with all of their senses to themselves and one another, they were able to really show up for the conversation. "Giving each other feedback is an investment into a better future together," says Jan Holan, Ropeworks' founder and CEO. "It should be welcomed as a gift. If we didn't care, we wouldn't go out on a limb and make the effort."

As they increased their capacity to handle embodied reactions to emotionally charged moments, Ropeworks team members became better equipped to have these important conversations. The more present they were with each other, the easier these previously missing performance assessments became. And the whole tone of the interaction changed for the better.

Human Code, a software-development firm focused on media and broadband applications, faced a similar-but-different challenge. CEO

Ed Perry was already a highly successful leader. By his early forties he had built and sold two companies, one of them to Apple. But he knew he was inadvertently placing limits on his vision and his potential.

When three of his most trusted advisors, none of whom knew each other, suggested he try an embodied approach to leadership development, he was intrigued. He enlisted Richard Strozzi-Heckler, one of the founders of the field, as his coach. During the two years he worked with Strozzi, Ed stepped into the floundering company that was Human Code, turned it around, and grew it to ten times the revenue and number of employees of his previous companies. "People say you can't go from running a company of a few million in revenue to one that's $30 to $50 million. To make a 10x jump in a single leap," says Ed, "there's some big change that's occurred in that person's life that allowed that to happen."

When Ed came on board as CEO, Human Code was fraught with problems. Politics, power moves, passive-aggressive behavior, and unproductive bickering were standard fare. As much effort was dedicated to protecting personal turf internally as to protecting turf in the marketplace—a waste of energy the faltering company could ill afford. Ed gamely began his job full of hope and optimism, but within thirty days Human Code was on the brink of bankruptcy, employees divided into clashing camps, fear and desperation on the rise.

Working with Strozzi, Ed had already substantially expanded his capacity to center under pressure and take action from that more resourceful and resilient state. The rocky start at Human Code put all of his training to the test. "The practices of maintaining center and deciding how to take right action from that place of centeredness is what allowed me to get through," Ed says. Despite the highly charged emotional atmosphere, Ed's newly cultivated equanimity created a calm port in the storm. Gradually his mood infected the leadership team, and over time they started to converge on Ed's positive outlook and centered presence. Working together under Ed's leadership, the team built the faltering company up to $80 million in value.

But the bickering and passive-aggressive behaviors were still taking a toll. And while Human Code staff wasn't necessarily any worse than other teams facing challenges like these, it wasn't any better, either.

Ed thought the practices he had been learning with Strozzi might knit the leadership team into a tighter unit. "I wanted to see if it was possible to use somatics to build the value of the company," he says. On their own, the Human Code team projected they could go from $80 million to $100 million over the next six months. When Ed brought Strozzi in to work with his staff, the charge was simple and direct: get us beyond $100 million.

Strozzi worked with team members to help them sense more, center themselves, get present, and build their capacity to put embodied mindfulness into action in their everyday interactions. In particular, developing team members' emotional, social, and physiological capacity to give and receive performance feedback created a "very, very powerful shift," according to Ed. "It created a different atmosphere on the team. We moved from a presumption of negative intentions to the point where there was clarity about positive intentions. With enough practice, assessments were delivered and received from a place of 'You've got my back,' and 'You're trying to help me be more successful at my area of the business.' That orientation produces high trust, and when there's high trust, everybody is lock-armed, moving together down the same road."

Because mood contagion affects results so profoundly, the level of rapport in a group really makes a difference to its success. I happen to be illustrating that with business examples here, but the same can be said of any group trying to get things done together: sports teams, church volunteers, the PTA, your family.

You're probably already familiar with this experience yourself. Think back to a time when you were part of a group where things just clicked. Perhaps there was a certain flow to your actions, like the feel of a bucket brigade in perfect rhythm, seamlessly handing off tasks one after another. Maybe what comes to mind for you is a professional situation, but it might just as easily be a rare moment of ease when packing the car for a family trip, or when your soccer team nailed every move perfectly, or when you were setting up for an important fundraiser and everything slid into place perfectly right as the doors opened.

Experiences like these often seem like one-offs, unrepeatable magic moments that are hard to come by and impossible to reproduce. But researchers actually know a bit about what goes into them. Three things characterize the kind of rapport that underlies that seamlessly operating bucket brigade: shared attention on a common objective, shared positive mood, and a biological effect known as synchrony.[5]

Synchrony is another word for biological entrainment—a state where the rhythmic systems in one person's autonomic nervous system sync up with the rhythmic systems in another's. Breathing, heart rate, blink rate... even brain waves are all subject to this kind of unconscious synchrony.

Synchrony plays out in conversations as well, where researchers have observed a dance of responsive timing that's tightly tied to rapport. Hand gestures, tilts of the head, turning toward or away... all of these factors and more contribute to the slow, below-awareness rhythmic physical dance that occurs during all communication.

This kind of synchrony is not unique to humans; it happens throughout the animal kingdom.[6] Across many species, behavioral and autonomic synchrony are vital components of clear communication, collaboration, and rapport. And the capacity for this kind of embodied alignment can be built.

Ropeworks had another challenge: teams were rarely intact for long. The company had a distributed workforce living all around the country, and each project required them to travel to a new location. Given the realities of scheduling people with different skill sets across multiple time zones, oftentimes employees wouldn't meet the members of their project team until they arrived at the job site. Sometimes the team included people they'd worked with extensively; just as often it included colleagues they had never met before. They needed a way to quickly sync up and get to work.

On the second day of our training, we went outside to a large grassy spot down by the river. I divided the company into small teams of half a dozen people each. Earlier in the day, my training partner Sally and I had taught the team how to do a series of five simple moves. Now we had each team make those five moves together, over and over, until they got into a rhythm with it. At intervals, I had them stop and give each other feedback in order to improve the team's performance. Using everything they had learned the day before, they practiced centering and settling their psychobiology for those intimate conversations. Their job was to deliver clear and direct feedback so they could get into an easy, smooth rhythm, working together seamlessly. When the team finally fell into step, the participants could all feel it. Something just clicked. It was the recognizable feeling of a high-functioning team.

Once each team had reached a high level of performance, I started to shake things up. I might remove a team member and assign him to a different team. I might break up a whole team and have the members sit on the sidelines for a bit, as sometimes happened in Ropeworks's business when a project ended. I might construct a new team out of two teams working at different ends of the field.

All of this mimicked their real life and everyday environment, and they saw the relevance immediately. Every time a new team member joined an existing group, the members had to adjust their collective rhythm to accommodate the new arrival. Giving and receiving performance feedback grounded in their shared objective and void of emotional charge allowed them to get into step together faster. Team Ropeworks got a real-time experience of how embodying the capacity to offer timely and relevant feedback could increase rather than diminish what they affectionately referred to as their "mojo"—the spirit of camaraderie that pervaded their delightful company. We ended the day on a high note.

We are wired to pick up on this kind of rhythmic conversational flow, and we're deeply disturbed by its absence. You know how sometimes you come up to someone in a hallway and you can't figure out how to pass? You both go one way, then the other, back and forth until one of you laughs or gets annoyed. Sometimes people "bump into each other" with their conversational rhythms as well. A stilted conversation feels altogether different from one that flows easily. In fact if someone's conversational rhythm is unlike your own, you may have a hard time connecting at all.

This is something we experience from birth. Over several decades, researchers have conducted multiple variations on a study protocol now known as the "still-face" experiment. This kind of study looks into conversational rhythms between mothers and their infants. To investigate the phenomenon, researchers ask mothers to respond to their baby's gurgles and coos as they normally do. When the mother responds to the child in real time like this, babies are typically at ease.

But when researchers ask mothers to fall silent and hold their face still, infants become distressed by this expressionless response. In less than a minute, they begin to fuss and cry, quickly escalating to shrieks of dismay.[7]

Our bodies move in a coordinated, synchronized rhythm as we communicate. Even before we can engage with language, we already know the steps to this dance of responsive timing. The dance occurs not only through words, but also through gestures, movement, and facial expression. Right from the get-go we can sense whether our rhythms are attuned or asynchronous, stilted or flowing.

This sense is thanks in part to the oscillating nature of the cells in a human body. Living cells have countless vibrating molecular structures, each with its own inner rhythm. The circadian rhythm that controls our sleep and wake cycles is fueled by oscillators such as these; so is the gradual convergence of women's menstrual cycles when they live together. Oscillators also help us coordinate the timing of our speech, actions, and gestures with the people around us. And they influence the biological entrainment of blink rate, heart rate, brainwaves, and more.[8]

In fact, a study conduced by Johanna Sänger of the Max Planck Institute in Berlin showed that the brainwaves of guitarists sync up when they are playing the same piece of music, even if they each take on different parts of the piece and play different notes. In other words, rhythm connects.[9]

Rhythm affects rapport, and as we have seen, mood and rapport affect results. Fortunately we can cultivate this, as military forces and marching bands have illustrated for centuries (although not always to happy effect). Like the timing exercise I did with Ropeworks, or the string quartet playing a piece, coordinated rhythmic action supports shared effort in a way that few other things do. Drumming, rowing, and some kinds of dance can all foster this kind of coordination and rapport. But it's also possible to just go through the motions. Unless you are sensing your internal state, centering, and listening to others with all of your senses, this deceptively simple rhythmic practice has less of an effect. But when you have the right foundations, moving together in time supports conversational synchrony and allows you to do better work together.

Practices such as these have helped Ropeworks, Human Code, and many other leaders, teams, and organizations dramatically improve performance. The results of moving together more effectively as a team? Ropeworks was acquired by a publicly traded company for a premium price. In just four years, Ropeworks leaders grew the business from thirty-five team members and $3.5 million in revenue into a division with over 400 rope-access technicians generating over $50 million in revenue. Their average annual growth rate exceeded 100 percent. "This would not have been possible," says CEO Jan, "without exceptional feedback, effective teamwork, continuous improvement, and internal training."

For Human Code, the answer was a 30 percent increase in valuation. In 1999, Human Code sold to Sapient for $135 million.[10] "The management team felt confident that we were able to achieve an additional $35 million above and beyond what we would have been able to achieve on our own," says Ed of the embodied training they did. "That's a 30 percent value difference in six months. When we asked the buyer 'why us,' they told us they paid a premium in large part because of the quality and integration of employees across the entire company. We do believe that training in embodied leadership had a significant impact on the valuation of Human Code."

16

Convert Conflict to Consensus

Mel: Building Backbone

Sometimes you just know when someone's lying to you. That's how Mel Szarek felt when she visited her contractor's office to make sure the workers scheduled to fix her front steps would arrive the next day as planned. They were meant to have called to confirm, but she hadn't heard from them. Were they still coming, she wanted to know?

"Uhhh... yes, yes, of course," the flustered contractor reassured her, while looking frantically for her paperwork. "They'll be there tomorrow." But despite this glib promise he appeared to have all but forgotten about the appointment.

Mel was worried. She had been careful to ask around before hiring one of the most reputable and well-respected contractors in town. She had spent the entire week prior moving storage boxes and heavy laundry appliances out of the basement in anticipation of the crew's arrival. The cracks in the front steps had become a hazard, and the basement below had begun to mildew from the leaks. She really needed this fixed.

When the crew arrived the next day, she breathed a sigh of relief. They got straight to work, and she went about her business as they toiled away for the next three days. But when she went to inspect their finished work, her heart sank.

Bricks were misaligned. Paint stains marred the basement, which had also been flooded by a power wash. Window latches had been painted shut. There was a chemical burn on the lawn and hazardous materials in the trash. And to top it all off, on the front steps several large, leaky cracks still remained.

Mel was furious. But she was also anxious. She had always been timid about conflict, and confronting contentious issues filled her with a sense of dread. Typically she would wait until the last possible minute to lodge a service complaint or to return a defective product, delaying the unpleasantness as long as she could. She avoided conflict in her personal relationships, too, letting resentments simmer and stew until she boiled over in an embarrassing explosion that she would later regret. But she knew she was going to have to call the contractor. She knew it couldn't wait. And she wasn't happy about it.

Ironically, Mel is actually a conflict-resolution specialist. As a retired internal organization development consultant for the IRS, she had hundreds of successfully resolved employee conflicts under her belt. Her work was well known and highly regarded all over the country, and for over two decades she was frequently sought out to resolve volatile and sometimes hostile workplace feuds. She even volunteered for the Better Business Bureau as an arbitrator in her free time.

So Mel certainly *knew* a lot about how to resolve conflict. And she was extraordinarily skilled at helping others come to successful resolution. But when it came to her own life, she had a biobehavioral blind spot. She simply didn't embody the capacity to step into conflict and resolve it gracefully.

Her years of conflict-resolution experience had taught her one thing, though: *always prepare*. So Mel wrote up a detailed list of fourteen issues that she wanted to review with the contractor. From the cracks in the masonry to the flooded basement to the acid burns on her lawn, she had a lot to bring to his attention. She didn't want to lose track of any of the details. So she wrote it all down and then set up an appointment for the contractor to come out and take a look.

For days, she rehearsed what she was going to say, turning it over and over in her mind. Although she was justified in her complaints and clear about her plan, Mel still felt anxious and vulnerable. Despite her constant rehearsal, she continued to feel underprepared. Her words never flowed well when she was filled with pent-up disappointment and anger. Plus the contractor was a big burly man, successful in the community, with a strong reputation. Considerably smaller and already timid about conflict, Mel felt like the underdog. She was afraid she'd be steamrolled.

The day of the meeting dawned, and Mel started the morning with her usual exercise routine. She did some forward bends, back bends, and side bends. Then she picked up a wooden staff called a jo—a martial arts weapon that resembles a sword—and stepped through a series of simple movements.

A couple of months earlier, as a student in one of my classes, she had added something new to these exercises. After learning about the importance of emotional engagement in supporting neural and behavioral change (see Chapter 3), Mel began to connect her daily exercises to a sense of meaning. "I'm building *backbone*," she would say to herself as she stretched and strengthened her back.

Today she paused and put her hand on her heart. She silently asked herself a soul-searching question. "Why am I doing this practice? What do I *really* care about?" Out loud she answered, "I'm taking a stand." As she sliced through the air with the jo, she said, "I'm taking a strong stand for my safety, for the safety and respect of my home, and for my dignity as a paying customer." She repeated these simple phrases aloud as she moved, linking her deeply felt care with movements to build "backbone."

Then she went about her day. Much to her surprise, she had quite a stress-free morning. Ordinarily she would have ruminated on the upcoming confrontation, unable to concentrate on anything else. But today her mind was quiet. All the rehearsal and rumination had mysteriously ceased.

She surprised herself again that afternoon by going out to the curb to greet the contractor as he pulled up in his truck. Normally she would have waited for him to ring the bell, backing away from the confrontation until she could avoid it no longer. But "I found myself totally without fear," Mel told me. "I remember feeling 'I can do this.' I just felt complete confidence and commitment. I was entering the ring, but I didn't feel like the underdog. That just didn't even come up." Greeting him at his truck was a way of stepping into the conflict rather than waiting for it to come to her. It wasn't something she had planned, but in the moment it felt like the most natural thing in the world.

With her list in hand, she led the contractor up to the front steps and started pointing out the first of the many issues and errors that she had found. Together they inspected the steps, the lawn, and the basement. Although Mel had expected to stammer and stutter her way through the conversation with shaky hands and voice, she instead felt "grounded, strong, respectful, and respected. I really felt no effort at all—no strain, no tension, no fear." The contractor had seemed tense when he arrived, but Mel's calm demeanor and clear communication seemed to put him at ease. He agreed to return to fix the problems, and according to Mel, "We both left with our dignity intact."

After he left, Mel went back inside. "Wow, that was so easy!" she thought. "But ... why?" It may seem obvious reading her story in retrospect, but that afternoon it took Mel a bit of time to put it together. "Oh right, I did those practices earlier in the day!" she finally realized. "I prepared my *body* for the confrontation, as well as my mind." Mel had always prepared her list. She had always rehearsed (and re-rehearsed) what she wanted to say. But she had never before prepared her body to enter into conflict with a powerful, centered, and clear presence.

Of course, this new type of preparation requires practice. Mel had been doing her morning exercises for years, and for the past several months she had been deliberately cultivating a link between her movements and what mattered to her by speaking aloud the qualities she wanted to embody. So she was already well-primed for her morning practice to have an effect on the afternoon's events. But it was only just this morning she had thought to tie her practice to the conflict at hand. Fortunately, it worked. By consistently building backbone over time, that quality was there for her to call on when she needed it most.

The contractor returned to make the repairs, and then had to return a third time because the job still wasn't done right. He tried to charge a higher price. But Mel had the backbone to insist on their prior agreement. Her life had been disrupted for weeks, and she had already put extra time and money into cleaning up the original mess. When she explained her position with the same calmly powerful demeanor that she had during his inspection, the contractor relented. The crew finished the job, did one final cleanup, and finally, after nearly a month, Mel had the repair she had originally contracted for, at the originally agreed-on price.

Mel is hardly alone in having a difficult time addressing conflict. Of course, some of us relish it, finding a good confrontation exhilarating. But for many, conflict raises all manner of discomfort: the churning stomach, the sweating brow, the wringing of hands. And even when conflict feels enlivening, it still has a physiological impact. Our psychobiology is at play in every interaction, whether or not we recognize that fact or know how to work with it. Every frustration with your teenager, disagreement with your coworkers, or disappointment in your friend involves your body and brain in ways you cannot see, but are unavoidably subject to.

That's because conflict lodges a potential threat against any or all of those essential nutrients of safety, connection, and respect. And our capacity to successfully address conflict has at least as much to do with how we handle our own embodied reactions as with what we plan to say, as Mel's case amply demonstrates.

When I teach courses, participants are often champing at the bit to get to the section on conflict. The reason it comes last in both my programs and this book is because the capacity to engage in and successfully resolve conflict builds on everything we've covered so far.

To review:

Any kind of perceived threat, conflict included, activates our body-wide danger-detecting neuroceptive networks and initiates the polyvagal response. Subtle changes in heart rate, muscular contraction, sweat, digestion, and more are all part of our perceptual process and indicate danger. In response, we either mobilize (fight/flight), immobilize (freeze, withdraw, or dissociate), or move into an ingratiating, eager-to-please mode (appease). These are automatic whole-body responses that lie largely outside of conscious control. And they can easily hijack your most sincere attempts to say what you mean.[1]

As we have seen, this response under pressure makes it harder to access the conscious awareness of interoception that characterizes embodied self-awareness. That may seem counterintuitive, because at times the gut-wrenching, anxiety-provoking nature of conflict may threaten to overwhelm you with intense emotions and sensations. But that is exactly the point. Those uncomfortable sensations become so demanding you simply *must* take action to relieve them. Whether you fight or withdraw, flee or appease, the action that's motivated by a blind attempt to reduce sensory discomfort is rarely your wisest, most well-considered move. This is the automatic, unconscious aspect of interoception—the origin of the knee-jerk reaction. This is how we "lose our heads" in the midst of conflict. When you're driven by a singular sense of discomfort, rather than guided by a full awareness of the present moment, you can literally lose access to the thinking part of your brain.

Conflict, like any stressor, can reduce access to the middle prefrontal cortex (MPFC), that part of the brain that plays such an important role in regulating emotions and extinguishing fear.[2] It's easy to imagine how diminished capacity in the MPFC might negatively affect highly charged conversations. Without the ability to manage your own mood, you'll quickly be pushed outside your capacity to handle strong sensations, and your behavior may become erratic and unpredictable. It becomes difficult or impossible to center yourself, and equally challenging to stay present. You may flip into fury about past transgressions or fantasize negatively about the future in ways that have nothing to do with what's happening right now. And all of that directly affects how you conduct yourself in highly charged conversations.

It also affects your ability—or not—to maintain a positive connection with the person or people you're fighting with. When you can't handle the agitated sensations you experience, it's very difficult to return yourself to center. And when you're not centered, it's virtually impossible to be present. This reduces your ability to convey respect to your adversary, to attune with them, and to truly listen for what legitimate concerns they might have. Embodied self-awareness, centering, and presence all directly affect empathy. When those internal states are absent, your ability to understand your opponent's perspective and see him or her as a reasonable person with legitimate concerns declines. Again, this affects how you handle yourself in the conversation.

Now, your adversary may not be reasonable. Not everyone is. But sometimes, otherwise reasonable people become quite unreasonable when they find themselves under threat. (Warning: This includes you!) Mood is contagious; so when you vent anger and blame in directly aggressive or passive-aggressive ways, it is much more likely that your partner in conflict will feel their own sense of safety, connection, or respect being threatened. When you can't find any way to empathize with your enemy, conflict rapidly escalates in a never-ending, self-perpetuating cycle.

This conundrum is why Mel's long list and incessant rehearsal left her feeling underprepared. Good ideas—no matter how good they may be—are insufficient to successfully address the psychobiological realities of conflict. They are a necessary aspect of conflict resolution, to be sure. But without the skill of managing your embodied response to stress, ideas often fail. Because language alone does not and cannot address the physiological arousal that is a natural part of high-conflict situations.

I asked Mel what she noticed about her body while she walked the contractor through the sloppy job. "I felt taller, bigger than I normally do," Mel told me. "Not just taller, but I felt length all the way through my spine and down to the ground. I didn't back away. There was a sense of effortless flow, without hesitation, tension, or strain. I really felt no effort at all. I also think my body displayed a readiness to engage—my shoulders were open; I didn't have my arms folded, that kind of thing. But it wasn't something I did on purpose, and I didn't really notice it at the time. It just felt natural.

"People tell you to take a breath, don't get stressed out. That's not the same. It just doesn't have the same impact as doing a physical movement that's related to what I care about."

Mel referred to her gentle karate class to describe how this conflict felt. In karate, "when I do a technique correctly, it's not only extremely powerful, but it feels effortless," Mel told me. "It's amazing how powerful you can be in your body with very little effort. This confrontation felt like the same thing. What blew my mind was I didn't have to think for the words. The words just came to me really naturally. And I think that was because I had prepared my body."

I've heard this from countless clients and experienced it myself: When your body is prepared, the words you need come naturally. That's because when you're centered, grounded, and calm, you have more use of the higher-level parts of your brain and intellect. Greater psychophysiological coherence is associated with better mental performance, even in difficult and challenging situations. Getting centered and present allows you to say what you really mean, with more clarity and less emotional charge. Your words just flow.

This points to a way out of high-conflict situations—a vital comple-
ment to the sort of conflict resolution skills to which Mel had devoted
her career. But while the way out is fairly simple to *describe*, I can't
promise that it's easy to *do*. Managing your own embodied reaction to
conflict is a tall order for anyone, and I've watched some of the most
practiced people I know get thrown off when the emotional charge is
high. Still, learning to manage your embodied response to conflict is
well worth the effort. When you can stay fully present and take wise
action, your internal experience changes for the better and the chance
for a successful resolution grows.

So how to do it? It will perhaps come as no surprise that the answer
lies in the culmination of the four fundamental competencies I've
already shared.

To begin with, SENSE more. Pay deliberate attention to your sensations. Familiarize yourself with their subtle nuances. Learn to sense
every part of your body, from the inside. Be aware of how you're standing, sitting, moving. Connect to your *feeling* of care—truly *experience*
caring about who and what you love. What's important for you to care
for and protect in this situation?

Also, CENTER. Cultivate the capacity to experience intense sensations without having to immediately react to them. Instead of letting
your discomfort drive you, learn how to return yourself to a state of
psychophysiological coherence, so that you can access your full intelligence under pressure. Coherence is contagious. Your centered presence (or alternatively, your spun-up psychophysiological incoherence)
affects other people's actions and the outcome of disagreements far
more than you might imagine.

Build PRESENCE. Stay connected to those you're in conflict with.
Respect their inherent worth and dignity as much as you can. (This is
nearly impossible if you're not centered yourself.) Keep your attention
simultaneously on yourself and your own needs and desires, along
with the other individual(s) and their legitimate concerns. Genuinely

attune to them so you can build trust and rapport. When people feel seen and heard, they are naturally more cooperative.

GALVANIZE others. When you've mastered your own internal state and connected with the other person to the degree that you're able, then it's time to take action. Embody the skill of making a clear request, rather than stammering it out. Build the capacity to say no, if that's something that's difficult for you. Learn how to insist on what's important to you with courage, composure, and kindness, and to give on the things that don't matter. Use the power of contagion to inspire others with you on behalf of the collective good.

Conflict resolution is the pièce de résistance of embodied learning, because it requires everything we've touched on thus far: the ability to feel your own cares, center yourself in the face of pressure, be fully present with yourself and others, compassionately legitimize another person's perspective even when you don't agree, communicate clearly, and collaborate well. When you embody all of these skills, you can approach conflict in a way that has the potential to build rather than destroy relationships.

Of course, none of this is a panacea or a guarantee. But you considerably up the odds by building embodied self-awareness and learning how to engage in embodied mindfulness in action. People can sense respect and attunement—as well as disrespect and distance—from miles away. The more safe, connected, and respected people feel, the more readily an agreeable resolution reveals itself. Your centered presence, predicated on your capacity to sense your own inner state, can help others stay calm and work with you rather than against you.

But of course, it's nearly impossible to employ these skills in a high stakes situation if you've rarely experienced them before. The only way to access these skills when you most need them is to practice them when you don't. This is how you build the muscle memory that makes a strong, centered, and compelling presence automatic. As Mel and many others will attest, it's very much worth the effort.

Imagine if you and everyone around you could negotiate conflict in a centered way: connected to core principles and committed to compassion and clear communication. What would become possible that isn't possible now? What would change in your life? How might disagreements at work or family legal disputes unfold differently? What might happen to online bullying, for example, or to our polarized political divides? When I imagine a world where more of us embody the skill of turning conflict toward consensus, I feel optimistic about the challenges ahead.

At the end of our conversation, Mel said "There's something magical about it." Ed Perry, Peter Maynard, Denise Rundle, and countless others have used those exact same words to describe their experience of this kind of embodied leadership learning. I'm sure I've used them myself.

But I maintain it's no more magical than any other technology you don't fully understand. The internet is magical; so is electricity. But we have magicians who are masters of those realms and who understand how to make the bits and bytes and electrons flow so that we can use them day to day without giving it so much as a passing thought.

Embodied leadership learning is the same. Masters of this realm can help you tap the best in yourself, make a contribution you truly care about, build better relationships, and handle stress, conflict, and pressure with more ease[†].

Is it mysterious? Yes. Powerful beyond all expectation? Yes. But magical? No. We now have the tools to peer under the hood and understand—or at least make some reasonably close educated guesses about—what's going on when you engage in meaningful embodied practice that's embedded in the context of your everyday life. When you do that repeatedly, you come to embody more love in action. It's really that simple.

[†] Visit yourbodyisyourbrain.com for a list of practitioners.

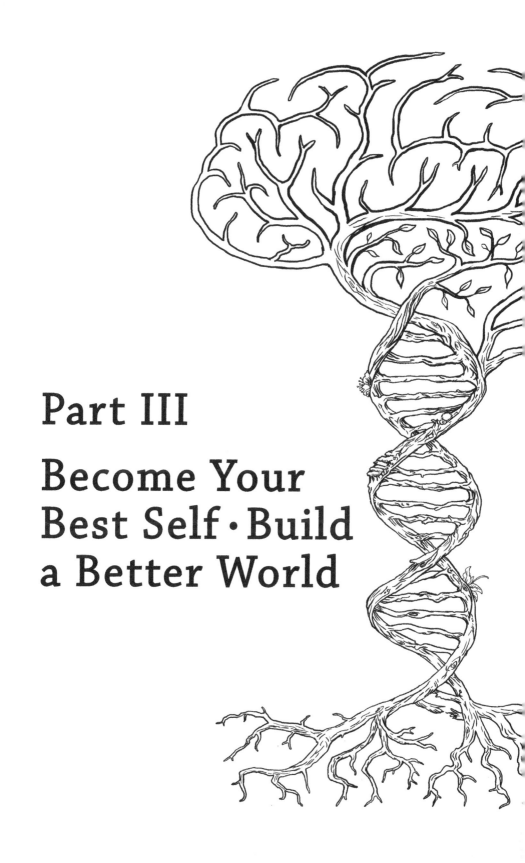

Part III

Become Your Best Self · Build a Better World

17

The Promise of Embodied Learning

If we can get in touch with what's really happening inside of us and we can communicate that to other people, then there will be peace in the world. At some level I really trust that. I realize it's not so easy. But people who attack each other, whether metaphorically in a corporation, or literally between warring tribes and nations, they all share the same inner gut feelings. The problem is that we can't feel ourselves because we're threatened and we're fighting. So instead we dehumanize others. The hope for me would be to get people to a place where they can feel their own feelings. If you can really feel your own true inner condition, then you immediately empathize with others.

—Dr. Alan Fogel

Healthy living systems are characterized by differentiation and integration. This is easiest to see in ecosystems. For instance, a large field planted in a single crop is far more vulnerable to a devastating invasion of pests or disease than a diversified farm growing multiple species on the same plot of land. The simple fact that pests have a harder time navigating their way to their favorite food in a more diverse ecosystem is an inherent buffer against catastrophe.

Healthy, mature ecosystems are characterized by a wide variety of species, each filling a different niche. This is differentiation. Each species also has links and mutually beneficial relationships with other species. This is integration. This relationship between differentiation, integration, health, and maturity holds true across all living systems, from ecosystems to cultures to individual organisms.

What this means for us is that to develop greater health and maturity, we must differentiate among our various intelligences, gaining finer and more nuanced distinctions in each. Pulling embodied self-awareness out of the background by learning to identify and fully feel your physical sensations leads to greater differentiation. Linking this growing embodied self-awareness with conceptual self-awareness leads to greater integration. Amplifying both conceptual and embodied self-awareness while in action, embedded in relationship, in the context of your daily life, leads to still further integration. This is how embodied mindfulness in action leads to greater health, maturity, wisdom, and skillful action.

Embodied mindfulness in action is qualitatively distinct from athletics, yoga asana, dance, and other physical practices that you add to your life a few times a week. The difference is that embodied mindfulness in action is *embedded in* your ever-present day-to-day activities and interactions. The result of engaging in this kind of experiential leadership learning is a growing integration, maturity, and wholeness.

As I collected stories for this book, a hidden theme that illustrates the power of this integration began to emerge. The people I interviewed often shared stories about reclaiming some aspect of themselves that had been sacrificed to broadly held social norms. Often this fell along gender lines. Over and over again I heard stories about men getting more in touch with their emotions, and women getting more comfortable claiming greater authority. Although I never set out to write about this pattern, as it came into view it gradually validated something I had long suspected:

I believe we live in a time when men are stepping more and more into their hearts, and women are stepping more and more into their power. For instance:

- Marianne Elliot used her yoga practice to call up the courage to lead when she was in over her head.
- Nichole Dunn relies on embodied practice to dial up her capacity for influence at the Women's Fund.
- Denise Rundle stopped striving for an A+ and became a more respected and trusted leader as a result.
- Malika Tremont learned how to make clear, unambiguous requests on behalf of herself and her organization.
- Mel Szarek stepped calmly into a confrontation that would have ordinarily made her run.

- Brian Fippinger melted the walls of his long-held fortress and developed the capacity for true intimacy.
- Peter Maynard learned to *feel* his care before he established the Environmental Council at Capital One.
- Rich Low stepped outside his comfort zone to do something totally woo-woo, and made a measurable difference in his startle response and short-temperedness.
- Claus Wieser transformed himself from a "brutally competent" boss into an empathetic and listening leader.
- The mostly male staff at Ropeworks increased their capacity for intimate conversations at work and at home.

In so doing, *each of these people became a more effective leader*. In building a more whole and integrated version of themselves, each of them came to have a more powerfully positive impact within their sphere of influence.

Of course, this gender-based pattern doesn't hold universally true. Every individual has his or her own biobehavioral blind spots and each person's journey of embodied learning is unique. But this pattern repeats itself often enough to suggest something notable: When you move toward greater integration, you begin to reclaim aspects of your humanity that may have been forfeited not only to the idiosyncrasies of your upbringing but also to broadly held societal norms. This holds true not just for gender norms, but also for constraining norms around other aspects of your life experience: race, religion, sexual orientation, age, class, and more. As more and more people reclaim these lost aspects of their humanity, this has the potential to make significant impacts on the world at large.

I want to be clear that this movement toward wholeness is not a movement toward sameness. It's not about men and women becoming more alike, or about people of different cultures or backgrounds giving up what makes them unique. It is about all of us gaining more access to the full breadth of our shared humanity. The capacity to love, to connect, and to care; to lead, to influence, and to achieve—these are neither masculine nor feminine qualities, but *human* qualities. And the more of us that embody the fullness of our humanity, the better off we all will be.

In this book I have tried to demonstrate that Dr. Fogel's statement above is not only true, but also inevitable. The more you sense yourself, the more you immediately, easily, and automatically empathize with others. This connection is simply a neurobiological reality; it is how our psychobiology is designed. The more you connect to your own felt sense of love, care, and desire to make a positive difference, the more powerfully and effectively you can take action. The more you center yourself and get present in the face of challenge, the better you become at communicating, leading teams, and resolving conflict. These qualities and capabilities are the hallmark of powerful, trusted, and effective leadership.

The world we want and the leaders we need *require* this kind of integration. I am not talking about gender-based integration, per se, but rather about wholeness. I am talking about the ability to consistently connect your actions to love and to take powerful action from a foundation of respect for all life.

Despite vast differences in belief systems, most people the world over long for similar things: Peace. Reliable safety for themselves and their loved ones. Comfortable shelter. Freedom and autonomy. Clean water and ample food. Justice. Creativity. Love.

I believe that the world we collectively long for—the one where peace, justice, and beauty reign—depends on each one of us embodying courageous, purposeful, love in action. I have seen, over and over again, how these potent qualities can become second nature. And I have found that the best and most lasting route to developing them is to train your _whole_ self to embody your _best_ self.

How do you get there? Deepen embodied self-awareness and integrate it with conceptual self-awareness. Sense more. Center yourself. Get present. *Practice.* And then and only then, take action.

Everywhere you go, you take your body with you. Your gestures, comportment, and sensations affect every action you take and even the very fabric of your worldview. Your body is an instrument—your *only* instrument—of both perception and action. It affects every last thing you see, say, and do.

As you become more whole by integrating embodied mindfulness into your everyday life and actions, you begin to heal first yourself, and then the shattered fragments and torn tapestries and painful rifts in the part of the world that is available to your influence. Embodying your leadership potential is an inside-out game.

This is the healing of our time and the task of our generation. I hope you'll join us.

Concluding Thoughts

Appendix A: Putting It Into Practice

Interest in mindfulness and the mind-body connection is becoming more and more commonplace. There's just one problem with this breezy mainstream enthusiasm: it makes it easy to mistake passing familiarity for true understanding, surface knowledge for genuine experience.

As much as I want you to have the learning I have offered you in this book, there's a reason I haven't addressed put-it-into-action practices until now. The reality is, experiential learning doesn't readily lend itself to the page.

You can read a book about swimming, but if you want to learn how to swim, you'll have to actually get wet. And once you dive in, can you teach yourself how to swim? Perhaps. On the other hand, you could drown trying.

My point here is not to suggest that you'll drown trying to embody leadership qualities on your own. My point is simply that nothing substitutes for real-world experience coupled with competent guidance. Those things will take you further, faster. Every time.

If you are inspired by what you've read in this book, I strongly recommend you find a competent teacher to help you put your learning into practice. Some of my favorite resources are listed on this book's companion website. † That being said, I can share a few things here that will help you get started on your own.

---

† Visit yourbodyisyourbrain.com.

Why Practice?

Musicians, athletes, actors, and artists of every stripe know this truth: The body only learns through practice. Most artists—including artists of athleticism—spend upwards of 80 percent of their time in practice or rehearsal. Reading a book or attending an afternoon workshop is the equivalent of going to the gym and learning how to do sit-ups. You can't walk out of that initial session and say, "Check it out, now I have abs!" If you want six-pack abs, you're going to have to do those sit-ups again and again, first to build and then to maintain the body you want.

Building the body of a leader is no different (although typically it's a little less sweaty). Repetition, focused attention, directed movement, and emotional engagement are all essential for embodied learning to take place. These core elements of neuroplasticity support the structural and chemical changes in neurons that result in long-term learning and durable change. And because leadership is ultimately a relational set of skills, you must be embedded in connection and community for them to successfully take root.

Embodied practice creates *durable* change, because it rewires your entire neuromusculature and creates new embodied patterns that affect your day-to-day actions. If you take the time to build the muscle memory for key personal and interpersonal qualities such as the ability to maintain composure, access compassion, resolve conflict, and act from care, those qualities become accessible to you *for the rest of your life.*

Suggestions for a Successful Practice

Harnessing the benefits of embodied self-awareness in an *applied* way requires far more than just paying attention to sensation. This is where many coaching methodologies, yoga classes, mindfulness practices, and self-help books fall short. Real learning and lasting change must go beyond producing awareness to actually produce new actions.

Make Your Practice Relevant

Know why you're practicing, and keep what you're hoping to achieve front and center. Truly *feel* your sense of care. Successful practice requires sustained effort over time. Keep your motivation high by staying connected to why your practice matters.

Practice Early, Practice Often

There are two good ways to teach your body a new skill: repetition and immersion. Practice five, ten, fifteen times a day. Short bursts and frequent reinforcement are essential to embodied learning. Or try a retreat. A weeklong immersion in deep daily practice can speed your body's learning. If supported by regular follow-up practice to maintain it, this kind of focused learning can really accelerate your progress.

Locate Your Practice in Space and Time

Practice new skills when you don't need them, so that they're available when you do. Don't wait until you're in a high-stakes situation to try to remember to take a deep breath—I guarantee you'll forget. Instead, teach your body to stand differently so you can breathe more deeply without having to think about it. Do this ten times a day for ten weeks, so that when a challenging situation arises, your *body* remembers for you.

Find a low-stakes time, location, or trigger for your practice. Choose something that happens multiple times a day, and tie your practice to that. Every stoplight. Every time the phone rings. Every time you walk through your office door. Set a reminder on your phone, tie a band around your wrist, put a note on your mirror. Whatever you need to do to help you remember. Typically, the hardest part of practicing embodied mindfulness in action is remembering to do it!

Extra Practice or Embedded Practice

There are practices that you add to your daily life, like meditation, or yoga, or Mel's back bends, or the Maynard family's daily run. And then there are practices that are embedded in your life, woven into the tapestry of your everyday activities. Helena leaned back from her to-do list to remind herself "I am enough." Another client of mine challenged herself to say no three times a day. In addition to her "extra" morning exercises, Mel now practices sensing her backbone at multiple points throughout the day.

Both kinds of practice are important. But one of the reasons people often struggle to practice is they try to add a significant new activity into an already packed schedule. Those new activities may be valuable, but if you can't consistently show up for them, they won't do you any good. So when in doubt, opt for micro-practices embedded in your daily life. They're usually easier to incorporate, and they're often more effective.

With these tips in mind, let's take a look at some practices.

Reveal Biobehavioral Blind Spots

Inventory Your Embodied Strengths + Limitations

This process is an opportunity to explore the origins of who you've become. What has shaped you: your personality, your strengths, your identity, your worldview, your habits? What events or circumstances contributed to who you are today? Questions like these can help you gain perspective on the gifts your life has brought you.

Choose two of your strengths that you are most proud of, and one thing about yourself that consistently trips you up. You can choose a second limitation if you like, but don't get carried away. Two is more than enough.

Remember that the limitation or challenge *is not how you're broken.* Your body and brain are vastly intelligent—far more so than you've probably given yourself credit for. If you developed this trait, you can trust it was for a very good reason. How did it originally help you get those essential nutrients of safety, connection, and respect—even if it's not doing such a good job getting you those things now?

	Strength #1	Strength #2	Chief Limitation or Challenge
Name it	*Example: determination*		
How has this trait helped you in your life? How was it intelligent? Why was it a good idea?	*I accomplish a lot. I can see projects through to completion, even hard ones. I know how to keep going when things are hard.*		
How did it protect or take care of essential nutrients? safety connection respect	*Gained me a lot of respect growing up. My peers and colleagues tend to be impressed.*		
How has it affected who you've become? worldview way of relating reactivity default behaviors	*I don't believe in giving up. I judge people who don't see things through, including myself. I support friends who are more flaky, but I also get impatient with them.*		

What were the key events, stories, relationships, and circumstances that contributed to its development? relationships activities institutions culture community	*My coaches pushed me hard. I grew up in a high-achieving community where excellence was expected. In high school I was very determined to win that debate with my teacher, and I did. This gained me a lot of respect with peers & staff.*		
How does it get expressed through your body? what is the predominant... sensation posture gesture facial expression mood Note: *If this is hard to see at first, that's normal! It may become clear as you look more deeply, so come back to this later if you like.*	*I grit my teeth & furrow my brow. My jaw gets tight & my eyes get narrow & focused. I breathe more shallowly. I lean forward slightly. But also... sometimes I get into a relaxed, calm, focused state, where everything feels quiet inside and I am just moving forward step-by-step.*		
What is the predominant mood associated with this quality?	*insistence resolve pride*		

What is your under-lying perspective or view of the world when it's at play? What do you say to yourself?	I _have to_ do this. I can. I must. I am capable. I will. Even if I don't want to, I will.		
How does this quality affect your relationships?	Sometimes it's connecting and sometimes it's distancing. I can get pretty single-minded and that can make it harder to connect.		
How does it affect your actions?	I get s*** done!		

After you've completed this exercise, consider finding a trustworthy friend with whom you can share your discoveries. Here are some suggested ground rules for that conversation:

First, decide on an amount of time the speaker will speak. Give yourself ample time—anywhere between fifteen and twenty minutes is usually good. Set a timer that will ring when you have a few minutes remaining, so you'll know when to start wrapping up.

Speaker:
- Tell your story. How have your life experiences built your biobehavioral strengths and limitations?
- Instead of talking _about_ what you've discovered on this worksheet, tell your _story_. "First this happened, and then this, and because of those experiences I developed this or that strength or limitation."

- You won't have time for everything, so emphasize the most important highlights and key turning points.

Listener:
- Your job is simply to listen. Don't interrupt, don't speak, and above all don't offer any advice. Just be a silent and attentive witness to the life that your friend has lived. Approach this opportunity like the sacred privilege that it is.
- **Make this a completely, 100 percent advice-free zone.** This is not a problem-solving conversation; it's a witnessing conversation. You may have advice, but that is not helpful now. If you like you can make note of your ideas, and if your friend is open to hearing them, perhaps you'll want to discuss them at a later time. But do not offer that now.
- You may want to make note of key insights you have along the way, but as much as possible leave paper and pen aside. It is much more important for you to *be present* with your friend. Just listen.
- When your friend is finished speaking, share what you see.
  - How is their story coherent? Consistent with who you know them to be? Intelligent?
  - What is most striking about your friend's resilience, humanity, or courage?
  - What are the gifts your friend has developed from his or her most difficult life challenges? Share what you see.
- Your perspective here can be invaluable. Offer your friend the best you've got. Help them see their own brilliance.

This kind of conversation can deepen intimacy and be very healing.

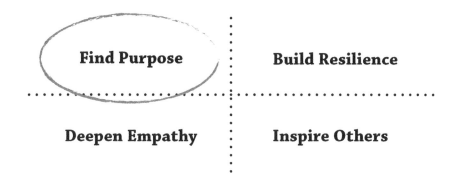

Find Purpose: Embody Your Commitment

This practice is similar to the one Peter Maynard did each day.

Emotional Engagement

Begin by wiggling your fingers. Imagine your hands to be full of kindness and love. Imagine that from the center of your heart love is flowing out your arms and into your hands. Really *feel* your hands—become aware of the sensations there as you wiggle and move, perhaps stretching your arms as you do so.

Now place one hand, or maybe both hands, gently over your heart. Bring with you all the kindness and love that you just invited into your hands. Offer yourself genuine appreciation for the struggles you've overcome, the strengths you've built, and the person you are today.

Call to heart the smile of someone you love. There is nothing special to do here, just allow that person to occupy your imagination. It doesn't matter if they are living or dead, present in your life now or not. They need not even be human; if you have a furry or four-legged friend who occupies an important place in your heart, he or she is welcome here, too. As you imagine this being, sense what happens in your heart. Notice if there is any more warmth, openness, or softness than there was before.

Continue calling to mind people, places, and activities that you love. Truly *feel* your feeling of care. Get intimately familiar with it. What happens in your heart and body as care arises? Take note.

Body

Keep opening to the sensations that accompany care. As you do so, shift your body into a stance that feels powerful for you. For many of us, this will be an open, expansive posture of some sort. You might experiment with different ways of standing until you find one that feels right to you. Perhaps your arms will be lifted to the sky. If you're a yogi, you might find that warrior pose, tree pose, or another powerful pose suits you. Maybe you'll find yourself just standing with your spine fully extended and relaxed.

Whatever it is for you, find that posture and invite in the feeling of care. Then hold it for a few moments. Then shift to something else. Then shift back. Pay attention to the difference between what we might call your current "normal" state, and your more powerful and care-filled state. Practice moving between the two states so that you become really aware of the differences.

The purpose of this exercise is to discover what you need to do to shift into care-based strength. It may be shifting the way you stand. Or it may be reminding yourself of a particular moment or memory. Or it may be relaxing your jaw, or softening your eyes, or straightening your back, or unlocking your knees. See if you can find one thing that serves as a "gear shift" that helps you enter into the felt sense of strength and care.

Movement

When you have a sense of both the feeling of care and the feeling of strength in your body, begin walking around the room. Concentrate on returning to the felt sense of care and power as you walk. Invariably, this feeling will slip away—that's to be expected. You are not "winning" if you never lose track of the feeling. Instead, *expect* to lose track of it. Just keep walking and returning to the feeling, walking and returning to the feeling. You may have to start out slowly at first. With practice, see if you can move more and more toward walking at your normal pace. If you practice this repeatedly over time, you will eventually come to embody a sense of strength and care more and more as you move through the world.

Meaning

Add to this a simple statement of who you are becoming, where you are steering your ship, the future you would like to create.

It's often a good idea to begin with the words "I am." These words are statements of being—of who and how we are. I *am* a woman. I *am* intelligent. I *am* kind. Simple, factual statements like these send a powerful message to your body and unconscious mind, drawing you inexorably toward the future you intend. Using the words "I am" amplifies that power. (But beware... the path and the ultimate outcome may not look anything like what you imagined!)

Keep it very simple, and try for ten words or fewer. Nothing is magical about the number ten—it's just a guideline to help you stay succinct and clear.

It might sound something like this:

I am deeply committed to living in harmony with nature.
I am doubling sales this year.
I embody wise action.
I am committed to completing a marathon.
I am raising $40,000 to combat lung cancer.
I am committed to being truly authentic at work and at home.
I am changing the signage in my neighborhood to secure safer roadways.

Of course, you can certainly choose something that you already know how to do and are doing... but this path is not where you'll find your most powerful results. Instead, see if you can really focus this statement on who you are becoming, where you want your life to go next, and the future you want to create. Allow yourself to be informed by your longing, by your deepest cares and desires.

Don't worry if it takes a while to land on the right words. Many people take days or weeks, and get help from coaches or friends, before they arrive at clear, concise wording that feels resonant to them. Take your time.

Once you find the right words, stick with them. Changing your commitment over and over will prevent you from getting traction. Choose something that will fuel you for six months, a year, a lifetime. This is a practice to support the big things that are important in your life. I spent the better part of a decade embodying my commitment to publish this book, for example.

We all have multiple cares and commitments. You may have commitments for love, home, work, family, friendships, hobbies, volunteer work, and so on. To begin with, choose the one—or maybe two at the most—that will make the biggest difference in your life. When you have embodied your first commitment and are taking consistent action on it, there will be ample time and opportunity to add more.

All Together Now

Once you have practice with each of these pieces, weave them together into a whole. Speak your commitment aloud as you call a sense of care into your heart. Enter into a power pose and invite in a feeling of strength and assurance. Walk into your future from here.

Repeat this daily, many times a day, and you will soon come to embody your commitment consistently and fiercely. It will be with you everywhere you go, woven into the fabric of your awareness and alive in every cell of your body. Success breeds success, so keep your attention focused on all the ways your commitment is coming into being, even if they're quite small. You will soon find yourself noticing previously invisible opportunities and tapping greater confidence to take action on them.[†]

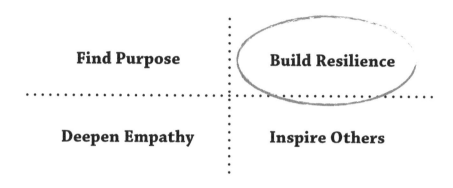

Build Resilience: Embody Confidence, Courage, and Composure

Get to Know Your Triggered Self

Identify a place in your life where you perpetually get stuck. This spot might be the limitation that you explored in the practice above. It could be something like procrastination, or maybe it's jumping into action too quickly that trips you up. It could be shrinking from offering your opinion, or being too brash. Whatever it is, look for something that happens several times a week so that you can track it easily and gather information about it quickly.

[†] If you'd like help doing this, please feel free to download the free Stress to Serenity Guide at the embright website: embright.org/centering-challenge.

Pay close attention to the sensations, gestures, and postures associated with this behavior. Do you notice yourself looking down, or up? Feeling queasy inside, or tense? When this behavior comes up, put your hand on the strongest sensation. Where in your body do you feel it the most? How would you describe that sensation? Aim to use *physical* words, rather than words about emotions. (For example, rather than saying "I'm anxious," say, "I feel fluttering in my chest.") There's no problem with naming emotions, too; just be sure to distinguish them from your sensations.

You might find this difficult to do. If so, that's normal. Remember that a lot of your internal sensations happen below conscious awareness, and that's by design. You'll probably want to set a reminder or keep a list like the one below to help you pay attention. Furthermore, most of us don't have a very rich vocabulary about our sensations, because we're just not taught to look for them. So if this work of paying attention is challenging, that doesn't mean you're failing. In fact, it probably means you're on precisely the right track.

Get to Know Your Best Self

When you've got a good feel for what your triggered state is like, identify what quality or way of being you want to move toward instead. If you could no longer experience this triggered state, what would you want to experience in its place? Name that. Look for places in your life where you already experience that state, or something like it.

Then ask the same set of questions about you at your best. What are the sensations, postures, and gestures that accompany this state of being? What is your mood? What is your overall interpretation of the world around you when you are in this mood? What background assumptions do you operate from?

	Triggered Self	Best self
What's this state called?	pre-presentation anxiety	confident golf swing
Sensation, Posture, Gesture	churning in my gut grinding my teeth a little hunched over	solid stance, shoulders relaxed breathing deeply, standing tall looking ahead, down the green
Mood, Emotions	scared, anxious afraid of being judged	focused, relaxed mildly excited, eager anticipation
Thoughts, Assumptions	I don't want to I can't do this I'm not good enough	I've got this If I blow it I can easily recover This is fun!

Know the Difference Between Them

Start to really get clear about the difference between these two states—not just in your mind but in your *body*. What does it *feel like* to be in your triggered state, in all the attendant sensations and movements that go along with it? How does that *feel different* from being at your best, with all of *its* attendant movements and sensations? Find a point of leverage in your body; a physical location that brings everything else—mood, thinking, sensations—along with it when it shifts. Then practice shifting gears with that lever as your focal point. In the example above, one possibility might be the focus of your gaze. If you were this (fictional) person, you might move from a hunched-over stance with a downcast gaze to lift your eyes and look down the green toward your goal.

Stop three times a day and spend a few minutes moving from your triggered self to your best self. Remind yourself what you are building and why this practice is important to you. Do this for a month or more, and start to see if your pre-presentation anxiety (or whatever it is for you) doesn't gradually start to subside. Even if not, you've now built an embodied habit of moving toward your best. So when anxiety arises, you have somewhere else to go—and the muscle memory to do it without a second thought.

A (Hopeful) Note of Caution

Let's not pretend that this isn't hard work. It takes dedication, attention, and perpetual self-forgiveness. And it takes time. Not a lot of time out of your day, perhaps, but consistent practice over weeks and months if you want to see a real change.

The good news is, if you choose this challenging path you will be rewarded by durable learning. If you want to embody new skills, new actions, and new ways of being—in short, if you want change that lasts—your dedication will pay off. You'll be able to call up your best self without a second thought. Because once you've wired in this kind of biobehavioral learning, you won't ever forget how. Just like riding a bike.

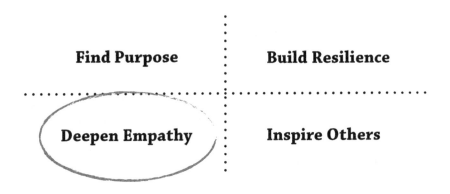

Find Purpose   **Build Resilience**

Deepen Empathy   **Inspire Others**

Deepen Empathy: Embody Compassion

Connect the Breath

You'll need a friend for this practice. Choose one person to lead and one to follow. Decide who will go first. When you've done this one way, you can switch roles.

Breather

Close your eyes. Notice how connected you do or don't feel with your friend. As you go through this exercise, simply pay attention to your sense of connection. That's your only job. If sensations arise, notice them. There is no need to pay attention to or try to change or control your breath, or anything else, for that matter. In fact it's better if you don't.

Sensor

Keep your eyes open. Notice how connected you do or don't feel to your friend right now. With a soft, diffuse awareness, take in the pattern and quality of her breath. Just become aware of how she is breathing, right now, in this moment.

Gradually, gently begin to match your breath to hers. Over the course of several breaths, make your way toward the pace, rhythm, and depth of your friend's breath. See what it feels like to breathe with her for a bit. What sensations arise? How connected do you feel? Is it the same as before, or different? If it's different in some way, what has changed?

Once you've spent a few moments doing this, avert your eyes and see if you can just *feel* your friend breathing. You might hear her, but pay more attention to your other sensations. Can you sense the pace of her breath, and continue to match it even as you are not looking?

Spend about two or three minutes doing this. That will probably seem like a long time, but you are certainly welcome to go longer if you like. When you've gotten a feel for this experience, let your friend know that you've finished. At that point, the Breather can gently open her eyes.

Debrief

Have a conversation about what you each noticed. Some useful questions to explore might include:

What happened to your level of connection? Did it stay steady, or did anything change? If it changed, what shifted? When did it shift? What made you aware of the shift?

What physical sensations or changes in posture occurred? Did those seem to be associated with any particular moment or mood?

What does this experience have to teach you about presence? Was it hard or easy to stay present? If hard, what made it hard? If easy, what made it so?

What did you learn here that you'd like to take into your day-to-day life?

Advanced Experimentation

Breather, turn your back to your friend. Sensor, gradually move toward matching your friend's breath, as you did before. Once you have a feel for the pace of her breath, turn your back to your friend.

Sitting back to back and slightly apart, place your attention on your breathing and simultaneously on your friend's breathing.[†] Start like this: Imagine your attention is like a sphere that has a bright point at the center. Place this central point of attention in the center of your own chest. Just pay attention to your own breathing. Then let that sphere of attention gradually expand to encompass more and more of your own body and sensations. Let your sphere of attention continue to expand until you are including your friend and their breathing along with your own. See if you can *sense* the rhythm of your friend's breath, rather than listen for it. Her breathing, and your breathing. Her breathing, and your breathing. Continue to explore what it feels like to match your breath to hers.

To do this, you must heighten your sensitivity to your own sensations and expand your attention outside the boundary of your own skin to include your friend. It's a tricky thing to do, and if you haven't spent much time training your attention (which usually acts like a puppy, jumping from one new thing to the next), or learning to feel your sensations, this exercise may seem difficult or impossible. Don't

---

[†] As an alternative, you can also try starting back to back, either with your backs touching, or sitting slightly apart.

fret; you just need more practice. Keep tracking your sensations in your daily life using the practices above. The more you do this, the more you'll be able to "feel with" others as well.

Debrief

Discuss what's different when you're relying on visual cues versus when you're not. How do you have to pay attention differently in order to feel "synced up" with your friend when you can't see them?

Apply It to Your Life

In your daily life, pay attention to where you feel "synced up" with someone, and where you feel out of sync. How do you know when you're in sync? What are the subtle physical cues that let you know? How does that feel different from being out of sync?

Experiment with noticing other people's breath. What does their breath reveal about their mood? What happens if you silently sync up your breath with theirs? What happens when you fall out of sync, deliberately or inadvertently? Just quietly experiment and see how your sense of connection is affected.

Note: You can find more practices at yourbodyisyourbrain.com.

Appendix B: Embodiment Versus...

There is often some confusion about what embodiment is, and what it is not. So I thought it might be useful to distinguish the term embodiment from some other things it might easily be confused with.

Embodiment Is Not Yoga. Or Athletics.

(Although either can potentially lead to deeper embodiment.)

Binky Mendoza, a yoga teacher in the Philippines, once asked me, "Why does it seem like yoga sometimes 'works' and sometimes it doesn't? Personally, I've learned so much that I can apply directly to my day-to-day life. But still, there are some yoga teachers and students who are just... jerks. What gives?"

Binky's right. Some yoga devotees *are* jerks. How can that be, when they are so clearly dedicated to practicing their pretzel-like poses? Isn't yoga supposed to make you happier, kinder, and more calm?

And we all see the news stories about the bad behavior of professional athletes. If the body is so intelligent, then why do celebrity athletes who have dedicated their lives to peak physical performance continue to act out?

It's true that the body has a brilliance all its own. But we have so little experience accessing it that even yoga doesn't automatically help. This is especially true when physical movement and spiritual platitudes are overemphasized at the expense of true self-cultivation, as is often the case with the mainstream asana-based version of yoga that has become popular in recent years.

The body is wise, but it is not all-knowing. We spend decades in school learning the skills of logic, critical thinking, analysis, and the many other distinctions necessary for skillful use of our intellect. Conversely, we spend virtually no time at all learning how to accurately discern and wisely use the intelligent messages present in our postures, gestures, and sensations.

What makes yoga so powerful are not the poses themselves. Some magic lies in the particular twists and turns of yoga, to be sure. But the heart of the personal and spiritual growth that is yoga's true potential lies less in the specific movement sequences and more in *how you pay attention* as you move, and how you apply the resulting insights to your daily life. And when you learn to pay attention in this way, you can do so just as easily walking down the street as you can in the studio.

As you've by now amply seen, embodiment training as I speak about it in this book is not simply about training the physical body. Training your body in isolation is useful if what you are aiming to do is build a stronger, more agile body. But where embodiment training really shines is when it *includes* the body and *integrates* embodied learning with mental, spiritual, emotional, and behavioral learning. This is holistic, experiential leadership learning at its finest.

Embodiment Is Not Body Language.

Embodiment is about what emanates from you and what emerges naturally and automatically from the inside, whereas body language is about picking and choosing from among a wide array of techniques in order to have the impact you want.

In the police academy, cops learn to stand in a way that intimidates.

A standoffish person might be told "don't cross your arms so much."

On the West Coast of the United States eye contact might signal connection and intimacy, whereas in a more deferential culture across the Pacific it might come across as inappropriate or even aggressive.

Body language varies by culture, gender, region, and role. It tends to be culturally bound and gesture-specific. Frequently it is taught as a way to secretly attempt to control the outcome of a situation. (As if you ever could!)

Teachers of body language tips and tricks have much to offer in terms of helping you be more effective in a number of areas, such as delivering presentations or meeting new people. At its best, adopting new body language through ongoing practice can lead you toward deeper embodiment of new ways of being.

But for the most part, learning "body language" tends to stay on the surface. It becomes a tool that you pick up and put down, a coat that you put on and remove. When it's used as a manipulative trick—a way to get someone else to do what you would like—it can easily come off as the inauthentic move that it is.

That's a far cry from a comportment that just naturally emerges from inside of you. Nelson Mandela *embodied* dignity. You could see it in his straight spine and his lifted chin, but that's not something he did to convince you that he was dignified. Rather, his life experiences built an unshakable dignity in him, and anyone could easily pick up on that inner state of being simply by watching him move. The Dalai Lama embodies kindness, and he moves quite differently from Mandela, in ways that reveal his own inner state. *Our bodies naturally express the qualities of the person living inside.* That is embodiment.

When you embody a way of being, you don't make a conscious choice to enact a technique: to fold your arms or to leave them uncrossed, for example. Instead, you *naturally engage with life.* Your body conveys your dignity, care, courage, compassion, and so on because it unselfconsciously reveals what you're experiencing on the inside.

Practicing new moves may feel like a trick or a technique at first. But once you embody the skill you're aiming to develop, it becomes a predisposition built deep into your neuromusculature, and the move you need arises at just the right moment, precisely when called for. Unlike body language tips and shortcuts, embodiment practice has the potential to shift your way of being from the inside out.

Embodiment Is Not Body Image.

(Although it can support a more positive body image.)

Throughout history, different societies have put particular value judgments on differently shaped bodies. Certain types of bodies are deemed good, acceptable, attractive—even morally virtuous—whereas others are not. Of course, which bodies are most in favor has changed constantly throughout history, which is one way we can know for sure that these value judgments are simply that—a temporary judgment rather than a deep truth. Michelangelo's *David* emerged in an era when the strong, lithe bodies of young men were seen as the height of beauty. In Reuben's era, larger bodies were in vogue. Today we are living in an era that idealizes the dangerously thin.

And that's only looking briefly at Western culture. If we look more broadly, we see cultures where long necks are preferred, or where piercing and scarring are signs of manhood, or where long hair is a sign of true bravery.

These fictional—but very powerful—cultural idealizations can lead to deep insecurities. And often we will furiously polish and primp and preen in a vain attempt to keep these insecurities at bay. But here's the rock-bottom truth:

Every body is an utterly and infinitely astonishing *miracle*.

Every. Last. One.

I realized this in an unforgettable way one afternoon. I was sitting on the edge of the bed clipping my fingernails, when suddenly I flashed on the tender and terrifying task of clipping an infant's fingernails—those impossibly tiny, dearly precious, razor-sharp claws that all babies seem to come equipped with. In my mind's eye, I imagined my nephew's tiny fist, and the way I marveled at the miracle of him—the extraordinary fact of his very existence.

And then it occurred to me with a shock: *I am just such a miracle myself.*

I once had fingernails that small. Someone once gazed at me through amazed and adoring auntie eyes. And although my fingernails and all the rest of me are larger now, that fact makes me no less a miracle. Nay, perhaps even more so.

It was arresting to see myself in this way—as the true miracle that I am, that you are, that each one of us is. I was not accustomed to feeling such tenderness toward myself. But the experience of that moment irrevocably changed me. I am kinder to myself now, and more openhearted. I am less concerned with fitting into society's restrictive norms. I am more interested in celebrating my gifts.

Embodiment is not about whether you are tall or short, thin or thick, soft or hard. It is about how the miracle that you inherently are gets expressed in and through physical form. It is about how the unique *you* of you shows up clothed in all the magnificent glory that is your body. It is about letting more and more of your truest, deepest, most miraculous self have expression in and positive impact on the world.

May you embody all of the magnificent glory that you already inherently are.

Acknowledgments

Before I publicly thank the long list of people who helped make this book a reality, I first wish to acknowledge the three mountain ranges that provided me with the silence and solitude I needed to write it. First and always, the Range of Light—my beloved Sierra Nevada mountains that sustain me with clear rivers, quiet lakes, and endless vistas and views. The Blue Ridge mountains and the Sierra de Gredos also played an important part in the life of this book. I'm grateful to Scott Reese, Laurie Reese, Robert Poynton, and Beatriz Sierra for providing me with such exquisite dwelling places and writing retreats in those mountains-far-from-home.

To the early and ongoing champions of this project who have had my back every step of the way, I offer a deep bow and (another!) box of chocolates: Renee Gregorio at River of Words coaching gently spurred me on as the book resisted my every ambitious deadline, and helped me develop the custom-made, right-for-me writing practice that finally delivered *Your Body is Your Brain* into your hands. Eunice Aquilina, friend and writing companion across the miles, helped me find my ground and own the value of what I had to say. Robyn McCullough blew the trumpet at every opportunity, consistently celebrating my efforts and spreading the word. Juliet Bradley and Luann Barndt volunteered themselves as my unofficial research assistants, unearthing endless fascinating studies to send my way. Dr. Chris Johnson read early drafts and helped me broaden my vision; her comments proved invaluable to the shape of the book. And my dear friend and colleague Jay Fields provided unyielding care and support at every step, including making some of the most valuable editorial comments.

In the daunting decade-long marathon of crafting this book, I was sustained through the inevitable lulls of productivity and moments of self-doubt by a few vital instances of encouragement. Pulitzer Prize-winning editor Jack Hart did me the great honor of lending a sharp eye, a sharp mind, and a sharp red pen to the manuscript—as well as offering much-needed applause at critical junctures. Publishing industry insider Linda Sivertson insisted I broaden my vision to encompass a much wider audience. If you waited a long time for this book, you have Linda to thank; meeting her radically changed my approach to the project and my ambition for the impact it might have. Bethany Kelly and her team at Publishing Partner stepped in towards the end of the project to usher these words into print, and provided support and expertise I didn't even know to ask for.

To the extraordinary community that has gathered around my Body = Brain® course, I wish to offer my deepest gratitude. Your trust in me to guide you through complex and sometimes mind-bending material has meant the world to me. Believe me when I say I have learned more from all of you than you ever learned from me. This book is very much a product of your questions and contributions over many years of teaching this material. Thank you.

Dr. Neil Randawa reviewed the Body = Brain® materials upon which this book is based and gave them a thumbs up from a medical perspective. He put my mind greatly at ease when he told me "at a certain point I stopped evaluating whether you knew what you were talking about and just immersed myself in learning from you." His words and our many conversations helped me trust myself as I found my way. Dr. Srikanth Sola and Dr. Gideon Besson provided similar reassurance at key junctures.

In many ways, this book is the culmination of a lifetime of study. Professors Bill Durham and Robert Sapolsky inspired my early interest in psychobiology and taught me the value of interdisciplinary approaches to complex problems. Similarly, Joel Westheimer sparked an interest in experiential learning that remains with me to this day. I had the good fortune to learn from these creative and thoughtful professors at an impressionable age, and I am grateful for the ways their teachings reverberate in my life even still. Their influence is all over this book, because their influence is all over my way of understanding the world. I would be a different person were it not for the Human Biology program at Stanford University.

Nearly any success I have in life can be attributed to the lessons of discipline, rigor, excellence, and persistence taught to me by Chris Carver and Betty Hazel of the United States Synchronized Swimming program. Certainly completing this book relied heavily on those important lessons. My life has been indelibly impacted by these two women, and I will never be able to thank them properly or appreciate them enough.

Richard Strozzi-Heckler once taught me a Japanese word which means "a debt of gratitude which you can never repay." It is this sort of gratitude I feel for what I have learned from him. I am also grateful to Richard Boyatzis for a life-changing cup of coffee that resulted in critical tweaks to the final draft, as well as an unexpected and exciting new trajectory in my career.

I want to acknowledge the undaunted experimental leaders who have pioneered the field of somatics and upon whose shoulders I stand. Alan Fogel, Wendy Palmer, Peter Levine, Bessel van der Kolk, Staci Haines, and Pat Ogden have all influenced my work through their teaching and writing. Indirectly the work of Ida Rolf, Moshe Feldenkrais, and Dr. Randolph Stone have also inspired me. And I am grateful for all I have learned from my friends and colleagues Suzanne Roberts and Ginny Whitelaw.

I also wish to thank the thousands of researchers on the frontiers of mind-body science who are exploring what we don't yet understand in the hopes of enriching people's lives with their discoveries. I am deeply indebted to their work. To those whose research I have featured in this book, I have endeavored to represent it accurately, and I hope I have both inspired your curiosity and done you proud.

And to those brave souls who shared their stories of embodied transformation with me and with you, I offer my deepest and most heartfelt appreciation. My fervent hope is that their willingness to share their experience will positively impact many people's lives, including your own.

Finally, I wish to acknowledge Lawrence Randle, whose belief in me surpasses my own and whose endless patience seems to know no bounds. He quietly endured the repeated complaints of a frustrated writer—not to mention many a boring weekend as I labored away in the writing cave—and yet his faith and support never wavered for an instant. My life is immeasurably richer with him in it.

About the Author

Amanda Blake is the creator of the popular Body = Brain® course on the neurobiology of experiential learning. In addition to teaching about the art and science of embodiment, she works with leaders worldwide to help them become their best self, enjoy life more, and make a bigger contribution. Once an internationally competitive athlete, Mandy is skilled at cultivating high performance in herself and others. She is a Master Somatic Leadership Coach and holds a degree in Human Biology from Stanford University. When she's not teaching people practical ways to leverage the links between body, brain, and behavior, you can find her swing dancing with her sweetie to corny country songs, backcountry skiing in the Sierras, or learning cool ninja tricks from her nephews.

Learn more at embright.org.

Endnotes

Introduction
1. This is documented in his wonderfully readable journal of the experience: *In Search of the Warrior Spirit*. (Strozzi-Heckler, 2003).
2. Bennis, 2009.

Chapter 1: Biobehavioral Blind Spots
1. Siegel, 1999.
2. Siegel, 1999.
3. LeDoux, 2003; Lewis, Amini, & Lannon, 2001.
4. LeDoux, 2003; Lewis et al., 2001; Sapolsky, 2005.
5. Carter et al., 2009; Gogtay et al., 2004; LeDoux, 2003; Siegel, 1999.
6. Carter et al., 2009.
7. Carter et al., 2009.
8. Gogtay et al., 2004.
9. Siegel, 1999.
10. Gogtay et al., 2004.
11. Most, Chun, Widders, & Zald, 2005; Young, Fishman, & Chen, 1980.

Chapter 2: Vision: Restored
1. Carter et al., 2009.
2. Siegel, 1999.
3. Siegel, 1999.
4. Many thanks to the authors of the exquisite book *A General Theory of Love* for pointing this out to me for the first time. (Lewis et al., 2001).
5. Many organs have smooth muscle fibers (as opposed to the striated muscle fibers of your voluntary muscles) that are also affected by this process of neuromuscular patterning. Armoring can affect how your heart beats, how your gut digests, and how your lungs breathe. (Fogel, 2009).
6. Fogel, 2009.
7. Fogel, 2009.
8. Fogel, 2009.
9. Like dopamine in the case of pleasure, and norepinephrine and cortisol in the case of stress or fear. (Arias-Carrión & Pöppel, 2007; Hamid et al., 2015; Hassert, Miyashita, & Williams, 2004; Tully & Bolshakov, 2010).
10. Levine & Frederick, 1997; Levine & Mate, 2010; Van der Kolk, 2015.

Chapter 3: Embodied Self-Awareness

1. Fogel, 2009.
2. The Sea Gypsies live their entire lives on the ocean. Because they are so keenly attuned to their environment, they were the only people who suffered no losses in the tragic 2004 tsunami in that region. (Doidge, 2007).
3. Craig, 2015; Fogel, 2009.
4. Fogel, 2009.
5. Hassert et al., 2004; Zhang, Harper, & Frysinger, 1986.
6. Gutkowska, Jankowski, Mukaddam-Daher, & McCann, 2000.
7. McCraty, 2008.
8. Pearsall, 1999.
9. Gershon, 2003.
10. Mayer, 2011.
11. Mayer, 2011.
12. Mayer, 2011.
13. Gershon, 2003.
14. Carter et al., 2009; Kaminoff & Matthews, 2012.
15. Philippot, Chapelle, & Blairy, 2002.
16. Philippot et al., 2002.
17. Berthoud & Neuhuber, 2000.
18. Dawson, Schell, & Filion, 2007.
19. Carter et al., 2009.
20. Pang et al., 2011.
21. Field, 2003.
22. Olausson et al., 2002.
23. Schleip, 2003.
24. Schleip, Findley, & Huijing, 2012.
25. Varela & Frenk, 1987.
26. Schleip, 2003.
27. Schleip et al., 2012.
28. Gladwell, 2002.
29. Fogel, 2009.
30. Craig, 2010; Fogel, 2009.
31. Sensations travel faster to the brain than conceptual awareness, which is one reason why our good ideas about how to respond can be hijacked by our body's quick sensory-emotional response. (Carter et al., 2009; Fogel, 2009).
32. Blakeslee & Blakeslee, 2008.
33. Blakeslee & Blakeslee, 2008.
34. Blakeslee & Blakeslee, 2008.
35. Carney, Cuddy, & Yap, 2010.
36. Fogel, 2009.
37. Davidson & Lutz, 2008; Doidge, 2007; Schwartz & Begley, 2002.

38. Lommel, 2011.
39. Doidge, 2007.
40. Schwartz & Begley, 2002.
41. Lewis et al., 2001.
42. Merzenich in Doidge, 2007.
43. Hamid et al., 2015; Tully & Bolshakov, 2010.
44. Lazar et al., 2005.
45. Doidge, 2007.
46. Doidge, 2007; LeDoux, 2003; Sapolsky, 2005; Siegel, 1999.
47. Doidge, 2007; Hamid et al., 2015; Rothschild, 2000; Tully & Bolshakov, 2010.
48. Anand, Malhotra, Singh, & Dua, 1959; Schmahmann & Caplan, 2006; Schutter & Honk, 2005, 2009.
49. Casasanto, 2009; Casasanto & Dijkstra, 2010; Dijkstra, Kaschak, & Zwaan, 2007.
50. Doidge, 2007; Ecker, Ticic, & Hulley, 2012.
51. Doidge, 2007; Ecker et al., 2012.
52. Goleman, 2005, 2007.

Section 1: Find Purpose

1. Bar-On, Tranel, Denburg, & Bechara, 2003.

Chapter 4: Care

1. Seligman, 2004.
2. Boyatzis & Akrivou, 2006; Buse & Bilimoria, 2014; Neff, 2015; Passarelli, 2015.
3. Christakis & Fowler, 2011.
4. McCraty, Atkinson, & Tomasino, 2001.
5. Berthoud & Neuhuber, 2000.
6. McCraty et al., 2001.
7. McCraty et al., 2001.
8. Hassert et al., 2004.
9. In fact, in 1983 the heart was reclassified to be included as part of the endo-crine system—a curt scientific nod to the physiology of love. (McCraty et al., 2001).
10. Torrent-Guasp et al., 2001, 2005.
11. McCraty, 2008.
12. Sylvia & Novak, 1998.
13. Pearsall, Schwartz, & Russek, 1999.

Chapter 5: Choose

1. Bar-On et al., 2003.
2. Bar-On et al., 2003; Fogel, 2009.
3. Goleman, 2005.

Chapter 7: Contribute

1. "Capital One Environmental Metrics," 2014.

Chapter 8: Courage

1. Porges, 2004.
2. Porges, 2004, 2009.
3. Porges, 2007.
4. Porges & Furman, 2011.
5. Carney et al., 2010.
6. Carney et al., 2010; Cuddy, Wilmuth, Yap, & Carney, 2015; Cuddy, 2015.
7. Cuddy, Schultz, & Fosse, 2017.
8. Porges, 1992, 1995.
9. Cottingham, Porges, & Richmond, 1988.
10. Schleip, 2003.
11. Parker, 2007.
12. Cuddy et al., 2015.
13. Barrios-Choplin, McCraty, Sundram, & Atkinson, 1999; McCraty et al., 2001; McCraty, Tomasino, Atkinson, & Sundram, 1999.

Chapter 9: Composure

1. Seppälä, 2013.
2. Philippot et al., 2002.
3. Fogel, 2009; Kaminoff & Matthews, 2012; Van der Kolk, 2015.
4. Schleip, 2003.
5. Seppälä et al., 2014.
6. Seppälä et al., 2014.
7. Massery, Hagins, Stafford, Moerchen, & Hodges, 2013.
8. Kaminoff & Matthews, 2012; Massery et al., 2013; Massery & Hodges, 2011.
9. M. J. Taylor, 2011.
10. M. J. Taylor, 2011.

Chapter 10: Confidence

1. Whitelaw & Wetzig, 2008.
2. Whitelaw & Wetzig, 2008.

Chapter 11: Credibility

1. Brown, 2007.

Chapter 12: Connection

1. Siegel, 2010.

2. I am trained in the Strozzi Somatics lineage of bodywork, which combines Rolfing, Feldenkrais, and polarity therapy with coaching to produce powerful personal breakthroughs like the one Laila experienced.
3. Olausson et al., 2002.
4. Keltner, 2010.
5. Triplett & Arneson, 1979.
6. Coan, Schaefer, & Davidson, 2006.
7. Fogel, 2009.
8. Field, 2003.
9. Flinn & Olson, 2009.

Chapter 13: Compassion
1. Iacoboni, 2009.
2. Gallese, 2001; Gallese & Goldman, 1998.
3. Ferrari, Gallese, Rizzolatti, & Fogassi, 2003; Rizzolatti & Craighero, 2004.
4. Iacoboni, 2009.
5. Jospe et al., 2018.

Chapter 14: Communicate
1. Siegel, 2010.
2. Siegel, 2010.
3. Brothers, 2005.

Chapter 15: Collaborate
1. Barsade, 2002.
2. Barsade, 2002.
3. Fredrickson, 2013; Fredrickson & Losada, 2005.
4. Gottman & Silver, 2000.
5. Tickle-Degnen & Rosenthal, 1990.
6. Ravignani, 2015.
7. Adamson & Frick, 2003; Tronick, 1989.
8. Nakano & Kitazawa, 2010; Vacharkulksemsuk & Fredrickson, 2012.
9. Sänger, Müller, & Lindenberger, 2012.
10. "TMF: Human Code Acquisition/Sapient Corporation," 2000.

Chapter 16: Convert Conflict to Consensus
1. Porges, 2004; Sapolsky, 2005; Siegel, 2010.
2. Siegel, 2010.

References

Adamson, L. B., & Frick, J. E. (2003). The still face: A history of a shared experimental paradigm. *Infancy, 4*(4), 451–473.

Anand, B. K., Malhotra, C. L., Singh, B., & Dua, S. (1959). Cerebellar projections to limbic system. *Journal of Neurophysiology, 22*(4), 451–457.

Arias-Carrión, O., & Pöppel, E. (2007). Dopamine, learning, and reward-seeking behavior. *Acta Neurobiologiae Experimentalis, 67*(4), 481–488.

Bar-On, R., Tranel, D., Denburg, N. L., & Bechara, A. (2003). Exploring the neurological substrate of emotional and social intelligence. *Brain, 126*(8), 1790–1800.

Barrios-Choplin, B., McCraty, R., Sundram, J., & Atkinson, M. (1999). The effect of employee self-management training on personal and organizational quality. HeartMath Research Center, HeartMath Institute.

Barsade, S. G. (2002). The ripple effect: Emotional contagion and its influence on group behavior. *Administrative Science Quarterly, 47*(4), 644.

Begley, S. (2007). *Train your mind, change your brain: How a new science reveals our extraordinary potential to transform ourselves.* New York, NY: Ballantine Books.

Bennis, W. G. (2009). *On becoming a leader* (Revised and updated). New York, NY: Basic Books.

Berthoud, H.-R., & Neuhuber, W. L. (2000). Functional and chemical anatomy of the afferent vagal system. *Autonomic Neuroscience, 85*(1), 1–17.

Blackmore, S. J. (2004). *Consciousness: An introduction.* Oxford, UK: Oxford University Press.

Blackmore, S. J. (2005). *Consciousness: A very short introduction.* Oxford, UK: Oxford University Press.

Blakeslee, S., & Blakeslee, M. (2008). *The body has a mind of its own: New discoveries about how the mind-body connection helps us master the world.* New York, NY: Random House.

Boyatzis, R. E., & Akrivou, K. (2006). The ideal self as the driver of intentional change. *Journal of Management Development, 25*(7), 624–642.

Boyatzis, R. E., & McKee, A. (2005). *Resonant leadership: Renewing yourself and connecting with others through mindfulness, hope, and compassion.* Boston, MA: Harvard Business School Press.

Brothers, W. C. (2005). *Language and the pursuit of happiness: A new foundation for designing your life, your relationships & your results.* Naples, FL: New Possibilities Press.

Brown, B. (2007). *I thought it was just me: Women reclaiming power and courage in a culture of shame.* New York, NY: Gotham Books.

Buse, K. R., & Bilimoria, D. (2014). Personal vision: enhancing work engagement and the retention of women in the engineering profession. *Frontiers in Psychology, 5,* 1400.

Capital One Environmental Metrics. (2014).

Capra, F. (1997). *The web of life: A new scientific understanding of living systems.* New York, NY: Anchor Books.

Carney, D. R., Cuddy, A. J. C., & Yap, A. J. (2010). Power posing: Brief nonverbal displays affect neuroendocrine levels and risk tolerance. *Psychological Science, 21*(10), 1363–1368.

Carter, R., Aldridge, S., Page, M., Parker, S., Frith, C. D., Frith, U., & Shulman, M. B. (2009). *The human brain book* (1st American ed.). New York, NY: DK Publishing.

Casasanto, D. (2009). Embodiment of abstract concepts: Good and bad in right- and left-handers. *Journal of Experimental Psychology: General, 138*(3), 351–367.

Casasanto, D., & Dijkstra, K. (2010). Motor action and emotional memory. *Cognition, 115*(1), 179–185.

Christakis, N. A., & Fowler, J. H. (2011). *Connected: The surprising power of our social networks and how they shape our lives; how your friends' friends' friends affect everything you feel, think, and do.* New York, NY: Back Bay Books.

Coan, J. A., Schaefer, H. S., & Davidson, R. J. (2006). Lending a hand: Social regulation of the neural response to threat. *Psychological Science, 17*(12), 1032–1039.

Cottingham, J. T., Porges, S. W., & Richmond, K. (1988). Shifts in pelvic inclination angle and parasympathetic tone produced by Rolfing soft tissue manipulation. *Physical Therapy, 68*(9), 1364–1370.

Craig, A. D. (2010). Interoception and emotion: A neuroanatomical perspective. In M. Lewis, J. M. Haviland-Jones, & L. F. Barrett (Eds.), *Handbook of emotions* (Vol. 3, pp. 272–292). New York, NY: Guilford Press.

Craig, A. D. (2015). *How do you feel? An interoceptive moment with your neurobiological self.* Princeton, NJ: Princeton University Press.

Cuddy, A. J. C. (2015). *Presence: Bringing your boldest self to your biggest challenges* (1st ed.). New York, NY: Little, Brown and Company.

Cuddy, A. J. C., Schultz, J. S., & Fosse, N. E. (2017). P-curving a more comprehensive body of research on postural feedback reveals clear evidential value for "power posing" effects: Reply to Simmons and Simonsohn. *Psychological Science.* In press, Nov. 2017.

Cuddy, A. J. C., Wilmuth, C. A., Yap, A. J., & Carney, D. R. (2015). Preparatory power posing affects nonverbal presence and job interview performance. *Journal of Applied Psychology, 100*(4), 1286–1295.

Damasio, A. R. (2000). *The feeling of what happens: Body and emotion in the making of consciousness* (1st Harvest ed.). San Diego, CA: Harcourt.

Davidson, R. J., & Lutz, A. (2008). Buddha's brain: Neuroplasticity and meditation [in the spotlight]. *IEEE Signal Processing Magazine, 25*(1), 176–174.

Dawson, M. E., Schell, A. M., & Filion, D. L. (2007). The electrodermal system. In J. Cacioppo, L. G. Tassinary, & G. G. Berntson (Eds.), *Principles of psychophysiology: Physical, social, and inferential elements* (pp. 159–181). Cambridge, UK: Cambridge University Press.

Dijkstra, K., Kaschak, M. P., & Zwaan, R. A. (2007). Body posture facilitates retrieval of autobiographical memories. *Cognition, 102*(1), 139–149.

Doidge, N. (2007). *The brain that changes itself: Stories of personal triumph from the frontiers of brain science.* New York, NY: Viking.

Durham, W. H. (2000). *Coevolution: Genes, culture, and human diversity* (Nachdr.). Stanford, CA: Stanford University Press.

Ecker, B., Ticic, R., & Hulley, L. (2012). *Unlocking the emotional brain: Eliminating symptoms at their roots using memory reconsolidation.* New York, NY: Routledge.

Emerson, D., & Hopper, E. (2011). *Overcoming trauma through yoga: Reclaiming your body.* Berkeley, CA: North Atlantic Books.

Ferrari, P. F., Gallese, V., Rizzolatti, G., & Fogassi, L. (2003). Mirror neurons responding to the observation of ingestive and communicative mouth actions in the monkey ventral premotor cortex: Mirror neurons for mouth actions in F5. *European Journal of Neuroscience, 17*(8), 1703–1714.

Field, T. (2003). *Touch* (2nd revised ed.). Cambridge, MA: Bradford Books.

Flinn, N. & Olsen, J. (2009, October). *Courage Center Project Summary.* Presented at the American Medical Rehabilitation Providers Association.

Fogel, A. (2009). *The psychophysiology of self-awareness: Rediscovering the lost art of body sense* (1st ed.). New York, NY: W.W. Norton.

Fredrickson, B. L. (2013). Updated thinking on positivity ratios. *American Psychologist, 68*(9), 814–822.

Fredrickson, B. L., & Losada, M. F. (2005). Positive affect and the complex dynamics of human flourishing. *American Psychologist, 60*(7), 678–686.

Gallese, V. (2001). The "shared manifold" hypothesis. From mirror neurons to empathy. *Journal of Consciousness Studies, 8*(5–6), 33–50.

Gallese, V., & Goldman, A. (1998). Mirror neurons and the simulation theory of mind-reading. *Trends in Cognitive Sciences, 2*(12), 493–501.

Gershon, M. D. (2003). *The second brain: A groundbreaking new understanding of nervous disorders of the stomach and intestine.* New York, NY: Quill.

Gladwell, M. (2002, August 5). The naked face. *The New Yorker.*

Gogtay, N., Giedd, J. N., Lusk, L., Hayashi, K. M., Greenstein, D., Vaituzis, A. C., ... Thompson, P. M. (2004). Dynamic mapping of human cortical development during childhood through early adulthood. *Proceedings of the National Academy of Sciences of the United States of America, 101*(21), 8174–8179.

Goleman, D. (2005). *Emotional intelligence* (10th anniversary ed.). New York, NY: Bantam Books.

Goleman, D. (2007). *Social intelligence: The new science of human relationships.* New York, NY: Bantam Books.

Gottman, J. M., & Silver, N. (2000). *The seven principles for making marriage work.* New York, NY: Three Rivers Press.

Gutkowska, J., Jankowski, M., Mukaddam-Daher, S., & McCann, S. M. (2000). Oxytocin is a cardiovascular hormone. *Brazilian Journal of Medical and Biological Research, 33*(6), 625–633.

Hamid, A. A., Pettibone, J. R., Mabrouk, O. S., Hetrick, V. L., Schmidt, R., Weele, C. M. V., ... Berke, J. D. (2015). Mesolimbic dopamine signals the value of work. *Nature Neuroscience, 19*(1), 117–126.

Hanson, R., & Mendius, R. (2009). *Buddha's brain: The practical neuroscience of happiness, love & wisdom.* Oakland, CA: New Harbinger Publications.

Hassert, D. L., Miyashita, T., & Williams, C. L. (2004). The effects of peripheral vagal nerve stimulation at a memory-modulating intensity on norepinephrine output in the basolateral amygdala. *Behavioral Neuroscience, 118*(1), 79–88.

Iacoboni, M. (2009). *Mirroring people: The science of empathy and how we connect with others.* New York, NY: Picador, Farrar, Straus and Giroux.

Jospe, K., Flöel, A., & Lavidor, M. (2018). The interaction between embodiment and empathy in facial expression recognition. *Social Cognitive and Affective Neuroscience, 13*(2), 203–215.

Judith, A. (2004). *Eastern body, Western mind: Psychology and the chakra system as a path to the self* (Rev. ed). Berkeley, CA: Celestial Arts.

Kaminoff, L., & Matthews, A. (2012). *Yoga anatomy* (2nd ed.). Champaign, IL: Human Kinetics.

Keltner, D. (2010, September). Hands on research: The science of touch. *Greater Good.* Retrieved from https://greatergood.berkeley.edu/article/item/hands_on_research

Kornfield, J. (2009). *The wise heart: A guide to the universal teachings of Buddhist psychology.* New York, NY: Bantam Books.

Lanza, R., & Berman, B. (2010). *Biocentrism: How life and consciousness are the keys to understanding the true nature of the universe.* Dallas, TX: BenBella.

Lazar, S. W., Kerr, C. E., Wasserman, R. H., Gray, J. R., Greve, D. N., Treadway, M. T., ... Fischl, B. (2005). Meditation experience is associated with increased cortical thickness. *Neuroreport, 16*(17), 1893–1897.

LeDoux, J. E. (1998). *The emotional brain: The mysterious underpinnings of emotional life* (1st. Touchstone ed.). New York, NY: Simon & Schuster.

LeDoux, J. E. (2003). *Synaptic self: How our brains become who we are.* New York, NY: Penguin.

Levine, P. A., & Frederick, A. (1997). *Waking the tiger: Healing trauma* (1st ed.). Berkeley, CA: North Atlantic Books.

Levine, P. A., & Mate, G. (2010). *In an unspoken voice: How the body releases trauma and restores goodness* (1st ed.). Berkeley, CA: North Atlantic Books.

Lewis, T., Amini, F., & Lannon, R. (2001). *A general theory of love* (1st Vintage ed.). New York, NY: Vintage.

Linden, D. J. (2016). *Touch: The science of hand, heart, and mind.* London, UK: Penguin Books.

Lommel, P. van (2011). *Consciousness beyond life: The science of the near-death experience.* New York, NY: HarperOne.

Long, R., & Macivor, C. (2006). *The key muscles of yoga: Your guide to functional anatomy in yoga* (3rd ed.). Baldwinsville, NY: Bandha Yoga Publications.

Massery, M., Hagins, M., Stafford, R., Moerchen, V., & Hodges, P. W. (2013). Effect of airway control by glottal structures on postural stability. *Journal of Applied Physiology, 115*(4), 483–490.

Massery, M., & Hodges, P. W. (2011, February). *State of the art in postural control.* Presented at the American Physical Therapy Association Meeting, New Orleans, LA.

Maturana, H. R., & Varela, F. J. (1992). *The tree of knowledge: The biological roots of human understanding* (Rev. ed.). Boston, MA: Random House.

Mayer, E. A. (2011). Gut feelings: The emerging biology of gut–brain communication. *Nature Reviews Neuroscience, 12*(8), 453–466.

McCraty, R. (2008). *The science and research behind the HeartMath System.* HeartMath Institute.

McCraty, R., Atkinson, M., & Tomasino, D. (2001). *Science of the heart: Exploring the role of the heart in human performance.* HeartMath Research Center, HeartMath Institute.

McCraty, R., Tomasino, D., Atkinson, M., & Sundram, J. (1999). *Impact of the HeartMath self-management skills program on physiological and psychological stress in police officers.* HeartMath Research Center, HeartMath Institute.

Most, S. B., Chun, M. M., Widders, D. M., & Zald, D. H. (2005). Attentional rubbernecking: Cognitive control and personality in emotion-induced blindness. *Psychonomic Bulletin & Review, 12*(4), 654–661.

Nakano, T., & Kitazawa, S. (2010). Eyeblink entrainment at breakpoints of speech. *Experimental Brain Research*, *205*(4), 577–581.

Neff, J. E. (2015). Shared vision promotes family firm performance. *Frontiers in Psychology*, *6*, 1–16.

Noë, A. (2010). *Out of our heads: Why you are not your brain, and other lessons from the biology of consciousness* (1st paperback ed.). New York, NY: Hill and Wang.

Olausson, H., Lamarre, Y., Backlund, H., Morin, C., Wallin, B. G., Starck, G.,... Bushnell, M. C. (2002). Unmyelinated tactile afferents signal touch and project to insular cortex. *Nature Neuroscience*, *5*(9), 900–904.

Palmer, W., & Crawford, J. (2013). *Leadership embodiment: How the way we sit and stand can change the way we think and speak.* San Rafael, CA: Embodiment Foundation.

Pang, Z. P., Yang, N., Vierbuchen, T., Ostermeier, A., Fuentes, D. R., Yang, T. Q.,... Wernig, M. (2011). Induction of human neuronal cells by defined transcription factors. *Nature*, *476*(7359), 220–223.

Parker, S. (2007). *The human body book* (1st American ed.). New York, NY: DK Publishing.

Passarelli, A. M. (2015). Vision-based coaching: Optimizing resources for leader development. *Frontiers in Psychology*, *6*, 412.

Pearsall, P. (1999). *The heart's code: Tapping the wisdom and power of our heart energy.* New York, NY: Broadway Books.

Pearsall, P., Schwartz, G. E. R., & Russek, L. G. S. (1999). Changes in heart transplant recipients that parallel the personalities of their donors. *Integrative Medicine*, *2*(2/3), 65–72.

Pert, C. B. (2003). *Molecules of emotion: Why you feel the way you feel.* New York, NY: Scribner.

Peterson, C., & Seligman, M. E. P. (2004). *Character strengths and virtues: A handbook and classification.* Washington, DC: American Psychological Association.

Philippot, P., Chapelle, G., & Blairy, S. (2002). Respiratory feedback in the generation of emotion. *Cognition & Emotion*, *16*(5), 605–627.

Pinker, S. (1999). *How the mind works* (1st publ.). New York, NY: Norton.

Porges, S. W. (1992). Vagal tone: A physiologic marker of stress vulnerability. *Pediatrics, 90*(3), 498–504.

Porges, S. W. (1995). Cardiac vagal tone: A physiological index of stress. *Neuroscience and Biobehavioral Review, 19*(2), 225–233.

Porges, S. W. (2004). Neuroception: A subconscious system for detecting threats and safety. *Zero to Three, 24*(5), 19–24.

Porges, S. W. (2007). The polyvagal perspective. *Biological Psychology, 74*(2), 116–143.

Porges, S. W. (2009). The polyvagal theory: New insights into adaptive reactions of the autonomic nervous system. *Cleveland Clinic Journal of Medicine, 76*(Suppl 2), S86.

Porges, S. W., & Furman, S. A. (2011). The early development of the autonomic nervous system provides a neural platform for social behaviour: A polyvagal perspective. *Infant and Child Development, 20*(1), 106–118.

Ravignani, A. (2015). Evolving perceptual biases for antisynchrony: A form of temporal coordination beyond synchrony. *Frontiers in Neuroscience, 9,* 339.

Rizzolatti, G., & Craighero, L. (2004). The mirror-neuron system. *Annual Review of Neuroscience, 27*(1), 169–192.

Rock, D. (2009). *Your brain at work: Strategies for overcoming distraction, regaining focus, and working smarter all day long* (1st ed.). New York, NY: Harper Business.

Rosenblum, B., & Kuttner, F. (2008). *Quantum enigma: Physics encounters consciousness.* Oxford, UK: Oxford University Press.

Rothschild, B. (2000). *The body remembers.* New York, NY: Norton.

Sänger, J., Müller, V., & Lindenberger, U. (2012). Intra- and interbrain synchronization and network properties when playing guitar in duets. *Frontiers in Human Neuroscience, 6,* 312.

Sapolsky, R. M. (2005). *Biology and human behavior: The neurological origins of individuality.* Chantilly, VA: Teaching Company.

Schleip, R. (2003). Fascial plasticity—A new neurobiological explanation: Part 1. *Journal of Bodywork and Movement Therapies, 7*(1), 11–19.

Schleip, R., Findley, T. W., & Huijing, P. (Eds.). (2012). *Fascia: The tensional network of the human body: The science and clinical applications in manual and movement therapy, 1e* (1st ed.). Edinburgh: Churchill Livingstone/Elsevier.

Schmahmann, J. D., & Caplan, D. (2006). Cognition, emotion and the cerebellum. *Brain, 129*(2), 290–292.

Schutter, D. J. L. G., & Honk, J. V. (2005). The cerebellum on the rise in human emotion. *The Cerebellum, 4*(4), 290–294.

Schutter, D. J. L. G., & Honk, J. V. (2009). The cerebellum in emotion regulation: A repetitive transcranial magnetic stimulation study. *The Cerebellum, 8*(1), 28–34.

Schwartz, J., & Begley, S. (2002). *The mind and the brain: Neuroplasticity and the power of mental force.* New York, NY: Regan Books/HarperCollins.

Seligman, M. E. P. (2004). *Authentic happiness: Using the new positive psychology to realize your potential for lasting fulfillment* (Reprint ed.). New York, NY: Atria Books.

Seppälä, E. M. (2013, May). *Free the mind.* Phie Ambo (Director). Film showing, Stanford University.

Seppälä, E. M., Nitschke, J. B., Tudorascu, D. L., Hayes, A., Goldstein, M. R., Nguyen, D. T. H.,... Davidson, R. J. (2014). Breathing-based meditation decreases posttraumatic stress disorder symptoms in U.S. military veterans: A randomized controlled longitudinal study: Breathing meditation for PTSD. *Journal of Traumatic Stress, 27*(4), 397–405.

Siegel, D. J. (1999). *The developing mind: Toward a neurobiology of interpersonal experience.* New York, NY: Guilford Press.

Siegel, D. J. (2010). *Mindsight: The new science of personal transformation* (1st ed.). New York, NY: Bantam Books.

Staugaard-Jones, J. A. (2012). *The vital psoas muscle: Connecting physical, emotional, and spiritual well-being.* Chichester, UK: Lotus Publications.

Strozzi-Heckler, R. (2003). *In search of the warrior spirit: Teaching awareness disciplines to the Green Berets* (3rd ed.). Berkeley, CA: North Atlantic Books.

Strozzi-Heckler, R. (2011). *Being human at work: Bringing somatic intelligence into your professional life.* Berkeley, CA: North Atlantic Books.

Strozzi-Heckler, R. (2014). *The art of somatic coaching: Embodying skillful action, wisdom, and compassion.* Berkeley, CA: North Atlantic Books.

Sylvia, C., & Novak, W. (1998). *A change of heart: A memoir* (Reprint ed.). New York, NY: Grand Central Publishing.

Taylor, J. B. (2008). *My stroke of insight: A brain scientist's personal journey* (1st Viking ed.). New York, NY: Viking.

Taylor, M. J. (2011). *The 3 Diaphragms Model.* YouTube video, Matthew J. Taylor Institute. https://www.youtube.com/watch?v=HTkFuPLZ3Uk

Tickle-Degnen, L., & Rosenthal, R. (1990). The nature of rapport and its nonverbal correlates. *Psychological Inquiry, 1*(4), 285–293.

TMF: Human Code acquisition/Sapient Corporation. (2000, August 31). Retrieved from http://boards.fool.com/human-code-acquisition-13221079.aspx

Torrent-Guasp, F., Buckberg, G. D., Clemente, C., Cox, J. L., Coghlan, H. C., & Gharib, M. (2001). The structure and function of the helical heart and its buttress wrapping. I. The normal macroscopic structure of the heart. *Seminars in Thoracic and Cardiovascular Surgery, 13*(4), 301–319.

Torrent-Guasp, F., Kocica, M. J., Corno, A. F., Komeda, M., Carreras-Costa, F., Flotats, A.,... Wen, H. (2005). Towards new understanding of the heart structure and function. *European Journal of Cardio-Thoracic Surgery, 27*(2), 191–201.

Triplett, J. L., & Arneson, S. W. (1979). The use of verbal and tactile comfort to alleviate distress in young hospitalized children. *Research in Nursing & Health, 2*(1), 17–23.

Tronick, E. Z. (1989). Emotions and emotional communication in infants. *American Psychologist, 44*(2), 112.

Tully, K., & Bolshakov, V. Y. (2010). Emotional enhancement of memory: How norepinephrine enables synaptic plasticity. *Molecular Brain, 3*, 15.

Vacharkulksemsuk, T., & Fredrickson, B. L. (2012). Strangers in sync: Achieving embodied rapport through shared movements. *Journal of Experimental Social Psychology, 48*(1), 399–402.

Van der Kolk, B. A. (2015). *The body keeps the score: Brain, mind and body in the healing of trauma.* New York, NY: Penguin Books.

Varela, F. J., & Frenk, S. (1987). The organ of form: Towards a theory of biological shape. *Journal of Social Biology and Structure, 10*, 73–83.

Wheatley, M. J. (1996). *Leadership and the new science: Learning about organization from an orderly universe* (1st paperback ed.). San Francisco, CA: Berrett-Koehler Publications.

Whitelaw, G., & Wetzig, B. (2008). *Move to greatness: Focusing the four essential energies of a whole and balanced leader*. Boston, MA: Nicholas Brealey International.

Wilber, K. (2000). *A brief history of everything* (2nd rev. ed.). Boston, MA: Shambhala.

Wolynn, M. (2016). *It didn't start with you: How inherited family trauma shapes who we are and how to end the cycle*. New York, NY: Viking.

Young, R. S., Fishman, G. A., & Chen, F. (1980). Traumatically acquired color vision defect. *Investigative Ophthalmology & Visual Science*, *19*(5), 545–549.

Zhang, J.-X., Harper, R. M., & Frysinger, R. C. (1986). Respiratory modulation of neuronal discharge in the central nucleus of the amygdala during sleep and waking states. *Experimental Neurology*, *91*(1), 193–207.

Zull, J. E. (2002). *The art of changing the brain: Enriching teaching by exploring the biology of learning* (1st ed.). Sterling, VA: Stylus Publishing.

Index

A

Acevedo, Maria, 201–206
acquired color deficiency, 20
acting from centered care, 195–196
Afghanistan, 122–129
All-American Girls Professional Baseball
    League, 14
ambivalence. *See* decision-making
amygdala, 48, 75, 115
anger, 32–33, 39–41, 186–187,
    189–191, 233
anterior cingulate cortex (ACC), 85
anxiety, 38, 95–96, 144, 148, 206, 232
    See also fear
appease response, 116–117, 201–206,
    207–210, 232
armoring, 31–33, 35–36, 133–140, 176
Army Special Forces, 3, 73
artists' personalities, 151
asking for help, 160, 162, 177, 210–211
athletes, and proprioception, 54
Attan, Anthony, 149–154, 156
attention, 45–48, 88, 102, 173–174,
    198–199
    and brain development, 59–60
    selective, 46
    See also embodied mindfulness;
    self-awareness
attunement, 173–174, 236
authenticity, 158, 162–163
autonomic nervous system, 49, 51, 222
awareness. *See* self-awareness

B

balance, sense of, 53–54, 60
Barakzai, 126–127

Barndt, Luann, 40
Bauby, Jean-Dominique, 13
bees, vision, 12
Bennis, Warren, 6
Bepler, Tom, 40
biobehavioral blind spots, 11–26, 41,
    44, 160
    in communication, 211–212
    examples of
        Amanda, 82
        Anthony, 150
        Denise, 160–161
        Laila, 171–173
        Malika, 211
        Mel, 228
        Nichole, 141–142, 146–147
        Peter, 74
        Rich, 133–138
biology and perception, 12, 38–39, 42,
    45–47, 60–61, 97, 189
body-oriented psychology, 30, 34–35
brain
    amygdala, 48, 75, 115
    anterior cingulate cortex (ACC), 85
    cerebellum, 60
    children's, 19–20
    development of, 16–20, 59–61
    insula, 51, 85, 188
    middle prefrontal cortex (MPFC),
        232–233
    orbitofrontal cortex (OFC), 85
    pattern detection, 16
    somatosensory cortex, 19–20, 155
    ventromedial prefrontal cortex
        (VMPFC), 56, 84–85
brainstem, 17–18, 210

breathing/breathing practices,
143–145, 179–180
and emotions, 49, 137–138,
139–141
and stress, 125, 128–129
shallow, 144
Brothers, Chalmers, 211
Brown, Brené, 162
bully (Bob), 113–114, 116–117

C

C tactile afferent cells, 174
Capital One, 70–71, 79, 102–107
care, 69–80
caregiving, 175, 178–181
Centered Leadership program, 184–186
centering, 111, 117–119, 121, 134,
142, 144–145, 233–236
cerebellum, 60
choices. *See* decision-making
Christakis, Nicholas, 73
closed postures, 54, 118–119
See also posture and mood
collaboration, 102–105, 199, 215–226
Collaborator pattern, 152
color blindness, 12, 20, 41
commitment vs. intentions, 91–100
communication, 116–118, 201–213,
224
and conflict, 228–231
and touch, 174–175
feedback, 216–219, 221
problems, 211–213
compassion, 183–192
composure, 131–148, 161–163
confidence, 149–156, 229–231
conflict resolution, 196–197, 227–237
connection, 169–182
connective tissue. *See* fascia
Cottingham, John, 120
courage, 109–110, 113–130, 147–148
See also composure; confidence

Courage Center, 178–181
credibility, 157–163
Cuddy, Amy, 54–55, 118–119

D

dancers' personalities, 151
de-armoring, 35–36, 42, 61, 146, 148.
See also armoring
decision-making, 81–90, 94, 203–204,
210
Democratic National Convention of
1968, 15
diaphragms, role in breathing, 143–145
disconnection, 32–33, 170, 171
disruption, 35–36, 61
dissociation, 32–33, 115
Diving Bell and the Butterfly, 13
dorsal vagal complex, 115
Driver pattern, 152
Dunn, Nichole, 141–142, 144–147, 243

E

earthworms, 17, 18
ectoderm, 50
Einstein, Albert, 2
Ekman, Paul, 51, 54
Elliot, Marianne, 122–129, 243
embodied learning, 58–62, 237,
241–245
embodied mindfulness, 219, 221
in action, 196–199, 209, 236, 242
embodied reaction to conflict,
114–117, 228–236
embodied self-awareness, 43–62,
68, 79, 100, 173–174, 188–190,
235–236
embodiment, 6–8, 266–270
emotional brain. *See* limbic system
emotional contagion, 73, 204,
217–218, 221–222
emotional intelligence, 62, 66–67, 68,
89

emotions
  accessing, 187–188. *See also*
    self-awareness
  and armoring, 31–32, 35–36,
    133–140, 176
  and biobehavioral learning, 33–41,
    58, 61
  and culture, 31–32
  and memory, 59–60
  and touch, 174–175
  development of, 37–39
  disconnecting from, 133–139
empathy, 167, 184, 189
  See also compassion; connection
enoughness, 91–100
enteric nervous system, 48–49, 150
environmental council, 102–107
Equifax, 107
experience-dependent brain develop-
    ment, 16–20, 59–61
exteroception, 45–47, 55, 205–206
eye contact, 162, 183

F

fascia, 51–52, 54, 121
fear, 38, 116–117, 123–125, 128–130
  of conflict, 228–231
  of disappointing others, 209–210
  of failure, 161
FEBI assessments, 154
feedback, giving/receiving, 210–211,
    216–219, 221, 223
fight or flight response, 49, 51,
    115–116, 128, 232
  fight mode, 186–187
  freeze response, 115, 186
  See also appease response
Fippinger
  Brian, 11–15, 21–26, 27–37, 39–41,
    243
  Charlotte, 14–15, 22, 23
  Diana, 21–26

Fogel, Alan, 55–56, 241, 244
Fowler, James, 73
freeze response, 115, 186

G

gender norms, overcoming, 243–244
General Theory of Love, 59
Goldberg, Whoopi, 145
Goleman, Daniel, 62, 66
gorilla, invisible, 46
Gottman, John, 218
guided visualization, 179–180
gut, 48–49, 52, 55, 142, 150

H

habits. *See* armoring; memory, implicit
heart, 47–48, 75–77, 79, 124, 129,
    232
heart transplant recipients, 48, 76
Hebb's Law, 16
Herat, Afghanistan, 126–127
hippocampus, 28, 48
Holan, Jan, 219, 226
HPA axis, 115
Human Code, 219–221, 226
human rights workers, 122–123,
    125–129
Hunt, Valerie, 155

I

Illinois Bell, 22
immobilization. *See* freeze response
impostor syndrome, 145
Inconvenient Truth, An, 104
indecision. *See* decision-making
insula, 51, 85, 188
integration (wholeness), 242–245
interoception, 47–53, 58, 84, 100,
    189, 205, 232
intimacy, 24–25, 32–33, 37, 88–89
Iraq War, 132–137

J

Jempe Center, 184, 186
Johnson, Chris, 27–31, 33, 37, 39, 42
Johnson, Rick, 183–184
Jungian archetypes, 152

K

Keltner, Dacher, 174
keystone, 97
Khan, Amanullah, 126–127
knee-jerk reactions, 52–53, 94, 186, 195, 232

L

language acquisition, 37–38
leadership
    body-oriented, 3–4, 30, 34–36, 73–74, 151–152, 183, 226
    military, 131–132, 135
    need for, 1–2
    principled, 198–199
    qualities of, 5–6, 72, 103
League of Their Own, 14
left- and right-handers, 60
limbic resonance, 174, 180
limbic system, 18, 49, 59–60, 210
listening, 167, 173, 190, 205–206
lizard brain. *See* brainstem
long-term potentiation, 16
Lotas, Alex, 152
Love, Paula, 89
Low, Rich, 131–139, 243
lungs, 49
    See also breathing/breathing practices
Luzmore, Peter, 71–74, 101–102

M

mammals and social groups, 17–18
Mayer, Emeran, 49
Maynard, Peter, 69–80, 101–107, 243
McConnell, John, 159–160, 186–187
meditation, 35, 60, 95, 128–129

memory
    explicit, 28
    implicit, 28–29, 31–32
    of heart, 48, 76–77
Merzenich, Michael, 59
Microsoft, 159, 161–162, 184, 187, 192
middle prefrontal cortex (MPFC), 232–233
military veterans, 131–139
mindfulness, 43, 196–197
    See also embodied mindfulness
mirror neurons, 188–189, 217
modeling behavior, 188–189
monkeys and mirroring, 188–189
mood
    and breathing, 49, 125, 128–129, 139–141, 144
    and gut, 48–49, 150
    and posture, 38–39, 54–55, 116–119
mood contagion, 73, 204, 217–218, 221–222
movement patterns, 151–156
muscle memory, 29, 31–33, 144, 148, 236
muscular anatomy, 155

N

National Guard, 131
nervous system, 16–17, 56, 60, 75, 114–115, 144
    and touch, 174–175
    autonomic, 49, 51, 222
    enteric, 48–49, 150
    parasympathetic, 120–121
    networking, 153–154
    neural ganglia, 75
    neuroception, 45, 114–115
    neuromuscular behavior patterns. *See* memory, implicit
    neuromuscular signatures, 151–152
    neuroplasticity, 58–59
    nociception, 45

O

obsessive-compulsive disorder, 59, 60
open postures, 54, 118–119
   See also posture and mood
orbitofrontal cortex (OFC), 85
Organizer pattern, 152
oscillators, 224–225
oxytocin, 48, 76, 175

P

panic attacks, 187, 192
paper use, 104–105
parasympathetic nervous system,
   120–121
Peet's Coffee, 170, 178
pelvic floor, 143
pelvic tilt, 120–121
perception. *See* biology and perception
Perry, Ed, 220, 226, 237
personality testing tools, 154
polyvagal response, 232
polyvagal theory, 115–116
Porges, Stephen, 114–115, 120
positive psychology, 72
positivity vs. negativity, 218
posture and mood, 38–39, 54–55,
   116–119
presence, 167, 172–173, 176, 180–
   182, 219, 235–236
Project Welcome Home Troops, 139
proprioception, 53–55, 205–206
psoas muscles, 143–144
psychobiological learning, 59–61
psychophysiological coherence, 111,
   124–125, 134, 142, 148, 234–235
Psychophysiology of Self-Awareness, 55
PTSD treatment, 136–141
purpose, 65–68, 72–73, 78–79, 255–259

R

Ranger School, 132
rapport. *See* collaboration

Rathbone, Josephine, 155
Reich, Wilhelm, 31
resilience, 109–163
respiration. *See* breathing/breathing
   practices
rhythm
   among people, 222–225
   internal, 124, 174
Richmond, Kent, 120
right- and left-handers, 60
Roberts, Suzanne, 142, 145–147
Rolfing, 34, 120–121
Ropeworks, 215–217, 219, 222–226,
   243
ROTC, 131
Rundle, Denise, 159–162, 243

S

Sanford, Matthew, 178–180
Sänger, Johanna, 225
Schleip, Robert, 121
School of Embodied Leadership, 73
Sea Gypsies, 46
selective attention, 46
self-awareness, 67–68, 93–94, 99, 242
   conceptual, 55–56, 204, 206
   embodied, 43–62, 56–58, 68, 79,
      100, 173–174, 188–190, 204,
      235–236
senses, 45–55, 167, 175, 205–206
Seppälä, Emma, 136, 139–141
serotonin, 49
Siegel, Daniel, 173
Sinek, Simon, 72
skin, 50, 174–175
social connection, 169–182
social dexterity, 196
social intelligence, 66, 67, 166
social tendencies, embodiment, 17
   See also armoring; memory, implicit
Solomon, Helena, 95–99
somatic intelligence, 66, 67

See self-awareness
somatosensory cortex, 19–20, 155
South Kingstown, RI, 77–78
spindle cells, 54
Start with Why, 72
still-face experiment, 224
stomach/gut problems, 48–49, 141,
   149–150
stories
  Amanda (indecision), 81–90
  Amanda (with bully), 113–117
  Anthony, 149–154, 156
  Brian, 11–15, 21–26, 27–37, 39–41
  Claus, 184–187, 189–192
  Courage Center, 178–181
  Denise, 159–162
  Helena, 95–99
  Human Code, 219–221, 226
  Jennifer, 91–94, 99
  Laila, 170–178
  Malika, 207–210
  Maria, 201–206
  Marianne, 122–129
  Mel, 227–231, 234
  Nichole, 141–142, 144–147
  Peter, 69–80, 101–107
  Rich, 131–139
  Rick, 183–184
  Ropeworks, 215–217, 219, 222–226
stress, 49, 111, 120–121, 125, 142–
   144, 148, 149–150, 187, 259
  bodily response, 114–116
  PTSD, 136–141
stroke patients, 59, 60
Strozzi Institute, 34
Strozzi-Heckler, Richard, 3–4, 73, 220
sufficiency. *See* enoughness
sympathetic nervous system, 115, 120
synapses, 16–17
synchrony, 222, 225
Szarek, Mel, 227–231, 234, 243

T
Tarraf, Laila, 170–178
Taylor, Matthew, 143, 178–180
Tefft Hill, 77, 79, 102
tension, unconscious, 171–176
thoracic inlet, 143
Torrent-Guasp, Francisco, 76
touch, sensation of, 50, 174–175
trauma healing, 34–42, 136–141
Tremont, Malika, 207–210, 243
trust, 88–89, 158–159, 162, 221

U
unlearning (embodied), 35–36, 61

V
vagal tone, 120
vagus nerve, 49–50, 75, 115–116, 175
values, 71–73
ventral vagal complex, 116
ventromedial prefrontal cortex (VMP-
   FC), 56, 84–85
vestibular system, 54
veterans, 131–139
virtual connection, 170
Visionary pattern, 152
visualization, 179–180
vulnerability, 24, 157–159, 160–163

W
Wade, Madeline, 34
Weiser, Claus, 184–187, 189–192, 243
Wetzig, Betsy, 151–152
Whitelaw, Ginny, 151–153
wholeness, 241–245
Williams, Vanessa, 145
Women's Fund of Central Ohio,
   141–142, 145, 146–147
work-life balance, 91–94, 95–99

Y
yoga, 125–126, 127–129, 178–180